Financial Management

Han Kang Hong

Butterworths

Financial Management

Han Kang Hong B.Sc (Econ) London, ACIS, AIB, AASA, RAS, BBM

Associate Professor
School of Accountancy
National University of Singapore

SINGAPORE
BUTTERWORTHS
1984

THE BUTTERWORTH GROUP OF COMPANIES

SINGAPORE	BUTTERWORTH & CO (ASIA) PTE LTD Crawford P.O. Box 770, Singapore 9119
ENGLAND	BUTTERWORTH & CO (PUBLISHERS) LTD London
AUSTRALIA	BUTTERWORTHS PTY LIMITED Sydney, Melbourne, Brisbane, Adelaide and Perth
CANADA	BUTTERWORTH & CO (CANADA) LTD Toronto and Vancouver
NEW ZEALAND	BUTTERWORTHS OF NEW ZEALAND LTD Wellington and Auckland
SOUTH AFRICA	BUTTERWORTH & CO (SOUTH AFRICA) (PTY) LTD Durban and Pretoria
USA	MASON PUBLISHING CO St. Paul, Minnesota BUTTERWORTH LEGAL PUBLISHERS Seattle, Washington BUTTERWORTH LEGAL PUBLISHERS Boston, Massachusetts BUTTERWORTH LEGAL PUBLISHERS Austin, Texas D & S PUBLISHING COMPANY Clearwater, Florida

ISBN 0 406 18116 0

PREFACE

This book arises out of my many years of teaching the subject at the School of Accountancy, National University of Singapore. It covers most of the topics taught under the discipline as Business Finance, Financial Management or Managerial Finance. The book attempts to include succinctly the relevant up-to-date concepts and techniques in the field which is all the time increasing in scope and sophistication.

Though some parts of the book are rather theoretical in nature, there are many areas which are economically feasible for application by accountants, financial managers and other executives. In a few areas, a knowledge of mathematics of finance and statistics is desirable and so Appendixes A and B contain brief reviews on these subjects. A few useful tables are provided in Appendix C.

Writing the book necessitated making references to various sources: textbooks, monographs, research publications and articles. A general acknowledgement is hereby made to all. With the consent of The Singapore Institute of Management parts of my book, "Cost and Management Accounting" have been used. I wish to thank many colleagues, friends and students past and present for their help. Last but not least, I appreciate the encouragement and moral support of my wife, Katherine.

Han Kang Hong
1984

CONTENTS

CHAPTER 1

The Finance Function

1.1. THE FINANCE FUNCTION WITHOUT CONSTRAINTS

The finance function of any firm is to maximize its value, that is, to maximize its profitability. Profitability is measured by the income streams flowing from the operating activities of the firm. These activities include those relating to investments, finance and production. In its simple form the finance function may be expressed as:

$$\text{Maximize} \sum_{t=0}^{n} Y_t =$$

$$\text{Maximize} \sum_{t=0}^{n} \sum_{i=0}^{m} [p_{ti} f_{ti}(X_{ti}) - v_{ti} f_{ti}(X_{ti}) - F_t](1 - T_t)$$

$$\frac{1}{\prod_{j=0}^{t}(1 + k_j)} \qquad (1.1.1.)$$

where Y_t is the after-tax expected net present value of the cash income of period t

p_{ti} is the price of output i in period t

$f_{ti}(X_{ti})$ is the quantity of output i in period t and is a function of X_{ti},

X_{ti} is a vector of input factors for output i in period t,

F_t is the total fixed cost in period t,

k_j is the appropriate discount rate for $j = 1, \ldots, t$.

T_t is the income tax rate for period t,

n is the number of periods in the planning horizon of the firm and may tend to ∞.

m is the number of products or outputs in period t

v_{ti} is the unit variable cost of output i in period t

1.2. THE FINANCE FUNCTION WITH CONSTRAINTS

In the formulation of the finance function in Section 1.1 the assumption is made that the firm is operating under conditions of certainty and unlimited resources or without constraints. Should capital rationing be a limiting factor this could be introduced as a constraint. There may be other constraints such as debt-equity ratio, working capital, cash availability, and so on. The finance function may then be expressed as:

$$\text{Maximize} \quad \sum_{t=0}^{n} Y_t =$$

$$\text{Maximize} \quad \sum_{t=0}^{n}\sum_{i=0}^{m} [p_{ti}f_{ti}(X_{ti}) - v_{ti}f_{ti}(X_{ti}) - F_t](1 - T_t) \frac{1}{\prod_{j=0}^{t}(1 + k_j)}$$

Subject to

$$g_{ti}(X_{ti}) \leq 0$$
$$h_{ti}[f_{ti}(X_{ti})] \leq 0$$
$$u_{ti}(p_{ti}) \leq 0$$
$$w_{ti}(l_{ti}) \leq 0 \quad \text{where } l_{ti} \text{ is the price of input factor } i \text{ in period } t,$$
$$X_{ti} \geq 0$$
$$f_{ti}(X_{ti}) \geq 0$$
$$i = 0, 1, \ldots, m$$
$$t = 0, 1, \ldots, n \qquad (1.2.1.)$$

where the constraints are expressed as functions of input factors, of outputs, and of prices of input factors and outputs.

The finance function as expressed in (1.2.1.) emphasizes that the income streams must be discounted to their present values by appropriate discount rates. If the assumption of certainty is removed the finance function will have to consider the risks of the income streams and/or the attitude to risk of the owners of the firm, and all values and cash flows may be expressed as mathematical expectations. Problems of forecasting demands and prices must be solved. Financing problems, such as the proportions of debt and equity finance and the availability and requirements of cash and working capital, may be incorporated into the model as constraints, and so standards or targets for these must be established. Optimal production and marketing activities require decisions regarding investment in fixed and current assets. Maximum risks acceptable to the firm as well as minimum acceptable rate of return have to be determined. The model in (1.2.1.) illustrates the complexity of the finance problem as well as the interrelationships and interdependence of production, investment, finance and dividend policies.

1.3. EFFECTS OF APPLYING THE MODEL

The effects of applying the model (1.2.1.) ought to be reflected in the resultant periodic balance sheets of the firm. In other words, balance sheets as well as profit and loss statements will be prepared periodically to assess the operating results and financial positions of the firm. In the context of managerial finance, the balance sheet ought to convey an optimal mix of finance as well as an optimal portfolio of assets, both being consequences of optimizing decisions.

Such financial statements, if prepared periodically, should reveal the operating activities of the firm in terms of cash flows and asset transformations. Optimal decision making is essentially determining the size and timing of such flows and transformations. They should reflect interrelationships and interdependence such as those between the cost and supply characteristics of debt and equity and their market values, and between current and fixed assets in relation to production levels and their utilization.

1.4. SUB-OPTIMIZATION

The model in Section 1.2 may be modified in a number of ways. But the practical application of such models in the real world is beset with difficulties. Nevertheless the book will try to explain concepts and techniques which are useful and which are really sub-optimization models in the sense they do not cover every facet of the firm as a whole. In reading the book the reader is respectfully requested to keep in mind the fact that a decision relating to any one section or function of the firm affects the other sections or functions though this may not be obvious from the models that will be discussed.

Single-objective mathematical programming models may not be able to cope with the increasing complexities of modern organizations with conflicting multiple goals. Hence, in practice management policies may be aimed at satisficing rather than maximizing; conflicting goals are resolved very often by compromise and sub-optimals become acceptable practical propositions. Such compromises are also necessitated by insufficient information and uncertainty. Nevertheless, mathematical programming including multiple-goal programming certainly provides promising approaches, concepts and useful insights for decision making and control. Sometimes it is also a powerful and practical tool.

1.5. SELECTED BIBLIOGRAPHY

1. Krish Bhaskers: A Multiple Objective Approach to Capital Budgeting, *Accounting and Business Research*, Winter 1979, pp 25–46.
2. C.W. Haley and L.D. Schall: The Theory of Financial Decisions.
3. L.W. Hill: The Growth of the Corporate Finance Function, Financial Executive, July 1976.
4. James P. Ignizio: Goal Programming and Extensions.
5. Y. Ijiri: Management Goals and Accounting for Control.
6. Ezra Solomon: The Theory of Financial Management.
7. Douglas Vickers: The Theory of the Firm (Production, Capital and Finance).
8. H.M. Weingartner: Mathematical Programming and the Analysis of Capital Budgeting Problems.
9. J.F. Western: The Scope and Methodology of Finance.

CHAPTER 2

Concepts of Value

2.1. FIRM VALUE IS PRESENT VALUE

In maximizing the firm value, being the objective of the finance function, the cash income streams of the operating activities of the firm are discounted by appropriate interest rates to their present value. In symbolic form:

$$V = \sum_{t=0}^{n} \frac{y_t}{\prod_{j=0}^{t} (1 + k_j)} \tag{2.1.}$$

where V is the expected net present value of the cash income streams, that is, the firm value,
y_t is the expected net after-tax cash income in period t, and
k_j is the appropriate discount rate for period $j = 0, 1, \ldots, t$

The concept of value adopted is present value.

2.2. VALUE RELATIONSHIPS

The following relationships have been established for deciding whether to continue to use an asset or to sell it:

Use if
$$PV > RC > NRV, \text{ or}$$
$$PV > NRV > RC, \text{ or}$$
$$RC > PV > NRV \tag{2.2.1.}$$

Sell if
$$NRV > PV > RC, \text{ or}$$
$$NRV > RC > PV, \text{ or}$$
$$RC > NRV > PV \tag{2.2.2.}$$

where PV is the present value of the asset,
RC is the replacement cost of the asset, and
NRV is the net realizable value of the asset.

In the first two cases, the asset will continue to be used and replaced at the end of its economic life since using it benefits the firm and its replacement is also worthwhile. But in the third case, the asset will be used but will not be replaced since its replacement cost is higher than its use or present value which is more than the cash for selling it.

In the fourth and fifth cases the firm will sell the asset and replace it for sale again. This action will be repeated because it benefits the firm more in terms of present cash value than using it. In the last case the firm will sell the asset but will not replace it as replacing it will result in a loss to the firm.

2.3. JUSTIFICATION OF PRESENT VALUE

The most important function of managerial finance is to assist management in decision-making. Decision-making essentially involves the future. And the concept of value that must of necessity take the future into account is present value. This fact alone justifies its adoption in maximizing the firm value.

If all entrepreneurs make decisions in this manner they will anticipate future events and such actions and reactions among them will result in a perfect market dealing in assets in the absence of restrictions imposed exogeneously and in the absence of monopolistic power enjoyed by any of them. Under perfect market conditions entrepreneurs who have better predictive abilities are more likely to succeed. Their predictive abilities are embodied in their computations of expected net present values of assets and proposed investment projects. These expected net present values enable them to make rational decisions regarding investing in, using, holding or disposing of assets as well as rational decisions regarding related activities such as methods, sources and mixes of finance.

2.4. BALANCE SHEET VALUES

The assets in any balance sheet at any point of time must therefore be expressed as present values if they are to be useful and relevant for decision-making. But in determining the present value of an asset its net future cash flows must be forecasted with reasonable accuracy. Besides having to fathom the economic life of the asset one has to use a correct discount rate, and though this is generally agreed to be the minimum acceptable rate of return, it is by no means indisputable what the minimum acceptable rate of return should be nor is it easy to gauge the direction in which it will change over the years. Moreover, the amount and the timing of such cash flows are at least partly the result of how these assets are combined in their use together with other input factors by the acumen and entrepreneurial skills of management.

Despite the multifarious difficulties, the expected net present value of an asset must be made available before any decision can be made in respect of that asset. But such expected net present values may be highly subjective and while useful to management in their decision-making, may not have sufficient objectivity for external users.

It is contended that if there is a market dealing in the assets of the firm, their selling prices ought to reflect closely their present values. A seller will sell his asset only if his estimate of its expected net present value is not more than its selling price, and a buyer will buy it at that price only if his estimate of its expected net present value is not less than the given selling price. In symbols:

$$\begin{aligned} PV(S) &\leq NRV \\ PV(B) &\geq NRV \end{aligned} \qquad (2.4.1.)$$

where $PV(S)$ is the seller's estimate of the expected net present value of the asset,
$PV(B)$ is the buyer's estimate of the expected net present value of the asset, and
NRV is the given selling price determined by forces of demand and supply.

If both the buyer's and the seller's estimates are accurate and both are efficient entrepreneurs, the selling price is therefore a good surrogate of the expected net present value.

2.5. MAXIMIZING FIRM VALUE

If investors in a securities market behave like entrepreneurs in an assets market, the existence of a perfect capital market can be assumed. In such a market shares of companies represent their net assets. The prices of shares represent the prices of these assets. Maximizing the firm value is then equivalent to maximizing the share price of the company since the price of one share represents the selling price of a proportionate part of the company's net assets and its selling price is a surrogate of its present value.

2.6. SELECTED BIBLIOGRAPHY

1. W.T. Baxter: Accounting Values and Inflation.
2. J.C. Bonbright: The Valuation of Property.
3. R.J. Chambers: Accounting, Evaluation and Economic Behaviour; Accounting for Inflation (Exposure Draft), 1975.
4. Edward and Bell: The Theory and Measurement of Business Income.
5. M.J. Gordon: The Investment, Financing and Valuation of the Corporation.
6. R.S. Gynther: Accounting for Price—Level Changes: Theory and Procedures.
7. Han Kang Hong: Cost and Management Accounting.
8. Parker and Harcourt (ed.): Readings in Concept and Measurement of Income.
9. R.R. Sterling (ed.): Asset Valuation and Income Determination.

CHAPTER 3

Dividend Policy and Retained Earnings

3.1. DIVIDEND POLICY UNDER PERFECT MARKET CONDITIONS

In maximizing the firm value using equation (2.1.) of Chapter 2, there is an implicit assumption that the net cash flow of each period is reinvested in the firm. The question then arises as to whether the firm value is still maximized if cash dividend is paid out of the income streams. The value of the firm at time $t = 0$ is expressed as [equation (2.1.) repeated]:

$$V = \sum_{t=0}^{n} y_t(1 + k)^{-t} \qquad (3.1.1.)$$

where k is the minimum acceptable rate of return which is assumed constant.

If the assumptions of certainty and perfect market conditions and that the firm operates in the interest of the shareholders are made, it can be shown that given the investment policy dividend policy is irrelevant where the objective is to maximize the firm value.

If the firm operates in the interest of the shareholders, maximizing the firm value is equivalent to maximizing the dividends receivable by shareholders (including the liquidating dividends, that is, the proceeds from sale of their shares or the net assets of the company in liquidation). Equation (3.1.1.) may now be expressed as:

$$V = \sum_{t=0}^{n} D_t(1 + k)^{-t} \qquad (3.1.2.)$$

The dividend and financial flow of the firm may be represented by:

$$y_t + d_t = D_t + l_t + (1 + k)d_{t-1} \qquad (3.1.3.)$$

where D_t is the dividend receivable in period t,
d_t is the amount of debt-finance at the end of period t,
d_{t-1} is the amount of debt-finance at the beginning of period t,
y_t is the expected net cash income of period t, and
I_t is the incremental investment undertaken in period t.

It can be noted that incremental investments in equation (3.1.3.) are financed from income streams and debt but not from additional equity. This simplification is justified because under conditions of certainty there are no risks; hence at any point of time k is the same for equity and for debt.
From equation (3.1.3.)

$$D_t = y_t - I_t + d_t - (1 + k)d_{t-1} \qquad (3.1.4.)$$

Substituting equation (3.1.4.) into equation (3.1.2.) gives:

$$\begin{aligned} V &= \sum_{t=0}^{n} [y_t - I_t + d_t - (1 + k)d_{t-1}](1 + k)^{-t} \\ &= y_0 - I_0 + d_0 + [y_1 - I_1 + d_1 - (1 + k)d_0](1 + k)^{-1} \\ &\quad + \sum_{t=2}^{n} [y_t - I_t + d_t - (1 + k)d_{t-1}](1 + k)^{-t} \\ &= y_0 - I_0 + (y_1 - I_1 + d_1)(1 + k)^{-1} \\ &\quad + [y_2 - I_2 + d_2 - (1 + k)d_1](1 + k)^{-2} \\ &\quad + \sum_{t=3}^{n} [y_t - I_t + d_t - (1 + k)d_{t-1}](1 + k)^{-t} \qquad (3.1.5.) \end{aligned}$$

By induction, by deleting d_t in all future periods, V becomes:

$$V = \sum_{t=0}^{n} (y_t - I_t)(1 + k)^{-t} \qquad (3.1.6.)$$

Equation (3.1.6.) shows that V is not affected by dividend policy since y_t is affected by past investment policy which is independent of dividend policy by assumption, and k is not dependent on dividend policy since it is the interest rate in a perfect market. It may be noted that the assumption of a constant k, though convenient, is not necessary.

Even if the assumption of certainty is removed, the result still holds because in a perfect market, resorting to debt or equity finance does not affect the firm's cost of capital, k, or its value under the Modigliani-Miller proposition explained in Chapter 9.

3.2. ATTRACTIVENESS OF RETAINED EARNINGS UNDER UNCERTAINTY

In reality the attractiveness of capital gains which are tax exempt is one of the decisive factors influencing the company's decision regarding its dividend policy. Issues of bonus shares and rights issues (at prices much below the current market prices) are devices often used to take advantage of the tax-free capital gains which shareholders enjoy by disposing of some of their shares.

However, some shareholders may prefer cash dividends to future capital gains even though the expected net present value of the latter is greater than that of the former. The fluctuations of share prices under conditions of uncertainty together with transaction costs and the inconvenience of share disposal are reasons why some shareholders prefer constant streams of cash dividends.

Yet, ploughing back profits has been a popular means of finance adopted by companies for many reasons. Flotation and transaction costs of issues of shares and debentures may not be economical. Besides, unless the existing shareholders are able to take up a sufficient portion of a new issue, control of the company may be diluted.

3.3. DIVIDEND POLICY UNDER UNCERTAINTY

Since the dividend policy of a company affects its ability to retain earnngs as a source of finance, it is useful to know how a company arrives at this decision. It is to be expected that every company is influenced by the special circumstances of its own case. But there must be some broad principles which can serve as guide posts to individual companies in arriving at decisions on dividend policies.

First of all, the dividends declared by a company must have some co-variation with the profits earned. In other words, a ratio of dividends to earnings may be established which is considered to be appropriate for the individual company concerned. Since it is the long-term interest of the company that is of paramount importance, the profits taken into account should include not only past profits but also expected future profits. This conclusion is based on the reasoning that shareholders expect the rewards from their investment in the company to be closely related to its earnings. If this thesis is accepted the yearly dividends should vary strictly with the yearly profits, and if profits fluctuate from year to year so should the rates of dividends declared. But in practice most companies seem to attempt to stabilize their yearly rates of dividends. Rates of dividends are dividends declared expressed as a percentage of paid-up capital or the nominal value of issued capital. If profits increase rates of dividends may also increase but less than proportionately. Rates of dividends in practice do follow the movements of profits but gradually and progressively. The policy of a stabilized rate of dividend is generally accepted as a desirable one, perhaps because this is regarded by most investors as an indication of the stability of the company as a going-concern. Hence, once a rate of dividend has been established, the inertia tends to continue unless there are compelling reasons for change.

Another relevant factor to consider is the rate of return which the re-invested profits are expected to yield from the investment opportunities open to the company. If this rate is as attractive as those available from other similar businesses in which the shareholders can invest their money, then there is justification for retaining the profits. Otherwise the shareholders are entitled to have their profits so that they can invest them elsewhere.

The third factor is the effect the dividends declared may have on the market price of the company's shares. Logically, since the value of the business is reduced by the payment of dividend, the price of its shares which represents this value should decrease if the rate of dividend increases. In practice, however, the declaration of a higher rate of dividend often causes the share price to rise. This may be the result of investors' expectations that the higher rate of dividend will continue in the future. This observed relation between the rate of dividend and the market price of shares has important bearing on some financial decisions. For instance, if a company wishes to obtain new finance by the issue of shares, a higher dividend rate declared may mean a higher issue price for the new issue. However, one must not forget the different motives of different kinds of investors. There are companies which either declare very low rates of dividends or do not declare any dividends at all, and yet the prices of their shares rise steadily because they plough back their profits for financing expansion and growth, and hence, their shares become attractive to investors seeking after capital gains.

The payment of dividends in cash depletes the company's liquid resources. So in most cases, the dividend policy of a company is co-ordinated and related to its cash budget both for the current year and for future years. Sometimes, a dividend is not paid because of acute shortage of liquid funds. This is due to poor financial planning and is not to be always emulated. Some companies are simply followers as far as dividends are concerned. So they declare the rate of dividends at which other similar businesses may have been paying. In conclusion, the individual company must decide its own dividend policy and there is no one single formula or ratio which is universally correct.

In recent years the ability of companies in general to expand by auto-financing seems to decline. And capital contributions and debt-financing seem to be the only means by which expansion or growth of a large scale can take place. Nevertheless, retained earnings are still a common source of finance for increasing modestly the scale of business operations. Retained earnings are very popular because they do not involve the company in definite obligations as borrowed resources, and this is a great attraction especially if the returns from the expected projects or operations cannot be easily forecasted.

3.4. RESTRAINTS ON RETAINED EARNINGS AND DIVIDENDS

The amount of earnings which a company can retain is influenced by at least three main factors:

(1) Rate of income taxation on a company's profits,
(2) Changes in the price level, and
(3) Dividend policy of the company.

The rate of income taxation affects the company's capacity for auto-financing in two ways. First, a proportion of the company's profits will be used to pay income tax, thus depleting the amount available for dividend payment and re-investment. And secondly, high rates of income taxation reduce the incentives of income-seeking investors to hold shares in the company. They are induced to part with their shares if they can obtain capital gains. To compensate for the loss of income to these shareholders due to their higher payments of income tax, the company may have to declare higher rates of dividends, thus leaving little retained earnings, if any.

An increase in the general price level means that to carry on the same level of business operations, the company requires more working capital in terms of monetary units. Let us illustrate this with a simple example. Doing a certain volume of business requires the carrying of an average inventory of, say, 20,000 physical units. If the cost is $1 per unit, the working capital tied up in stock is $20,000. With a rise of 20% in price, the working capital required is now $24,000.

The company also requires more funds to replace fixed assets in periods of rising prices. Let us again illustrate with a simple example. A machine having a productive life of 5 years and no residual value was installed at a cost of $100,000. At the end of its life, the amount of depreciation provided is $100,000, the annual amount being $20,000 on a straight-line basis. With an increase in price of 50% over five years, the sum required to replace the machine with one similar in capacity and operating efficiency is $150,000. This is $50,000 more than the depreciation charge over this period. Hence, if all the profits after tax during this period calculated by orthodox accounting methods were distributed as dividends, the company would in effect be returning capital (in the economic sense) to the shareholders. And if all the companies follow the same dividend policy, there is capital erosion on an industrial-wide scale.

Price increases, therefore, affect the company's capacity for auto-financing. Sufficient money profits must be set aside not for business expansion or growth but just to maintain the company's level of operations. Under such conditions, the company must be conservative in its dividend payments if it wishes to finance its expansion or growth by retained earnings. On the other hand, in periods of falling prices, the profits as arrived at on the historical cost convention basis, are understated. Hence, orthodox accounting methods contribute to capital erosion in periods of rising prices and over-savings in periods of falling prices.

The dividend policy of the company also affects its capacity for auto-financing, because the more dividends it pays, the less it has for re-investment in the business. Dividend payments are taken to mean the distribution or paying out of a company's profits to the shareholders which will result in a reduction in the value of the business. The issue of bonus shares out of profits or reserves does not constitute a payment of dividend in this sense, since the net assets of the company remain intact. Dividends are usually paid in the form of cash, but may be paid in kinds, such as, the firm's own products or the shares of other companies held by the firm.

The payment of dividends is entirely at the discretion of the directors, though there are certain legal rules which must be observed. The amount of dividend on each class of shares is recommended by the board of directors, and once the shareholders declare it at the general meeting of members, the amount of dividend so declared becomes a legal debt of the company. The general legal requirement is that dividends can be paid only out of trading profits and must not constitute a return of paid-up capital. This is for the protection of the company's creditors. A company can legally pay a dividend out of its past years' profits, or out of the current year's profit though its past trading losses have not been written off. Sometimes a company's right to declare dividends is restricted by contracts entered into by the company with creditors or debenture holders. For instance, a bank may advance a sum of money to the company on the condition that its yearly payment of dividend must not exceed a certain amount.

The amount of dividends may also be restricted by the desire to use retained earnings as a source of finance (Please see Section 10.9 of Chapter 10) as well as the investment opportunities available to the company. Sometimes a company may pay out as dividends only residual profits, that is any profits that remain after all other claims on profits have been satisfied, such as income taxes and investment requirements. The residual-profit dividend policy is sometimes adopted if the independence hypothesis is held that the firm value is not affected by its dividend policy.

3.5 SELECTED BIBLIOGRAPHY

1. W.J. Baumol: On Dividend Policy and Market Imperfection, Journal of Business, January 1963.
2. F. Black and S. Myron: The Effects of Dividend Yield and Dividend Policy on Common Stock Prices and Returns, *Journal of Financial Economics*, May 1974.
3. J.A. Brittain: Corporate Dividend Policy
4. F. Modigliani and M.H. Miller: The Cost of Capital, Corporation Finance, and the Theory of Investment, American Economic Review, June 1958.
5. F. Modigliani and M.H. Miller: Dividend Policy, Growth and the Valuation of Shares, Journal of Business, October 1961.
6. J.E. Walter: Dividend Policy: Its Influence on the Value of the Enterprise, Journal of Finance, May 1963.
7. J.C. Van Horne: Financial Management and Policy.

CHAPTER 4

Investment in Fixed Assets Under Certainty and Unlimited Resources

4.1. THE INVESTMENT PROBLEM

Since funds from whatever sources can be obtained only at a cost, the investment of such funds must be made rationally so that the firm's resources are utilized effectively to yield maximum returns in increasing the value of the business. To carry out these functions efficiently, management must be constantly aware of the many alternative uses to which the firm's resources can be put and be familiar with all the techniques and criteria by which a choice can be made among the alternatives. Management must also be able to control the need for funds as well as to predict the flows of funds in the foreseeable future. The need for funds is so pervasive that every activity of the business affects it in one way or another. The need for funds is controlled by ensuring that every asset of the firm is essential for its operations and is put to work at the highest possible level of productivity. For instance, over-stocking reduces the effective use of resources which are tied up in stock but which could be used productively elsewhere. The main need for funds lies in investment in fixed assets, stock, receivables, and cash.

The types of fixed assets and their magnitudes are determined by the nature of the business and its present as well as expected future scale of operations. Some of these problems are engineering in nature, such as the design and type of machine, and perhaps even the minimum size of the plant in some cases. Investment in fixed assets needs long-term planning since once a decision is made it cannot be easily changed without incurring a financial loss.

Forecasting the present and future market of the firm's products is as essential as forecasting the supply conditions under which the firm will operate. The forecasted demand may determine not only the size of the plant but also the decision to go into business. In some cases the optimum size of the firm is so large and the fixed costs are so high that the firm will not be started at all if demand is restricted by keen competition. Though in some cases demand can be influenced by forceful salesmanship, advertising and other marketing techniques, the additional costs that will be incurred should be taken into account. If demand for the firm's products is small but expected to increase rapidly, the initial plant installed may have reserve productive capacity to meet the expected expansion of production.

The supply conditions must be studied because they affect the decision-making process in respect of plant size and type. The degree of competition in the market both present and future, the number of firms already in the market and likelihood of increase in this number, the present total demand of the industry and likely changes in the future, all these factors influence the size and type of plant to be installed. The rate of technological advance in the industry is relevant to such a decision. A delay in installing heavy equipment is usual in the light of an expectation of the development of better machines. The trend of service costs of manufacture, such as the trend of labour rates and availability of skilled labour, can influence the decision to invest in automated machines or to use labour-intensive equipment.

The location of the plant and the investment in land is determined generally by economic considerations. Here, the choice will be of the location that promises the maximum net returns or the minimum costs, and factors such as proximity to market, raw materials, power and water, availability of labour, cost and convenience of communication, ancillary services, facilities for workers, grants from government or governmental agencies, pioneer status (entitling so many years of taxfree profits), and other regulations—all these are pertinent for consideration.

4.2. THE NATURE OF CAPITAL BUDGETING

A firm must incur expenditure of various types in order to ensure its continuity as well as its growth and expansion. Some of these outflows of expenditure are expected to generate inflows of benefits to the firm in the same year as they are incurred. These are termed revenue expenditure. Others are expected to generate inflows of benefits to the firm over a period of years and are termed capital expenditure. Capital expenditure may be classified into three different categories, depending on the purpose of its incurrence:

(1) For expansion and growth,
(2) For replacement,
(3) For staff welfare facilities.

The outflows of these types of capital expenditure can be quantified. But while the inflows of benefits from expansion or replacement of plant can reasonably be quantified, the quantification of benefits from staff welfare facilities is beset with difficulties.

4.3. CONTINUOUS BUDGETING

The incurrence of a capital expenditure often commits the firm to a course of action over several years. Hence, it is considered to be of sufficient importance for decisions on capital expenditure to be made by the highest authority, very often the board of directors. Forecasting the inflows of benefits from a project increases in difficulty the longer the economic life of the project is. This means that capital expenditure planning should always be long-term, thus ensuring that the most economical resources are used. It is desirable that the capital budget should form part of an integrated overall development plan of the firm. For purposes of control and review, however, the long-term capital budget is very often divided into annual budgets. Continuous budgeting is recommended as a tool for attaining this objective. Suppose the firm has a five-year plan. At the end of the first year, the plan will be reviewed in the light of what has been achieved and the changed circumstances of the firm and its environment, the remaining four annual budgets may have to be revised and another year's programme is added. In this way the firm will have at any point of time an up-to-date five-year plan.

4.4. INVESTMENT MODEL

If an investment model is to be built, it should help management to obtain information in the following areas:

(1) the relative profitability in order of priority of prospective projects,

(2) the investment magnitude required to generate the expected profitability, and
(3) the best sources and methods of financing to adopt.

In its bare essentials, the investment model is simply a comparison of the outflows of expenditure and the inflows of benefits of projects:

(x)	Inflows of Benefits	+
(y)	Outflows of Expenditure	−
(z)	Result	+ or −

If management has to decide whether to invest in a project and there are no other projects to choose from, the criterion is simple: invest only if (z) is positive. However, investment opportunities are often numerous and management may have to decide on the degree of desirability of the different projects. In other words, management would like to place the prospective projects in the order of priority, and this must be in the order of profitability, if economic considerations alone are taken into account. The project on the top of the scale of preferences is the project having the highest profitability index obtained thus $\frac{x}{y}$. But the economic evaluation of capital expenditure is not so simple as the model would suggest, since there are different ways of measuring (x) and (y), and thus (z).

4.5. DIFFERENT TECHNIQUES OF EVALUATION

The main methods of evaluation are:

(1) Pay-back period,
(2) Annual Return on Average Investment,
(3) Cost-Volume-Profit
(4) Internal Rate of Return
(5) Net Present Value.

The example in Table 4.5.1 will be used to illustrate the different techniques.

Mr Lock proposes to invest his savings of $500,000 in a project that will yield an annual income of at least 10% after tax. He considers all the investment opportunities available to him and finally concludes that the three projects which he terms *A*, *B*, *C*

Table 4.5.1

Project	*Outflow of Expenditure at time Year 0 ($'000)*	*Economic Life (in years)*	*Scrap Value at end of Life*
A	500	5	nil
B	500	5	nil
C	500	5	nil

are worthy of further evaluation. Each of the project requires the same initial outlay of $500,000 and has an economic life of five years. The forecasted profit and loss statements and balance sheets, and the projected cash flows are given in Tables 4.5.2 and 4.5.3 respectively.

Income tax is paid at the rate of 40% of the annual net profit one year after the net profit is earned. Mr Lock intends to withdraw from or introduce into the business at the end of each year any cash necessary to ensure that no profits or losses are carried forward in the balance sheet. The original outlay of each project is depreciated over five years by the straight line method. Cash flows are assumed to take place only at the end of each year.

4.5.1. Pay-Back Period Method

Under this method, the entrepreneur attempts to ascertain the number of years the benefits derived from the project take to recover the outlay. The solution under this method is shown below:

Project			*Pay-back Period (Years)*	*Order of Priority*
A	(100 + 80 + 110 + 140 + 70 = 500)	$4\frac{70}{620} \simeq$	4.11	3
B	(200 + 260 − 170 + 210 = 500)	$3\frac{210}{580} \simeq$	3.36	1
C	(120 + 140 + 80 + 160 = 500)	$3\frac{160}{240} \simeq$	3.67	2

Table 4.5.2.

Forecasted Profit and Loss Statements for the Year Ended 31st December

	YEAR 1			*YEAR 2*			*YEAR 3*		
	A $'000	*B* $'000	*C* $'000	*A* $'000	*B* $'000	*C* $'000	*A* $'000	*B* $'000	*C* $'000
Sales revenue	450	600	550	800	1000	550	1200	350	550
Less Variable costs	280	390	340	570	550	340	900	190	340
Fixed costs	120	110	110	130	150	110	150	110	110
	400	500	450	700	700	450	1050	300	450
Net Profit	50	100	100	100	300	100	150	50	100
Drawing/ (Introducing of Cash)	50	100	100	80	260	60	110	(70)	60
Income tax (40%)	—	—	—	20	40	40	40	120	40
	50	100	100	100	300	100	150	50	100

Forecasted Balance Sheet as at 31st December

	A $'000	*B* $'000	*C* $'000	*A* $'000	*B* $'000	*C* $'000	*A* $'000	*B* $'000	*C* $'000
Proprietorship	500	500	500	500	500	500	500	500	500
Trade creditors	200	250	100	300	400	100	500	100	150
	700	750	600	800	900	600	1000	600	650
Fixed Asset	400	400	400	300	300	300	200	200	200
Stock	100	200	100	200	200	100	300	50	150
Trade debtors	150	50	80	250	300	100	450	350	180
Cash	50	100	20	50	100	100	50	0	120
	700	750	600	800	900	600	1000	600	650

YEAR 4			*YEAR 5*			*YEAR 6*		
A $'000	*B* $'000	*C* $'000	*A* $'000	*B* $'000	*C* $'000	*A* $'000	*B* $'000	*C* $'000
1600	350	550	1800	350	550			
1250	190	340	1400	190	340			
150	110	110	150	110	110			
1400	300	450	1550	300	450			
200	50	100	250	50	100			
140	30	60	170	30	60	(100)	(20)	(40)
60	20	40	80	20	40	100	20	40
200	50	100	250	50	100	0	0	0

A $'000	*B* $'000	*C* $'000	*A* $'000	*B* $'000	*C* $'000	*A* $'000	*B* $'000	*C* $'000
500	500	500	500	500	500			
800	400	100	0	0	0			
1300	900	600	500	500	500			
100	100	100	0	0	0			
350	50	100	0	0	0			
800	200	100	0	0	0			
50	550	300	500	500	500			
1300	900	600	500	500	500			

Table 4.5.3
Forecasted Cash Flows

	YEAR 1			YEAR 2			YEAR 3		
	A $'000	B $'000	C $'000	A $'000	B $'000	C $'000	A $'000	B $'000	C $'000
Net Profit	50	100	100	100	300	100	150	50	100
Add Depreciation	100	100	100	100	100	100	100	100	100
Increase/ (Decrease) in trade creditors	200	250	100	100	150	0	200	(300)	50
	300	350	200	200	250	100	300	(200)	150
Less Increase/ (Decrease) in trade debtors	150	50	80	100	250	20	200	50	80
Increase/ (Decrease) in stock	100	200	100	100	0	0	100	(150)	50
	250	250	180	200	250	20	300	(100)	130
Cash from Trading Operations	100	200	120	100	300	180	150	(50)	120
Less: Income tax paid	0	0	0	20	40	40	40	120	40
Net Cash Inflows from Project	100	200	120	80	260	140	110	(170)	80

YEAR 4			*YEAR 5*			*YEAR 6*		
A $'000	*B* $'000	*C* $'000	*A* $'000	*B* $'000	*C* $'000	*A* $'000	*B* $'000	*C* $'000
200	50	100	250	50	100			
100	100	100	100	100	100			
300	300	(50)	(800)	(400)	(100)			
400	400	50	(700)	(300)	0			
350	(150)	(80)	(800)	(200)	(100)			
50	0	(50)	(350)	(50)	(100)			
400	(150)	(130)	(1150)	(250)	(200)			
200	600	280	700	0	300			
60	20	40	80	20	40	100	20	40
140	580	240	620	(20)	260	(100)	(20)	(40)

One outstanding defect of this method is that it does not measure profitability. However, it may still be useful if it is used in conjunction with the other methods, especially if liquidity rather than profitability is of paramount importance. A project may not be as profitable as another, yet it may be chosen in preference to the more profitable one if it brings in cash at the time when the firm needs it badly or when the firm considers as important the speedy recovery of its outlay.

4.5.2. Annual Return on Average Investment

The mechanics of this method are shown below:

	PROJECTS		
	A	*B*	*C*
Total Profit	$750,000	$550,000	$500,000
Average Annual Profit	$150,000	$110,000	$100,000
Average Investment	$\frac{\$500,000}{2}$	$\frac{\$500,000}{2}$	$\frac{\$500,000}{2}$
	= $250,000	$250,000	$250,000
Rate of Return	$\frac{150,000}{250,000}$	$\frac{110,000}{250,000}$	$\frac{100,000}{250,000}$
	= 0.60	0.44	0.40
Order of Priority	1	2	3

This method has the defect that it does not recognise the timing of the inflow of benefits and of the outflow of expenditure. However, this defect is avoided if the following conditions hold true:

(1) The outflows of expenditure of the different projects occur at the same point of time,
(2) The inflows of benefits are even and constant,
(3) Their economic lives are the same.

4.5.3. Cost-Volume-Profit Method

This method is sometimes used to evaluate the viability of a proposed investment project and to compare the operating costs of different machines in either installing or replacing plant and equipment. For this analysis all costs involved, costs to manufacture and sell and other necessary operating costs, are segregated into their fixed and variable components. Fixed costs are defined as costs which remain constant within the relevant range of output and the predetermined period of time and variable costs as costs which vary proportionately and directly with outputs. The analysis is carried out as follows:

Sales revenue − variable costs − fixed costs = profit

$$S - V - F = P \qquad (4.5.3.1.)$$

where S is the dollar sales revenue
P is the total profit
V is the total variable cost
and F is the total fixed cost of the period.

At the break-even point neither profit nor loss is made, hence,

$$S - V = F \qquad (4.5.3.2.)$$

Multiplying both sides of the equation by S results in $S(S - V) = SF$. Therefore, the break-even point is:

$$S^* = \frac{FS}{S - V} \qquad (4.5.3.3.)$$

From the illustration given in Table 4.5.2., the break-even points are (using the first year's forecasts where the figures are in thousands):

For Project A,

$$S^* = \frac{(120)(450)}{450 - 280} \simeq \$317.647 \qquad (4.5.3.4.)$$

For Project B,

$$S_B^* = \frac{(110)(600)}{600 - 390} \simeq \$314.286 \qquad (4.5.3.5.)$$

For Project C,

$$S_C^* = \frac{(110)(550)}{550 - 340} \simeq \$288.095 \qquad (4.5.3.6.)$$

Thus cost-profit-volume analysis indicates the economic feasibility of the project if demand is a key factor. It also indicates the sensitivity of profit to sales volume changes. But the technique is a static device with the assumption of linear costs and revenue behaviour. It also ignores the time value of money. Nevertheless, it is a simple technique useful for small enterprises without strong financial resources. Such small businesses may not be able to withstand initial trading losses for too many years even though the net present value of the venture is positive when the planning horizon is extended many years into the future.

4.5.3.1. The Problem of Deciding Whether to Buy or to Manufacture

A product usually consists of many components. And a manufacturer may have to decide whether to buy a component from another firm or to manufacture it himself. Break-even techniques are useful in solving this kind of problem. Let us assume that the manufacturer estimates that to produce a particular component, he has to incur an additional fixed cost of $50,000 and a variable cost of $15 per component. If he buys it from another firm, he has to pay $20 per component. Should he buy or manufacture? The answer can be obtained from a break-even type of chart as shown.

If x is the number of units of the component required, $\$20x$ will be the total cost of purchasing it. The total cost of manufacturing it is the sum of the total fixed cost $50,000 and the total variable cost $15x$, that is $\$(50{,}000 + 15x)$. At the point of

Figure 4.5.3.1.

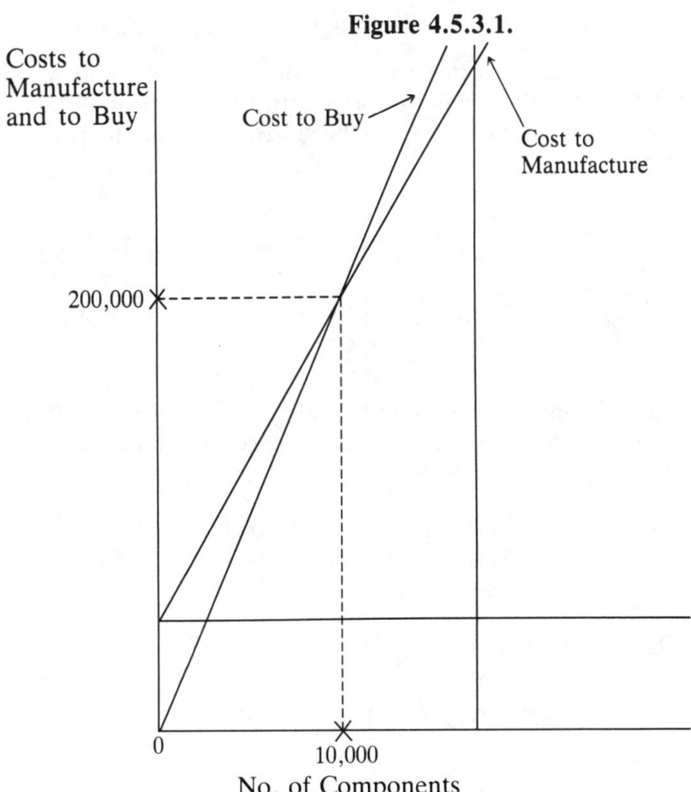

indifference whether to buy or manufacture, the total cost of purchase and that of manufacture must be the same, that is:

$$20x = 50{,}000 + 15x$$

$$\therefore \quad x^* = \frac{50{,}000}{5} = 10{,}000 \text{ units}$$

Hence, if the requirement exceeds 10,000 units it is cheaper to manufacture. Nevertheless, non-quantifiable factors, such as future prices and availability of supply, must always be considered.

4.5.3.2. The Problem of Replacing or Installing Machines

A manufacturer has often to choose one type of machine among alternatives which he will install or with which he will replace an old machine. The problem may be stated in a simplified form as follows:

	MACHINE		
	Type A	*Type B*	*Type C*
Annual Fixed Costs	$50,000	$100,000	$200,000
Variable Cost per Unit of Output	$20	$10	$5

Let x be the number of units of output at which the total costs of production are the same between any two machines. The total annual production costs are:

$$\begin{aligned} &\text{Machine } A\text{:} \quad 20x + 50{,}000 \\ &\text{Machine } B\text{:} \quad 10x + 100{,}000 \\ &\text{Machine } C\text{:} \quad 5x + 200{,}000 \end{aligned}$$

The indifference point x^* between Machine A and Machine B is obtained as follows:

$$20x + 50{,}000 = 10x + 100{,}000$$

$$\therefore \quad x^* = \frac{50{,}000}{10} = 5{,}000 \text{ units}$$

The break-even point between Machine B and C is derived from solving for x the following equation:

$$10x + 100{,}000 = 5x + 200{,}000$$

$$\therefore \quad x^* = \frac{100{,}000}{5} = 20{,}000 \text{ units}$$

And the indifference point between Machine A and C is:

$$20x + 50{,}000 = 5x + 200{,}000$$

$$\therefore \quad x^* = \frac{150{,}000}{15} = 10{,}000 \text{ units}$$

The choice of Machine is therefore *A* if requirement is below 5,000 units; *B* if requirement is between 5,000 and 20,000; and *C* if it exceeds 20,000 units.

Though cost-volume-profit is a useful technique its limitations must be recognized, and the assumptions that must be made should always be borne in mind so that misleading conclusions may be avoided.

4.5.4. Internal Rate of Return Method

Under this method a discount rate must be chosen which will discount all the incremental cash flows, both inflows and outflows, from a proposed project to their present values so that the algebraic sum of their present values is zero. This rate of interest is arrived at by trial and error. It is sometimes called the marginal efficiency of capital. With the same example from Table 4.5.3, the results are shown in Table 4.5.4.1. A project is acceptable if its internal rate of return is not less than the minimum acceptable rate of return.

Table 4.5.4.1.

Project	*Present Value of Cash Outflow*	*Internal Rate of Return*	*Ranking (Order of Priority)*
A	$500,000	0.19	2
B	$500,000	0.21	1
C	$500,000	0.16	3

The internal rate of return is compared with the minimum acceptable rate of return. If the internal rate of return is greater than the minimum acceptable rate of return, the project is accepted. If it is smaller than the minimum acceptable rate of return, the project is rejected. Ranking of projects in order of priority is in accordance with the internal rates of return. Sections 4.7.2 and 4.7.3 explain the likely problems with this method. The rates given in Table 4.5.4.1 are thus subject to the remarks made there.

4.5.5. Net Present Value Method

Under this method the cash inflows and cash outflows expected from a project are discounted to their present values at the minimum acceptable rate of return. If the algebraic sum of their present values is positive, the project is accepted. If it is negative, the project is rejected. The solution to the same example is given below:

Net Present Value Method
(Minimum Acceptable Rate = 10%)

Project	*Present Value of Cash Outflow*	*Present Value of Cash Inflow*	*Present Value of Net Cash Flow*	*Ranking*
A	500,000	663,815	163,815	1
B	500,000	641,411	141,411	2
C	500,000	587,682	87,682	3

4.5.6. A Comparison of the Five Methods

The first three methods fail to recognize that money has a time value. In other words, in order to have a valid basis of comparison, all cash flows must be reduced to their present values or values at the same point of time.

The internal rate of return method assumes that the cash generated from the investment is re-invested in the business at the internal rate of return whereas the net present value method assumes the cost of capital to be the re-investment rate. The two methods sometimes give different answers to the same problem.

4.6. ASSUMPTIONS OF THE FIVE METHODS

The above analysis is based on the assumption that all investment opportunities have been included for consideration. Investment opportunities are classified into independent investment projects in such a way that the acceptance or rejection of one project will not affect the other projects. This implies that two or more investment opportunities that are dependent on one another are classified as one project. For instance, the construction of a car park within the premises of a supermarket also to be constructed and the supermarket itself must be considered as one single investment project if the car park affects the cash flows of the supermarket. For each investment project all possible combinations of opportunities are taken into account and only the best combination is to be included for consideration as a proposed investment project.

The above five methods are based on the assumption of certainty and unlimited resources.

4.7. SOME PROBLEMS IN THE INTERNAL RATE OF RETURN METHOD

4.7.1. Cash Flows All of the Same Sign

The internal rate of return method cannot be used if the cash flows are either all positive or all negative, such as those relating to minimizing operating costs when selecting alternative machines to replace an existing one.

4.7.2. Multiple or Imaginary Rates of Return

The internal rate of return method involves solving the following equation for k:

$$\sum_{t=0}^{n} C_t \, (1 + k)^{-t} = 0 \qquad (4.7.2.1.)$$

which may be written as:

$$C_0 + C_1X^1 + C_2X^2 + \ldots + C_nX^n = 0 \qquad (4.7.2.2.)$$

where C_t is the net cash flow in period t, and
k is the internal rate of return.

This is a polynomial equation of degree n. Thus if there is more than one change of algebraic sign in the cash flows of a proposed project, there will be multiple or imaginary internal rates of return and the internal rate of return method may not sometimes be applicable.

4.7.3. Mutually Exclusive Investment Projects

Investment projects are independent if the acceptance or rejection of any one of them does not affect the desirability of another or the others. Investment projects are mutually exclusive if only one of them can be chosen, that is, the choice of one excludes all the others. For example, using coal, petroleum or nuclear energy as fuel for a power station. The use of internal rates of return for ranking these mutually exclusive investment projects may lead to an incorrect decision where there are unlimited resources. Table 4.7.3. illustrates this.

Table 4.7.3.
Net Cash Flows

Project	*Year 0*	*Year 1*	*Year 2*	*Year 3*	*10% Net Present Value*	*Internal Rate of Return*
	$	$	$	$	$	
A	− 800	250	250	1,040	415	0.31
B	−2,500	300	300	2,700	58	0.11
C	−3,100	740	760	3,900	1,130	0.25
B–A	−1,700	50	50	1,660		0.01
C–A	−2,300	490	510	2,860		0.22

According to the internal rates of return, project *A* should be chosen and projects *B* and *C* excluded. But according to the net present values, *C* should be selected. One may argue that the internal rate of return is the correct criterion since the difference of $(3,100–800 = 2,300) in the initial outlays between *A* and *C* can be invested elsewhere and together they will earn more net present value than project *C* alone. This argument is correct if the firm has only $3,100 to invest and the difference of $2,300 can be invested elsewhere yielding an internal rate of return of 25% or more. But in the absence of capital rationing new projects can still be undertaken together with project *C*. Hence, in the absence of capital rationing, the net present value method provides a better criterion.

However, the internal rate of return method can still be validly applied under the assumption of no capital rationing if one evaluates the differences in the cash flows of the mutually exclusive projects as illustrated in the last two rows of Table 4.7.3., where the internal rates of return of the cash flows of (*B*–*A*) and (*C*–*A*) indicate clearly that *C* is the preferred project.

4.8. PROJECTS WITH UNEQUAL ECONOMIC LIVES

Suppose a machine can be replaced by either a fully-automatic or semi-automatic one which have different economic lives, say 2 years and 3 years, respectively, but which can perform the given task equally well. To make them comparable entails deciding what should be done when the machines are no longer productive, whether they will be replaced with identical models and how many times they will be so replaced. No valid comparison is likely unless these are known, but they depend on a host of factors that will prevail in the future. A common way of evaluating investment projects with unequal economic lives is to assume that they will continue up to the least common multiple of their lives. Table 4.8 illustrates this.

Table 4.8.
Net Cash Flows

Protect	*Life*	*Year 0*	*Year 1*	*Year 2*	*Year 3*	*Year 4*	*Year 5*	*Year 6*	*10% Net Present Value*
	Years	$	$	$	$	$	$	$	$
A	2	−1,000		−1,000		−1,000			
			800	900	800	900	800	900	1,182
B	3	−2,000			−2,000				
			800	1,500	1,000	800	1,500	1,000	1,257

Project *B* is preferred to Project *A*

4.9. FOREIGN EXCHANGE REQUIREMENTS AND EARNINGS

In capital expenditure decisional analysis, the cash flows that must be discounted could contain foreign exchange requirements and earnings. For a country as a whole, especially one having difficulties of balance of payments, the expected cash flows of proposed projects should be examined in the light of their foreign exchange earnings and requirements. If this is done, one may select Project *B* though it is economically more beneficial to choose Project *A* because the former enjoys foreign exchange advantages over the latter. This is best illustrated with an example.

Table 4.9.
Expected Cash Flows

	PROJECT *A*		PROJECT *B*	
Year	*Local Currency*	*Foreign Exchange*	*Local Currency*	*Foreign Exchange*
0	−10,000	−15,000	−20,000	− 5,000
1	+ 5,000	+15,000	+ 5,000	+15,000
2	+15,000	+ 2,000	+ 1,000	+15,000
3	+10,000	+ 2,000	+ 1,000	+10,000
4	+10,000	+ 1,000	+ 1,000	+ 1,000

Using the net present value method, and assuming a minimum acceptable rate of return of 10%, the solutions are tabulated below:

Net Present Value Method
(without taking foreign exchange into consideration)

PROJECT *A*

Year	*Total Cash Flows*	*Discounting Factor (10%)*	*Present Value of Cash Flows*
0	−25,000	1.000	−25,000
1	+20,000	.909	+18,180
2	+17,000	.826	+14,042
3	+12,000	.751	+ 9,012
4	+11,000	.683	+ 7,513
		Net Cash Flow =	$ +23,747

Net Present Value Method
(without taking foreign exchange into consideration)

PROJECT *B*

Year	*Total Cash Flows*	*Discounting Factor (10%)*	*Present Value of Cash Flows*
0	−25,000	1.000	−25,000
1	+20,000	.909	+18,180
2	+16,000	.826	+13,216
3	+11,000	.751	+ 8,261
4	+ 2,000	.683	+ 1,366
		Net Cash Flow = $	+16,023

	Project *A*	Project *B*
Profitability Index =	$\frac{48,747}{25,000}$	$\frac{41,023}{25,000}$
	= 1.95	1.64

Economically, therefore Project A is preferable. If we take foreign exchange into account the position appears below:

Net Present Value Method
(From viewpoint of Foreign Exchange)

PROJECT *A*

Year	*Total Cash Flow*	*Discounting Factor (10%)*	*Present Value of Cash Flows of Foreign Exchange*
0	−15,000	1.000	−15,000
1	+15,000	.909	+13,635
2	+ 2,000	.826	+ 1,652
3	+ 2,000	.751	+ 1,502
4	+ 1,000	.683	+ 683
		Net Present Value = $	+ 2,472

Net Present Value Method
(From viewpoint of Foreign Exchange)

PROJECT *B*

Year	*Total Cash Flow*	*Discounting Factor (10%)*	*Present Value of Cash Flows of Foreign Exchange*
0	− 5,000	1.000	− 5,000
1	+15,000	.909	+13,635
2	+15,000	.826	+12,390
3	+10,000	.751	+ 7,510
4	+ 1,000	.683	+ 683
		Net Present Value =	$ +29,218

	Project *A*	Project *B*
Profitability Index =	$\frac{17,472}{15,000}$	$\frac{34,218}{5,000}$
=	1.16	6.84

Taking into account the foreign exchange requirements and earnings, we find that Project *B* is preferable. Perhaps, in evaluating proposed alternative investment projects, both angles must be scrutinized before a decision is made.

4.10. ANOTHER EXAMPLE

The Fuel Division of Lee Company (Private) Ltd has reported net sales of $800,000 for each of the past three years. The costs of operation during each of these years, including depreciation of $26,000, have amounted to $810,000. There is a little prospect for any improvement. The company's managing director, while not optimistic, believes that the present rate of operation can be continued for 10 years, thus enabling the division to recover a large portion if not all of its fixed investment. At the end of 10 years it is estimated that $20,000 can be realised in salvage value from the sale of the plant and equipment, which at the present time has an undepreciated cost of $280,000.

The Division's manager believes that the division should accept an offer of \$95,000 for the plant and equipment and discontinue operations, saying that other investment opportunities can give a 12% return.

The other four divisions of the company have been very profitable and are independent of the Fuel Division.

Annual Cash Flows from Continued Operations:

Annual sales revenue		\$800,000
Less Annual operating costs		\$810,000
Annual net operating loss		\$ 10,000
Add Annual depreciation		\$ 26,000
Annual net operating cash inflow		\$ 16,000
Annual tax savings from net loss (0.4)(10,000)		\$ 4,000
	Total	\$ 20,000

Net Present Value from Continued Operations:

Present value of net cash inflow for 10 years (20,000 × 5.65)	\$113,000
Present value of salvage value of plant and equipment (20,000 × 0.322)	\$ 6,440
Total Net Present Value from Continued Operations	\$119,440

Net Present Value from Discontinuing Operations:

Disposal of plant and equipment		\$ 96,000
Book (written-down) value of plant and equipment	\$280,000	
Disposal value at present	\$ 95,000	
Loss (entitled to balancing allowance)	\$185,000	
Tax savings from balancing allowance (0.4)(185,000)		\$ 74,000
	Total	\$170,000

It is thus better to discontinue operations, other things being equal. The present value of \$1 received annually at 12% for 10 years is \$5.65 (obtainable from Table 2 of Appendix C) and the present value of \$1 received at the end of 10 years at 12% is \$0.322 (obtainable from Table 1 of Appendix C).

4.11. SELECTED BIBLIOGRAPHY

1. P.W. Bacon: The Evaluation of Mutually Exclusive Investments, *Financial Management*, Summer, 1977.
2. H. Bierman, Jr. and S. Smidt: The Capital Budgeting Decision.
3. Han Kang Hong: Cost and Management Accounting
4. J.C.T. Mao: Quantitative Analysis of Financial Decisions.
5. J.C.T. Mao: Survey of Capital Budgeting: Theory and Practice, Journal of Finance, 1970.
6. A.J. Merrett and A. Sykes: Capital Budgeting and Company Finance.
7. K.A. Middleton: The Economics of Capital Expenditure.
8. A.A. Robichek and S.C. Myers: Optimal Financial Decisions.
9. Ezra Solomon: The Arithmetic of Capital Budgeting Decisions, *Journal of Business*, April 1956
10. J.C. Van Horne: Financial Management and Policy.

CHAPTER 5

Investment in Fixed Assets Under Certainty and Capital Rationing

5.1. THE FIRM OBJECTIVE

In the approach to capital budgeting in the last chapter, there is an implicit assumption that the firm's resources are unlimited. If that is the case, all investment projects which give a positive net present value under the present value method will be accepted. However if the firm is operating under constraining conditions of limiting resources, it is the profitability of the firm rather than that of individual projects which will be maximized by combining and using the limited resources optimally. Thus an individual project though more profitable than another may be rejected in favour of the latter which places less strain on the resources of the firm. Mathematical programming considers specifically all the limited resources. In fact, all constraints of the firm are embodied in the model so that the opportunity set may be identified. Besides narrowing down the number of possibilities, mathematical programming offers greater scope for realizing the objectives of the firm under realistic conditions in which the firm is operating. The objective of the firm is often taken to be maximizing profitability as measured by net present value.

5.2. LINEAR PROGRAMMING MODEL

One way of incorporating capital rationing into the capital budgeting model is to use a linear programming model where the limited sums available for investing are included as constraint constants. The following is an example:

Maximize $$\sum_{j=1}^{n} P_j x_j$$

Subject to $\sum_{j=1}^{n} R_{tj}x_j \le K_t,\ t = 1, \ldots, m$

$$0 \le x_j \le 1,\ j = 1, \ldots, n \qquad (5.2)$$

where R_{tj} is the cash requirement of project x_j in period t,
P_j is the net present value of project x_j,
K_t is the total amount of cash available in period t for investing in the proposed projects.

The constraints show that for any period t, the capital ration K_t cannot be exceeded. One obvious limitation of the above model is that it permits the admissibility of a fraction of a project. Unless every proposed investment has the property of divisibility, the linear programming model may not be appropriate for solving this kind of problems.

An illustration will clarify the problem.

$$P_1 = \$400{,}000; \quad P_2 = \$300{,}000$$
$$K_1 = \$200{,}000; \quad K_2 = \$210{,}000$$
$$R_{11} = \$200{,}000; \quad R_{12} = \$100{,}000$$
$$R_{21} = \$140{,}000; \quad R_{22} = \$210{,}000$$

Maximize $Z = 400{,}000x_1 + 300{,}000x_2$

Subject to

$$200{,}000x_1 + 100{,}000x_2 \le 200{,}000$$
$$140{,}000x_1 + 210{,}000x_2 \le 210{,}000$$
$$0 \le x_1 \le 1$$
$$0 \le x_2 \le 1$$

The optimal solutions are:

$$x_1^* = \tfrac{3}{4},\ x_2^* = \tfrac{1}{2}$$
$$Z^* = \tfrac{3}{4}(400{,}000) + \tfrac{1}{2}(300{,}000)$$
$$= \$450{,}000$$

The optimal solutions suggest investing in $\frac{3}{4}$ of project one and $\frac{1}{2}$ of project 2. This may not always be feasible. A zero-one programming model like the one in Section 5.4 will provide the optimal solutions:

$$x_1^* = 1,\ x_2^* = 0,\ Z^* = \$400{,}000.$$

5.3. INTEGER PROGRAMMING MODEL

Most of the investment projects possess the characteristic that they must be accepted in total. To avoid the admission of a fraction of a proposed project, integer programming may be employed. The following is an example:

$$\text{Maximize} \quad \sum_{j=1}^{n} P_j x_j$$

$$\text{Subject to} \quad \sum_{j=1}^{n} R_{tj} x_j \leq K_t,\ t = 1, \ldots, m, \tag{5.3}$$

$$x_j = 1, 2, \ldots, n \qquad j = 1, \ldots, n$$

where the symbols mean the same as in (5.2) except that x_j must be an integer.

The last constraint indicates that x_j can only take on integers. This integer programming model has the disadvantage that any project can be duplicated, for instance, if $x_3 = 2$.

5.4. ZERO-ONE PROGRAMMING MODEL

The objective of the firm could be to maximize profitability as measured by net present value. And the objective function will then be:

$$\text{Maximize} \quad \left[PX = \sum_{j=1}^{n} P_j x_j \right]$$

where P_j is the net present value of project x_j.

A zero-one programming model could have the following constraints:

$$
\begin{aligned}
& AX \leq B \\
& \sum_{i=\alpha+1}^{r} x_i \leq 1 \qquad\qquad\qquad\qquad\qquad\qquad (5.4) \\
& \sum_{i=\alpha+1}^{r} x_i \geqq 1 \qquad r \leqq n, \ \alpha \geqq 0 \\
& x_j = 0, 1 \qquad j = 1, 2, \ldots, n.
\end{aligned}
$$

Where A is a mxn matrix, X is a $nx1$ column vector, B is a $mx1$ column vector, J is a set of indexes where $j \in J$, and S is a subset of J where $i \in S$.

Writing out the constraints in full gives:

$$
\begin{aligned}
a_{11}x_1 + a_{12}x_2 + \cdots + a_{1n}x_n &\leqq b_1 \\
a_{21}x_1 + a_{22}x_2 + \cdots + a_{2n}x_n &\leqq b_2 \\
a_{31}x_1 + a_{32}x_2 + \cdots + a_{3n}x_n &\leqq b_3 \\
\vdots \qquad\qquad\qquad\qquad & \quad \vdots \\
a_{m1}x_1 + a_{m2}x_2 + \cdots + a_{mn}x_n &\leqq b_m \\
x_{\alpha+1} + x_{\alpha+2} + \cdots + x_r &\leqq 1 \\
x_{\alpha+1} + x_{\alpha+2} + \cdots + x_r &\geqq 1 \\
x_j = 0, 1 \qquad j = 1, 2, \ldots, n.
\end{aligned}
$$

The first constraint could mean that project x_1 requires a_{11} man-hours, x_2 requires a_{12} man-hours, ... , and x_n requires a_{1n} man-hours, and it must be ensured that the total available man-hours b_1 must not be exceeded. The other constraints mean that other kinds of resources must not be exceeded. For instance, suppose cash outflows required for the projects over the next three years must not exceed the following:

Year	*Maximum Cash Outflows*
1	b_2
2	b_3
3	b_4

The second constraint then means that in the first year project x_1 requires a cash outflow of a_{21}, x_2 requires a cash outflow of $a_{22}, \ldots, x_n$ requires a_{2n}, and the total cash outflow in the first year must not exceed b_2. The third constraint shows that in the second year project x_1 requires a cash outflow of a_{31}, x_2 requires $a_{32}, \ldots,$ x_n requires a_{3n}, and the total cash outflow in the second year must not exceed b_3. Similarly the fourth constraint explains that in the third year the total cash outflow must not exceed b_4. The remaining $m - 4$ constraints give the rest of the limited resources which must not be exceeded or other binding conditions.

The last two constraints show that projects numbering from $x_{\alpha+1}$ to x_r are mutually exclusive and that only one of them can and must be selected. For instance, if projects x_8 and x_9 are mutually exclusive in the sense that only one of the two must be selected, the two additional constraints will be: $x_8 + x_9 \leqq 1$ and $x_8 + x_9 \geqq 1$. If only one or none may be accepted, then only the first constraint is required, namely, $x_8 + x_9 \leqq 1$. If project x_{10} must be selected, this constraint will be $x_{10} = 1$. If project x_{11} is conditional on the acceptance of project x_{12}, this will necessitate the constraint $x_{11} \leqq x_{12}$.

And finally using a zero-one programming model ensures that if $x_j = 1$, the jth project is accepted, and if $x_j = 0$, the jth project is rejected.

The consideration of the relevant time period is involved in the application of the above model and this necessitates the determination of the firm's planning horizon. The model becomes very complicated if it incorporates a continuing series of projects extending indefinitely into the future. If the planning horizon is finite, the model could try to maximize the present value of all projects commenced at any time from initial time t_0 to terminal time, t_1 as well as the present value of the firm at terminal time. The model is a very useful one in that it gives not only the optimal allocation of the firm's resources, but also their marginal values as well as their relative scarcity. It may be useful to know that the number of programming models for capital budgeting is very large, including some which take into account conditions of risks and uncertainties.

5.4.1. An Example

Resors Limited has embarked upon an expansion programme and after a preliminary survey has decided that the following six projects whose net present values are all positive are worthy of further consideration:

Project Number	*Net Present Value ($'000)*	*Cash Requirements*			*Daily Maximum Production Capacity ('000 units)*
		1st Year ($'000)	*2nd Year ($'000)*	*3rd Year ($'000)*	
1	40	60	40	40	400
2	100	50	40	20	600
3	25	40	10	10	500
4	200	90	100	200	100
5	70	20	10	10	250
6	30	80	100	150	200

It is ascertained that the maximum cash that can be made available for the projects in each of the next three years without jeopardizing the liquidity position of the company is as follows:

Year 1 .... $250,000
Year 2 .... $200,000
Year 3 .... $200,000

The company has contractual obligations to supply at least 1,000,000 units of output per day. All the six proposed projects are able to supply units of an acceptable quality according to agreed specifications. However, Project 1 and Project 2 are mutually exclusive in the sense that only one or none of the two may be accepted. And Project 4 is contingent upon the acceptance of Project 3, that is, Project 4 can only be accepted if Project 3 is also accepted though Project 3 can be accepted on its own.

Maximize $Z = 40x_1 + 100x_2 + 25x_3 + 200x_4 + 70x_5 + 30x_6$
Subject to

$$60x_1 + 50x_2 + 40x_3 + 90x_4 + 20x_5 + 80x_6 \leqq 250$$
$$40x_1 + 40x_2 + 10x_3 + 100x_4 + 10x_5 + 100x_6 \leqq 200$$
$$40x_1 + 20x_2 + 10x_3 + 200x_4 + 10x_5 + 150x_6 \leqq 200$$
$$400x_1 + 600x_2 + 500x_3 + 100x_4 + 250x_5 + 200x_6 \geqq 1{,}000$$
$$x_1 + x_2 \leqq 1$$
$$-x_3 + x_4 \leqq 0$$
$$x_j = 0,\ 1,\ j = 1, 2, \ldots, 6$$

The optimal solutions are:

$$x_2^* = x_3^* = x_5^* = x_6^* = 1$$
$$x_1^* = x_4^* = 0$$
$$Z^* = \$225{,}000$$

So Projects 2, 3, 5 and 6 are accepted.

5.5. QUADRATIC PROGRAMMING MODEL

If the firm has a limited sum of money to be invested among a set of all available proposed investment projects, a quadratic programming model may be applied to decide on the fraction of the total sum to be invested in any of the proposed projects. This model is applicable if the amount of cash to be invested in any project can be varied at the discretion of the firm, and the risks of the proposed projects are appropriately quantified by their variances and covariances of returns.

The problem here is to choose a portfolio $X = [x_1 x_2 \cdots x_n]^T$ where x_j is the proportion of the total funds invested in the jth project, $j = 1, 2, \ldots n$. The return on the portfolio is EX where E is a given row vector of mean returns on the n projects. The risk on the portfolio is indicated by the quadratic form: X^TNX, where N is a given $n \times n$ matrix of variances and covariances of returns. N is assumed positive definite. The choice of an investment portfolio can then be expressed as a quadratic programming problem:

$$\begin{aligned} &\text{Minimize} && X^TNX \\ &\text{Subject to} && EX \geqq R \\ & && \sum_{j=1}^{n} x_j = 1 \qquad (5.5.1.) \\ & && X \geqq 0 \end{aligned}$$

where R is the minimum acceptable rate of return

This is a quadratic programming problem because the objective function contains no terms of degree higher than 2 and the constraints are all linear. The portfolio given by the programme will be efficient in the sense that no other portfolio can give a higher return without increasing risk nor the same return with less risk. It can be demonstrated that the following programme is also efficient:

$$\begin{aligned} &\text{Maximize} && E\ X \\ &\text{Subject to} && X^TNX \leqq D \\ & && \sum_{j=1}^{n} x_j = 1 \qquad (5.5.2.) \\ & && X \geqq 0 \end{aligned}$$

where D is the maximum acceptable risk

Let us illustrate with an example using the data: $E = [.2\ \ .3]$ $R = .2$ and

$$N = \begin{bmatrix} .1 & -.1 \\ -.1 & .3 \end{bmatrix}$$

Using (5.5.1.), we have the following quadratic programming problem:

$$\begin{aligned} \text{Minimize} \quad & F(X) = .1x_1^2 - .2x_1x_2 + .3x_2^2 \\ \text{Subject to} \quad & .2x_1 + .3x_2 \geqq .2 \\ & x_1 + x_2 = 1 \\ & x_1, x_2 \geqq 0 \end{aligned} \tag{5.5.3.}$$

The Kuhn-Tucker conditions are:

$$\begin{aligned} .2x_1 - .2x_2 - .2\lambda_1 - \lambda_2 &= 0 \\ -.2x_1 + .6x_2 - .3\lambda_1 - \lambda_2 &= 0 \\ \lambda_1(.2x_1 + .3x_2 - .2) &= 0 \\ \lambda_2(x_1 + x_2 - 1) &= 0 \\ .2x_1 + .3x_2 &\geqq .2 \\ x_1 + x_2 &= 1 \end{aligned}$$

Using the Kuhn-Tucker conditions and adding appropriate slack and artificial variables, we have the following linear programming problem, to which the simplex algorithm is applied:

$$\begin{aligned} \text{Maximize} \quad & Z = -a_1 - a_2 - a_3 - a_4 \\ \text{Subject to} \quad & .2x_1 - .2x_2 - .2\lambda_1 - \lambda_2 - S_1 + a_1 = 0 \\ & -.2x_1 + .6x_2 - .3\lambda_1 - \lambda_2 - S_2 + a_2 = 0 \\ & .2x_1 + .3x_2 - S_3 + a_3 = .2 \\ & x_1 + x_2 + a_4 = 1 \end{aligned} \tag{5.5.4.}$$

The optimal solution is therefore: $x_1 = .75, x_2 = .25, s_1 = .1$, and $s_3 = .025$.

This is global since $H_1 = \dfrac{\partial^2 F}{\partial x_1^2} = .2 > 0$, and $H_2 =$

$$\begin{vmatrix} \dfrac{\partial^2 F}{\partial x_1^2} & \dfrac{\partial^2 F}{\partial x_1\,\partial x_2} \\ \dfrac{\partial^2 F}{\partial x_2\,\partial x_1} & \dfrac{\partial^2 F}{\partial x_2^2} \end{vmatrix} = \begin{vmatrix} .2 & -.2 \\ -.2 & .6 \end{vmatrix} > 0$$

and the constraints are all linear.

Since the constraint $.2x_1 + .3x_2 = .225 > .2$ and hence ineffective, it implies that varying this constraint constant marginally will not affect the optimal value of the objective function. In other words our optimal solution remained valid even if we were inaccurate in estimating the minimum acceptable rate of return by a small margin.

Usually before a final decision is made further sensitivity analysis will be carried out, that is, the same programme will be run with some or all of the parameters changed, for instance, with different expected returns and variances and covariances. The final decision will usually be the result of the interplay between management's acumen, value judgment and experience and the optimal solutions obtained. Another way of coping with uncertainties of the future is to employ stochastic models where probabilities of the expected returns are incorporated.

5.6. CHOICE OF PRODUCTION METHODS AND HENCE INVESTMENT IN PLANT AND EQUIPMENT

In complicated types of manufacturing activities with many processes, there are often options among alternative methods of production. Before deciding on the types of equipment to install and before commencing production activities, it is desirable to have a feasibility study regarding the optimal combination of processes in order to minimize production costs. This information is useful in the choice of productive processes and hence the choice of plant and equipment. The following systems model will illustrate this.

Suppose all possible methods of production and processes are included in the following production set:

$$\{T | T = (B - A)X, X \geqq 0\} \tag{5.6.1.}$$

Where $B = (b_{ij})$ is the output matrix having positive components b_{ij} if i is an output of the system, and $A = (a_{ij})$ is the input matrix also having positive components a_{ij} if i is an input, both at unit level of operation of X. The other elements of A and B are zero. If the firm operates the processes at X level, $T = (t_1, t_2, \ldots; t_n)^T$ is the net outputs of the system. Both B and A of the firm's production technology are $m \times n$ matrixes and both joint production and substitution in the production process are permissible.

Since X is a closed convex set, T is closed and convex by linear transformation. And as the system is assumed to be operating at constant returns to scale, the following linear programming problem can be formed:

$$\begin{aligned} &\text{Minimize} && CX \\ &\text{Subject to} && (B - A)X = MX = T \\ &&& X \geqq 0 \end{aligned} \tag{5.6.2.}$$

Where C is a row vector of direct costs of the processes at unit level and T is the desired level of net outputs. T is thus determined by the demand conditions of the firm as well as the availability of input resources. The solution to this linear programming model is a global optimum since the objective function is convex and the feasibility set is convex, closed and bounded. Its dual is:

$$\begin{aligned} &\text{Maximize} && YT \\ &\text{Subject to} && YM \leqq C \end{aligned} \tag{5.6.3.}$$

The optimal solution to the dual, Y^*, is the shadow prices of the primal constraints. Hence, they measure the marginal prices the firm should be willing to pay to relax the constraints.

From the duality theorems of linear programming, sensitivity analysis can be carried out. Denoting the optimal solution of YT as

Y^*T and that of CX as CX^*, we have

$$CX^* = Y^*T, \text{ so that}$$

$$\frac{\partial(CX^*)}{\partial T} = Y^* \tag{5.6.4.}$$

Hence, given the resources of the firm and demand conditions, Y^* is the vector of shadow prices (opportunity costs) which is useful to management for deciding whether the firm should use any or all of its processes.

The sensitivities of the optimal values of the objective function to changes in the objective constraints are:

$$\frac{\partial(CX^*)}{\partial C} = X^*, \text{ and}$$

$$\frac{\partial(Y^*T)}{\partial T} = Y^* \tag{5.6.5.}$$

The meaningful economic interpretations of the analysis can be made concrete by the following numerical example with three commodities and four processes:

$$M = \begin{bmatrix} 1 & 2 & -3 & 4 \\ -2 & -\frac{1}{2} & 1 & -1 \\ -1 & 0 & 2 & -3 \end{bmatrix}$$

$$C = [3 \quad 1 \quad 4 \quad 2], \text{ and}$$

$$T = [80 \quad 60 \quad 70]^T$$

The first column of the matrix M indicates that Process 1 will use 2 units of Commodity 2 and 1 unit of Commodity 3 to produce 1 unit of Commodity 1. The third column of M shows that Process 3 will use 3 units of Commodity 1 to produce 1 unit of Commodity 2 and 2 units of Commodity 3. The other two columns have similar interpretations. The matrix M shows the various processes operating at unit level of activity. The row vector C gives the direct costs of operating the X processes at unit level of activity, and the column vector T is the given demand of the three commodities.

The primal programme can then be formulated as:

$$\begin{array}{ll} \text{Minimize} & 3x_1 + x_2 + 4x_3 + 2x_4 \\ \text{Subject to} & x_1 + 2x_2 - 3x_3 + 4x_4 = 80 \\ & -2x_1 - \tfrac{1}{2}x_2 + x_3 - x_4 = 60 \\ & -x_1 + 2x_3 - 3x_4 = 70 \\ & x_1, x_2, x_3 \geqq 0 \end{array} \qquad (5.6.6.)$$

And its dual is:

$$\begin{array}{ll} \text{Maximize} & Z = 80y_1 + 60y_2 + 70y_3 \\ \text{Subject to} & y_1 - 2y_2 - y_3 \leqq 3 \\ & 2y_1 - \tfrac{1}{2}y_2 \leqq 1 \\ & -3y_1 + y_2 + 2y_3 \leqq 4 \\ & 4y_1 - y_2 - 3y_3 \leqq 2 \end{array} \qquad (5.6.7.)$$

The solutions are:

$$X^* = [0 \quad 140 \quad 320 \quad 190]^T$$
$$Y^* = [y_1 \quad y_2 \quad y_3 \quad y_4 \quad y_5 \quad y_6 \quad y_7] = [6 \quad 22 \quad 0 \quad 41 \quad 0 \quad 0 \quad 0]$$

Analysis of Optimal Solution

	Produces			*Uses*			*Net Outputs*		
Activities	*Com. 1*	*Com. 2*	*Com. 3*	*Com. 1*	*Com. 2*	*Com. 3*	Com. 1	Com. 2	Com. 3
2	280	0	0	0	70	0			
3	0	320	640	960	0	0			
4	760	0	0	0	190	570			
Total	1,040	320	640	960	260	570	80	60	70

If we substitute the solution values into the dual constraints, we find that the first dual constraint is ineffective:

$$y_1 - 2y_2 - y_3 = 6 - 44 - 0 = -38 < 3$$

Process 1 will not be used since it is making a loss at shadow prices (6 − 44 − 3 = −41). The other three processes will be used since they make zero profits at shadow prices. Thus the method of production described by Process 1 will not be set up and no capital investment in Process 1 will be made.

The objective function as well as the constraints in the model can be modified to yield useful information for decision-making. The model presented here is supported by well-established mathematical programming theory, and it removes some of the undesirable consequences of classical marginal analysis which may ignore the fact that all firms operate under constraining conditions and that the identification of the opportunity set is vital for ensuring the feasibility of a solution as well as the existence of a global optimal solution.

5.7. MULTIPLE OBJECTIVE GOAL PROGRAMMING

In some situations, single-objective mathematical programming models may not be applicable if the constraints are inconsistent since in such cases there are no feasibility sets. Goal programming will overcome such problems by including all constraints as objectives including the objective function as in the case of a single-objective programming model. Since the objectives cannot all be achieved in these circumstances, they are ranked in order of priority. If an objective must be satisfied before all the others, it is placed at priority level one. And the less important objectives are placed at lower priority levels. In this way conflicting objectives are resolved by compromises and management policy is one of satisficing rather than optimizing. An example should clarify the issue.

Goal Ltd. has decided to invest a sum of $100,000 in two assets, X_1 and X_2. The company would like to invest at least $80,000 in X_1 and at least $50,000 in X_2 and to have an annual income of at least $12,000. X_1 yields a return of 9% and X_2 of 15%; the different rates of return are due to different risks of the two investments.

A linear programming formulation will be:

Maximize $Z = .09X_1 + .15X_2$

Subject to

$$\begin{aligned} X_1 + X_2 &\leqq 100{,}000 \\ X_1 &\geqq 80{,}000 \\ X_2 &\geqq 50{,}000 \\ X_1, X_2 &\geqq 0 \end{aligned}$$

The above linear programming problem has no solution since the constraints are inconsistent. A goal programming formulation is as follows:

Minimize $Z = [(Y_{+1}), (Y_{-4}), (Y_{-2} + Y_{-3})]$

$$\begin{aligned} X_1 + X_2 + Y_{-1} - Y_{+1} &= 100{,}000 \\ X_1 + Y_{-2} - Y_{+2} &= 80{,}000 \\ X_2 + Y_{-3} - Y_{+3} &= 50{,}000 \\ 0.09X_1 + 0.15X_2 + Y_{-4} - Y_{+4} &= 12{,}000 \\ X_1, X_2 &\geqq 0 \\ Y_{-i} &\geqq 0, i = 1, 2, \ldots, 4 \\ Y_{+i} &\geqq 0, i = 1, 2, \ldots, 4 \end{aligned}$$

The optimal solutions are:

$$X_1^* = 50{,}000;\ X_2^* = 50{,}000;\ Z^* = [(0), (0), (30{,}000)]$$

It can be seen that the optimal solutions are compromises; the objectives at the first and the second priority level are fully satisfied while the objectives at the third priority level partially satisfied. The first objective in the goal programming model is placed at priority level one to ensure that the sum of $100,000 is not exceeded; the objective at priority level two is to earn the desired income of $12,000; and the last one is to invest as much as possible in each of the two projects. At the optimal solutions, the full desired amount of $50,000 is invested in X_2 while only $50,000 out of the desired amount of $80,000 is invested in X_1. This must be so since X_2 is more profitable and the fact that $100,000 cannot be exceeded is at a higher priority level.

Other mathematical programming models such as stochastic and dynamic models are beyond the scope of this book.

5.8. SELECTED BIBLIOGRAPHY

1. J.C.G. Boot: Quadratic Programming
2. R. Dorfman, P.A. Samuelson, and R. Solow: Linear Programming and Economic Analysis
3. Saul I. Gass: Linear Programming
4. Han Kang Hong: (1) Cost and Management Accounting
   (2) Reciprocal Service Costs Allocation and Sensitivity Analysis, *Accounting and Business Research*, Spring 1981
5. J.P. Ignizio: Goal Programming and Extension
6. T.C. Koopmans (ed.): Activity Analysis of Production and Allocation
7. J. Lorie and L.J. Savage: Three Problems in Capital Rationing, Journal of Business, October 1955.
8. J.C.T. Mao: Survey of Capital Budgeting (Theory and Practice), Journal of Finance, May 1970
9. J.C.T. Mao and B.A. Wallingford: Extensions of Lawler and Bell's Method of Discrete Optimization, Management Science, October 1968.
10. H. Markowitz: Portfolio Selection, Cowles Foundation Monograph No. 16
11. Sang. M. Lee: Goal Programming for Decision Analysis.
12. W.F. Sharpe: A Simplified Model for Portfolio Selection Analysis, Management Science, January 1963

CHAPTER 6

Investment in Fixed Assets in Uncertainty

6.1. UNCERTAINTIES AND RISKS

Certainty and absence of risk have been assumed in the evaluation techniques so far explained. This is contrary to reality in practical business situations. Inaccuracy in forecasted cash flows could occur in the following areas:

(1) Demand forecast, such as the future growth of the market as well as the firm's share of such market and the expected selling prices of the products. These will affect the cash inflows from sales revenue.
(2) Expected economic lives of the proposed investment projects, which are affected by technological advances and the degree of competition in the market. This too affects cash inflows from sales revenue.
(3) Forecasted costs, such as labour, materials and factory as well as commercial overheads.

If risk is measured by the difference between actual and forecasted cash flows, it can be quantified through the help of statistical analysis. Uncertainty in its broadest sense which includes all unforeseen eventualities can hardly be quantified. The following paragraphs will explain the main statistical techniques dealing with risk in the forecasted cash flows.

6.2. THE ACTUARIAL APPROACH

The actuarial approach relies very heavily on the arithmetic mean or the expected value of the forecasted cash flows. Each of every possible cash flow is weighted by the probability that that cash flow will take place. The sum of all such weighted cash flows is called the mathematical expectation or expected value of the cash flows. Table 6.2 illustrates the calculations of the expected value for one period, ($t = 1$). [See Appendix B equations (18) and (19)]. The

Table 6.2.

	All Possible Cash Flows	*Probability*	*Expected Value*	
i	C_{ti}	p_{ti}	$\bar{C}_{ti}$	(10%) $\overline{NPV}_i$
	$		$	
1	2,000	0.5	1,000	909
2	3,000	0.2	600	545
3	4,000	0.3	1,200	1,091
		Expected Value =	$2,800	
		Expected Net Present Value =		$2,545

expected net present value of all possible cash flows of a proposed investment project is thus calculated as:

$$\overline{NPV} = \sum_{t=0}^{n} \sum_{i=1}^{m} C_{ti} p_{ti} (1 + k)^{-t} \qquad (6.2.)$$

where $\overline{NPV}$ is the expected net present value,
k is the minimum acceptable rate of return,
n is the economic life of the proposed project,
C_{ti} is the ith after-tax net cash flow with probability p_{ti} in period, t, and
m is the total number of possible cash flows in period t.

If the net present value criterion is relevant, then a project with a positive expected net present value is acceptable while one with a negative expected net present value is rejected.

The expected value is a measure of central tendency in the sense that the probability distribution of the cash flows tends towards this figure. As such the individual investor's attitude towards risk is ignored.

6.3. THE UTILITY FUNCTION

6.3.1. Inadequacy of Expected Values

Most people prefer getting $100,000 with certainty to a fifty-fifty chance of getting $250,000 though the expected value of the latter is \$125,000. Two proposals may have the same expected value as shown below, but a person may prefer one to the other.

		Probability	Outcome	Expected Value
Proposal	1	0.009	\$1,000,000	\$9,000
		0.991	0	0
		1.000		\$9,000
Proposal	2	0.900	\$ 10,000	\$9,000
		0.100	0	0
		1.000		\$9,000

Thus expected value may not always be an acceptable criterion for making a choice among alternatives. Personal psychology and the individual's attitude to risk may exert an influence on his choice.

6.3.2. Utility Index

The Neumann-Morgenstern utility index may be used to predict the choice of an individual among risky alternatives. If he prefers q to r then q is assigned a higher utility number than r. If an investor is willing to incur \$l for an investment which has two outcomes x with probability p and y with probability $(1 - p)$ and if their respective utilities are $U(x)$ and $U(y)$, then the utility of \$l is defined as:

$$U(1) = pU(x) + (1 - p)U(y) \qquad (6.3.2.)$$

But how are the utilities of x and y calculated? These are calculated from the utility function of the individual investor. If the investor is consistent in his preferences, his utility function may be derived by observing his behaviour in choice situations. Once his utility function is obtained, it can be used to infer which alternative he will select without asking him.

Suppose an investment project has two extreme outcomes: a probability of 0.5 of \$500,000 and a probability of 0.5 of zero dollars. If the investor is willing to pay $100,000 for this investment, he is indifferent between the sum of $100,000 and the investment project. Table 6.3.2. illustrates this.

Table 6.3.2.

Mr. Gambler is willing to pay	*For the Probability of*	*Of Winning*	*And the Probability of*	*Of Winning*
$		$		$
100,000	.5	500,000	.5	0
200,000	.4	100,000	.6	500,000
300,000	.6	500,000	.4	200,000

The table may be read in the following manner:

Row one: Mr. Gambler is willing to pay $100,000 for the probability of .5 of winning $500,000 and .5 of winning zero dollars.

Row two: Mr. Gambler is willing to pay $200,000 for the probability of .4 of winning $100,000 and 0.6 of winning $500,000.

Let $U(0) = 0$ and $U(500{,}000) = 1$, then the following utility numbers can be calculated using equation (6.3.2.):

$$\begin{aligned} U(100{,}000) &= (0.5)U(500{,}000) + (0.5)U(0) \\ &= (0.5)(1) + (0.5)(0) = 0.5 \end{aligned}$$

$$\begin{aligned} U(200{,}000) &= (0.4)U(100{,}000) + (0.6)U(500{,}000) \\ &= (0.4)(0.5) + (0.6)(1) = 0.8 \end{aligned}$$

$$\begin{aligned} U(300{,}000) &= (0.6)U(500{,}000) + (0.4)U(200{,}000) \\ &= (0.6)(1) + (0.4)(0.8) = 0.92 \end{aligned}$$

Figure 6.3.2. represents Mr. Gambler's utility function. The graph shows a concave function indicating that

Figure 6.3.2.

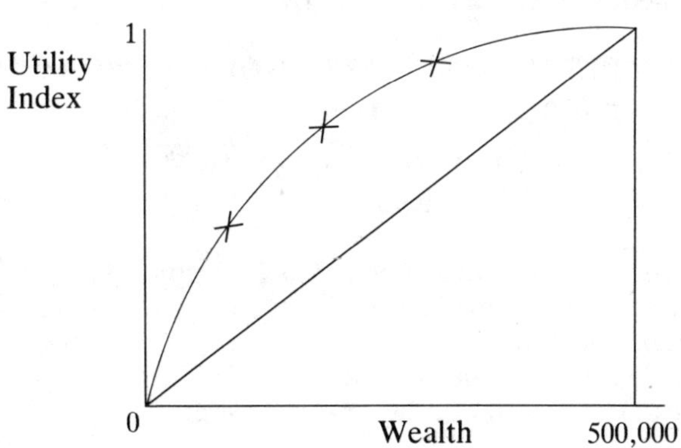

Mr. Gambler is averse to risk. His utility increases less than proportionately with every increase in wealth.

6.3.3. Use of Utility Index for Evaluating Investments

Both investments projects *X* and *Y* shown in Table 6.3.3. are acceptable under the net present value criterion.

Table 6.3.3.

Investment X			*Investment Y*		
Probability	*Present Value*	*Expected Present Value*	*Probability*	*Present Value*	*Expect Present Value*
	$	$		$	$
.3	0	0	.6	100,000	60,000
.2	500,000	100,000	.4	200,000	80,000
.5	200,000	100,000			
1.0		200,000	1.0		140,000

The utility of Investment X and of Y, using Mr. Gambler's utility function is calculated as follows:

$$\begin{aligned} U(X) &= (0.3)U(0) + (0.2)U(500{,}000) + (0.5)U(200{,}000) \\ &= 0 + 0.2 + 0.4 = 0.60 \\ U(Y) &= (0.6)U(100{,}000) + (0.4)U(200{,}000) \\ &= 0.3 + 0.32 = 0.62 \end{aligned}$$

To Mr. Gambler, Investment Y is preferred to Investment X in spite of the higher expected present value of X because Y has higher expected utility.

Mr. Gambler's choice is influenced by his risk aversion. The standard deviations of the two projects are:

The standard deviation of project X
(See Appendix B equation (22))

$$= \sqrt{\sum_{i=1}^{n} (r_i - \bar{r})^2 p_i}$$

$= \$173{,}205$

where r_i is the present value with the probability of p_i and $\bar{r}$ is the expected present value.

(6.3.3.1.)

And the standard deviation of project Y

$= \$48{,}988$ (6.3.3.2.)

Thus if risks are measured by variances, project X is more risky because its present value distribution is more widely spread.

6.3.4. Utility Curves

The utility function of any investor, inter alia, can be one of three types as depicted in Figure 6.3.4.

Mr. A, like our Mr. Gambler, is averse to risk while Mr. C is a risk-seeker and Mr. B is neutral to risk. For Mr. B his utility increases proportionately with wealth whereas Mr. C's utility increases more than proportionately with wealth.

Figure 6.3.4.

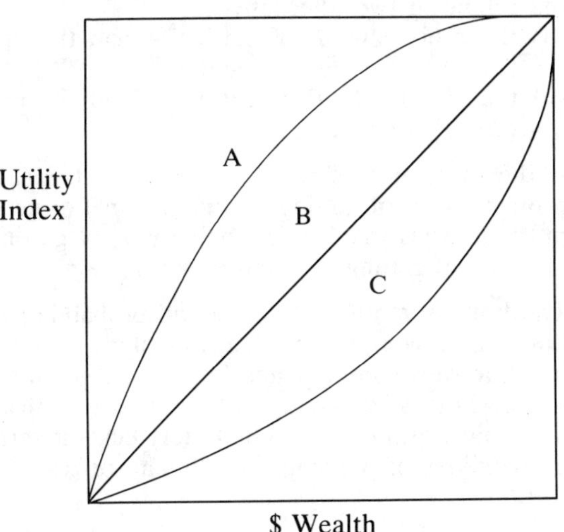

6.3.5. Assumptions of the Neumann-Morgenstern Utility Index

The usefulness of the Neumann-Morgenstern Utility Index for decision-making in risky situations depends very much on whether the underlying assumptions reflect realistically the behaviour of investors. There are five of them.

(1) If an investor is indifferent between outcomes X and Y and also indifferent between Y and Z, then he will be indifferent between X and Z.

(2) If the investor prefers outcomes D to E and also prefers E to F, then there exists a probability $0 < P < 1$ such that he is indifferent between the following two alternatives:
  (i) E, and
  (ii) the probability P of getting D and the probability $(1 - P)$ of getting F.

(3) If the investor is indifferent between outcomes A and B, and also indifferent between C and D, then there exists a

probability $0 < P < 1$ such that he is indifferent between the following two alternatives:
(i) the probability P of getting A and the probability $(1 - P)$ of getting C, and
(ii) the probability P of getting B and the probability $(1 - P)$ of getting D.

(4) If the investor prefers the outcome G to H, then the probability p_g of getting G and $(1 - p_g)$ of getting H is more desirous than the probability p_h of getting G and $(1 - p_h)$ of getting H if and only if $p_g > p_h$.

(5) The last assumption of compound probability computation is a bit complicated. But roughly it implies that the investor who contemplates buying a compound lottery ticket whose prizes are other lottery tickets will assess the desirability of this compound lottery ticket in terms of the probabilities of winning the ultimate prizes.

6.3.6. The utility function and the normal distribution

Expanding the utility function at the point Y_0 in a Taylor series gives:

$$U(Y) = U(Y_0) + \frac{dU(Y_0)}{dY}(Y - Y_0) + \frac{1}{2!}\frac{d^2U(Y_0)}{dY^2}(Y - Y_0)^2 + \ldots$$

$$= a + b(Y - Y_0) + c(Y - Y_0)^2 \qquad (6.3.6.1.)$$

Setting Y_0 = zero gives

$$U(Y) = a + bY + CY^2 \qquad (6.3.6.2.)$$

Hence, if the degree of accuracy is acceptable, the investor's utility function may be approximated by a quadratic equation.

Expressing the utility function in terms of rates of return gives:

$$U(r) = X + \psi r + Wr^2 \qquad (6.3.6.3.)$$

The expected value of this utility function is [See Appendix B equation (35)]:

$$E[U(r)] = X + \psi\bar{r} + W(\bar{r}^2 + \sigma_r^2) \qquad (6.3.6.4.)$$

where $E(r) = \bar{r}$ and $E(r^2) = \bar{r}^2 + \sigma_r^2$

[See Appendix B equation (21)]

If the investor is risk-averse, his utility function is concave and W in equation (6.3.6.3.) is negative. Hence, given the expected rate of return, the expected utility value varies inversely with the variance. If W is zero the investor is neutral to risk; his criterion for evaluating investment projects is expected rates of return. If W is positive, he is a risk-seeker.

The above analysis seems to suggest that the expected return and the variance of the returns are two useful criteria for evaluating different projects with different probability distributions. This appears reasonable if the utility function can be approximated by a quadratic equation and the probability distributions are normal so that they are adequately described by their means and variances.

If the assumption of nonsatiation holds, that is, given two possessions of wealth $\$X$ and $\$Y$, the expected utility of X is greater than that of Y if $\$X > \$Y$, then the quadratic utility function seems to pose a problem in the sense that there is a maximum r^* at which $U(r)$ has the highest value. Equating the first derivative of $U(r)$ with respect to r to zero gives:

$$\frac{dU(r)}{dr} = \psi - 2Wr = 0 \qquad (6.3.6.5.)$$

which gives

$$r^* = \frac{\psi}{2W} \qquad (6.3.6.6.)$$

Nevertheless, the above analysis does demonstrate strongly the close relation between the expected utility value and the variance of rates of returns from an investment. [See Example in Table 6.3.3. and Equations (6.3.3.1.) and (6.3.3.2.)]

6.4. USEFULNESS OF EXPECTED VALUE AND VARIANCE

It is mentioned in Section (6.3.6.) that expected value and variance seem to be two relevant criteria for evaluating investment projects. The following paragraphs explain how they can provide useful information to the investor. The expected net present value of an investment project is defined as:

$$\overline{NPV} = \sum_{t=0}^{n} \sum_{i=1}^{m} (C_{ti} p_{ti})(1 + r)^{-t} \qquad (6.4.)$$

where $\overline{NPV}$ is the expected net present value of an investment project,
r is the risk-free rate of discount,
n is the number of periods during which cash flows take place,
C_{ti} is the ith after-tax net cash flow with probability p_{ti} in period t, and
m is the number of discrete cash flows in period t.

6.4.1. Independence of Cash Flows

With the assumption of serial independence of cash flows, that is, the cash flows of one period are independent of the cash flows of another period, the standard deviation of the probability distribution of net cash flows in period t is:

$$\sigma_t = \sqrt{\sum_{i=1}^{m} (C_{ti} - \bar{C}_t)^2 p_{ti}} \qquad (6.4.1.1.)$$

The standard deviation of the probability distribution of NPV is:

$$\sigma_I = \sqrt{\sum_{t=0}^{n} \sigma_t^2 (1 + r)^{-2t}} \qquad (6.4.1.2.)$$

Table (6.4.1.) shows the cash flows and the associated probabilities from which the relevant useful information is obtained.

Table 6.4.1.
$r = 0.06$

Year 0			Year 1			Year 2		
C_{0i} $	P_{0i}	$\overline{C_{0i}}$ $	C_{1i} $	P_{1i}	$\overline{C_{1i}}$ $	C_{2i} $	P_{2i}	$\overline{C_{2i}}$ $
−5,000	1.0	−5,000	2,000	0.2	400	7,000	0.1	700
			5,000	0.3	1,500	4,000	0.3	1,200
			6,000	0.5	3,000	7,000	0.6	4,200
	1.0	−$5,000		1.0	$4,900		1.0	$6,100
		$\sigma_0 = 0$			$\sigma_1 = \$1,513$			$\sigma_2 = \$1,375$

Using equation (6.4) gives:

$$\overline{NPV} = -5,000 + 4,900\ (1.06)^{-1} + 6,100\ (1.06)^{-2}$$
$$= \$5,052 \qquad (6.4.1.3.)$$

Using equation (6.4.1.2.) gives:

$$\sigma_I = \$1,880 \qquad (6.4.1.4.)$$

The probability that $NPV \leq 0$ and hence that the internal rate of return will be less than r can be calculated as follows:

$$S = \frac{0 - NPV}{\sigma_I} = \frac{0 - 5,052}{1,880}$$
$$= -2.6872 \qquad (6.4.1.5.)$$

This means that the net present value of $0 lies 2.6872 standard deviations to the left of the expected value of the probability distribution of net present values. From Table 3 in Appendix C,

$$P(NPV \leq 0) = (1 - 0.9964) = 0.0036 \qquad (6.4.1.6.)$$

Thus there is a 0.0036 probability that the net present value will be zero or less.

The probability that $NPV \leq \$5{,}000$ is calculated as follows:

$$S = \frac{5{,}000 - 5{,}052}{1{,}880} = -0.028 \qquad (6.4.1.7.)$$

Table 3 in Appendix C gives:

$$P(NPV \leq 5{,}000) = (1 - .512) = .488 \qquad (6.4.1.8.)$$

Similarly the probability that $NPV \geq \$6{,}000$ is calculated as:

$$S = \frac{6{,}000 - 5{,}052}{1{,}880} = 0.504 \qquad (6.4.1.9.)$$

$$P(NPV \geq 6{,}000) = (1 - .6915) = .3085 \quad (6.4.1.10.)$$

From equations (6.4.1.3.) and (6.4.1.4.) one standard deviation from the mean is:

$$\$5{,}052 \pm \$1{,}880 \qquad (6.4.1.11.)$$

Thus there is a 0.683 probability that the net present value will be between \$3,172 and \$6,932, that is:

$$P(\$3{,}172 \leq NPV \leq \$6{,}932) = .683 \qquad (6.4.1.12.)$$

The probability figure [2(.8413 − .5) = .683] is obtained from Table 3 in Appendix C.

6.4.2. Perfect Correlation of Cash Flows

Because the cash flows of one period are perfectly correlated with those of another period, the variance of the probability distribution of net present values is greater than σ_I^2.

The standard deviation of a stream of cash flows which are perfectly correlated over time is:

$$\sigma_D = \sum_{t=0}^{n} \sigma_t(1 + r)^{-t} \qquad (6.4.2.)$$

With the new σ_D, similar analysis can be carried out as in the last section.

6.4.3. Partial Correlation of Cash Flows

When the stream of cash flows is partially correlated over time, that is, the cash flows of one period are partially correlated with those of another period, thc formula for the standard deviation of the probability distribution of the net present values becomes:

$$\sigma_p = \sqrt{\sum_{i=1}^{m} (NPV_i - \overline{NPV})^2 p_i} \qquad (6.4.3.1.)$$

where NPV_i is the net present value of the ith series of net cash flows of all periods, p_i is the joint probability of the occurrence of the ith series,
m is the total number of series, and
$\overline{NPV}$ is the expected net present value of the investment project.

Table 6.4.3. illustrates this case where

$$P[C_{t,i}/C_{t-1,i}] \qquad (6.4.3.2.)$$

is the conditional probability of the occurrence of the net cash flow in the ith series in period t given the occurrence of the net cash flow in the ith series in the previous period, $t - 1$.

Applying equation (6.4.3.1.) to the information obtained in Table (6.4.3.) gives:

$$\sigma_p = \$2,377 \qquad (6.4.3.3.)$$

Probability analysis can be carried out as in Section 6.4.1.

As the number of periods and probabilities increases, the computations involved can be enormous. Simulation techniques may prove more economical under such circumstances. It should be noted that in the above probability analysis, the rate of interest used for discounting the cash flows is the risk-free interest rate. A risk-adjusted discount rate is not suitable since using it for discounting incorporates the risk element in the resultant present values.

Table 6.4.3.
Risk-free interest rate = 0.06

Period 0			Period 1			Period 2					
$P(C_{0i})$	C_{0i}	Present Value of C_{0i}	$P[C_{1i}/C_{0i}]$	C_{1i}	Present Value of C_{1i}	$P[C_{2i}/C_{1i}]$	C_{2i}	Present Value of C_{2i}	Total Present Value NPV_i	Joint Probability $P[C_{0i}, C_{1i}, C_{2i}] = p_i$	$\overline{NPV}$
	$	$		$	$		$	$	$		$
1.0	−2,000	−2,000	.6	500	472	.3	1,000	890	−638	0.18	−115
						.7	500	445	−1,083	0.42	−455
			.4	2,000	1,887	.2	6,000	5,340	5,227	0.08	418
						.8	4,000	3,560	3,447	0.32	1,103
										1.00	
										$\overline{NPV}$ =	$951

6.5. THE CAPITAL ASSET PRICING MODEL

6.5.1. Diversification of Risk

Uncertainty exists when the actual cash flows associated with an investment project differ from its forecasted cash flows. The term risk refers to the risk of the investment project, and this risk is assumed to be capable of being measured by the dispersion or variance of the probability distribution of the cash flows. However, the risks of individual investments can be reduced by a well-diversified portfolio of investment projects. In other words risk is reduced by diversification. The amount of the risk that can be diversified away is termed diversifiable or unsystematic risk. Hence total risk is the sum of diversifiable and non-diversifiable or systematic risk. When diversification is possible and effective, only non-diversifiable risk remains, and only non-diversifiable risk is relevant to decision-making.

Prices of securities change for two reasons. The first reason is found in the economic forces of the environment, such as a change in the general interest rate. Such macro-economic variables cause share prices to vary together. But not all share prices change in the same direction or at the same rate. This second reason is found in the micro-economic variables of individual firms, such as the invention of a new product, design or method of production. If the co-efficient of correlation of returns of two investments is negative or if there is little co-variation between them, then holding one of them alone entails greater risk than holding both of them together.

Hence, if the risk of an investment is measured by the variability of the returns, such risk can be reduced by effective diversification. If one investment has the same expected rate of return as another but the variance of its probability distribution of returns is less, then the former is less risky than the latter. The example in Table 6.5.1. illustrates this conclusion.

The portfolio consists of, say 20% of available funds invested in A and 80% invested in B, instead of 100% of the available funds invested either totally in A or totally in B.

Equation (35) of Appendix B gives the expected rate of return of the portfolio as:

$$(.2)(.10) + (.8)(.25) = 0.22 \qquad (6.5.1.1.)$$

Table 6.5.1.

Investment	*Expected Rate of Return*	*Variance*	*Co-variance*
A	10%	10%	} −5%
B	25%	15%	
Portfolio: 20% of funds in *A* and 80% in *B*.	22%	8.4%	

Equation (36) of Appendix B gives the variance of the portfolio as:

$$(.2)^2(.10) + (.8)^2(.15) + (2)(.2)(.8)(-.05) = 0.084 \quad (6.5.1.2.)$$

Thus most investors would diversify away the diversifiable risk of investments. In other words, they would minimize risk subject to the minimum acceptable rate of return or maximize rate of return subject to maximum risk.

6.5.2. Non-diversifiable Risk and the Opportunity Line

Non-diversifiable risk is shown on the horizontal axis while expected return is shown on the vertical axis in Figure 6.5.2. This figure is drawn from the data provided by Table 6.5.2.1.

Table 6.5.2.1.

Project	*Expected Return*	*Non-diversificable Risk*
A	10%	5%
B	15%	15%
C	15%	20%
D	30%	20%

From Figure 6.5.2. it is seen that the projects are ranked in the following order:

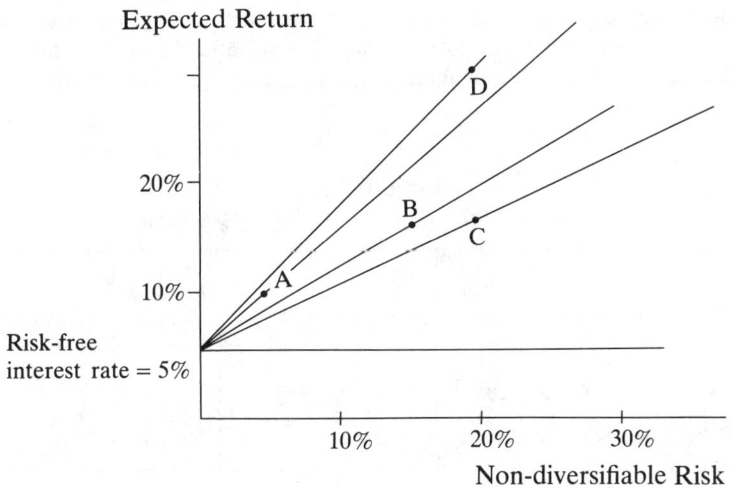

Figure 6.5.2.

Table 6.5.2.2.

Project	*Ranking*
A	2
B	3
C	4
D	1

It can be seen that at any given level of risk, Project *D* has the highest expected return followed by *A* and then *B* and *C* in that order. And at any given expected rate of return, Project *D* has the lowest risk, followed by *A* and *B* in that order; *C* has the highest risk.

6.5.3. Relation between Risk and Income

Moving up to the right of an opportunity line from the point, say *D*, represents increasing debt finance of the investment project and raises its expected return as well as its variance. Moving down and to the left represents lending or negative leverage and decreases expected return as well as variance. This illustrates the close dependence relation between risk and income. Tables 6.5.3.1. and 6.5.3.2. provide a good example of this relation.

Table 6.5.3.1.
Case of 20% Debt Finance at 10% rate of interest

	Cash Flows	*Equity Finance*	*Debt Finance*	*Internal Rate of Return*	*Probability of Return*	*Expected Return*	*Variance*
	$	$	$				
Outflows	$100,000	80,000	20,000				
Inflows	$120,000	98,000	22,000	0.225	0.6	0.135	0.006
Inflows	$140,000	118,000	22,000	0.475	0.4	0.190	0.009
					1.0	$\bar{R}_e = 0.325$	$\sigma_e^2 = 0.015$

Table 6.5.3.2
Case of 50% Debt Finance at 10% rate of interest

	Cash Flows	*Equity Finance*	*Debt Finance*	*Internal Rate of Return*	*Probability of Return*	*Expected Return*	*Variance*
	$	$	$				
Outflow	100,000	50,000	50,000				
Inflows	120,000	65,000	55,000	0.3	0.6	0.18	0.01536
Inflows	140,000	85,000	55,000	0.7	0.4	0.28	0.02304
					1.0	$\bar{R}_e = 0.46$	$\sigma_e^2 = 0.0384$

It can be seen that other things being equal, increasing the debt finance from 20% to 50% increases the expected return from 32.5% to 46%, at the same time raising the variance from 0.015 to 0.0384.

Thus increase in leverage increases both return and risk.

6.5.4. Non-Diversifiable Risk and the Market Line

In a perfect market where all investors have perfect knowledge, they will rank the investment projects in the same way as in Table 6.5.2.2. if they act rationally. Forces of supply and demand will then push up the price of *D* and push down the price of *C*, and so on. There will be an adjustment of prices and rates of return, forcing all the opportunity lines to arrive at the equilibrium position as depicted by the market line in Figure 6.5.4.1.

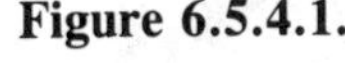

Figure 6.5.4.1.

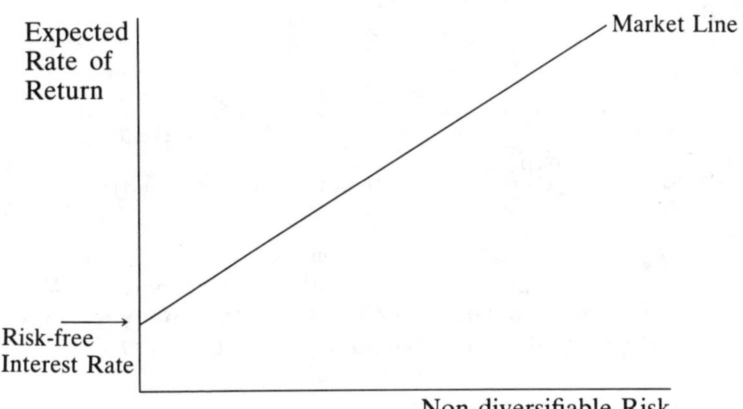

If the investor's portfolio is well diversified, the correlation coefficient of its return and that of the market portfolio is one and the market line can now be represented by Figure 6.5.4.2.

The non-diversifiable risk of the market portfolio is now σ_x since the correlation coefficient of its return and that of the investor, is one. From Figure 6.5.4.2. and the properties of the equation of a straight line, the market line equation for any investment project *Y* is therefore:

$$R_Y = I + \frac{(\bar{R}_X - I)}{\sigma_X} p_{XY}\sigma_Y \qquad (6.5.4.1.)$$

$$\bar{R}_Y = I + b(\bar{R}_X - I) \qquad (6.5.4.2.)$$

Figure 6.5.4.2.

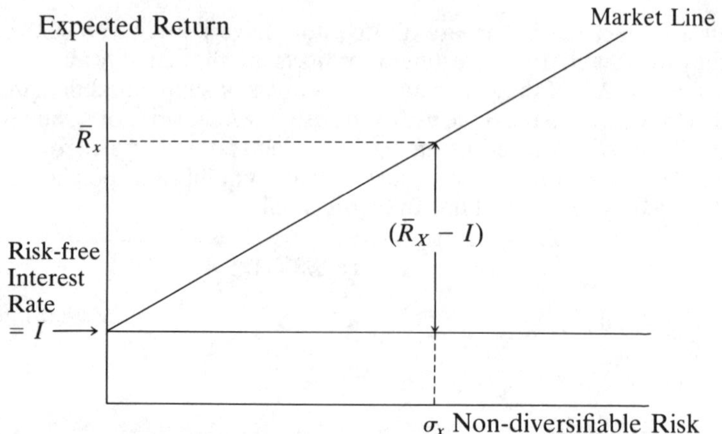

where $b = p_{XY} \dfrac{\sigma_Y}{\sigma_X}$ [See Appendix B equation (62)] (6.5.4.3.)

p_{XY} = the correlation coefficient between the return of the investment project Y and that of the portfolio X.
σ_X = the standard deviation of the return on portfolio X.
σ_Y = the standard deviation of the return on project Y.

6.5.5. The Risk Adjusted Discount Rate

Equation (6.5.4.2.) explains that the expected return $\bar{R}_Y$ on any investment project Y consists of two elements: the risk-free interest rate I and the premium for risk, $b(\bar{R}_X - I)$. The risk premium being objectively determined has no dependence relation with the individual investor's attitude to risk.

R_Y is often called the risk-adjusted discount rate or the minimum acceptable rate of return and is used for evaluating risky investment projects under perfect market conditions. In the world of certainty and perfect market conditions there is only one interest rate, I and it is used for making decisions on investment projects. In the world of uncertainty, the market line is used for the same purpose; it is a range of minimum acceptable rates of return for investment projects at different risk levels.

6.5.6. Assumptions of the Market Line and Efficiency Theory

The usefulness of the market line for evaluating investment projects depends on whether its underlying assumptions reflect realistically the practical situations where such decisions are made. The basic assumptions are:

(1) The market for investment opportunities is perfect and efficient.
(2) Borrowing and lending can be done at the same rate of interest.
(3) All investors have homogeneous expectations, that is, they hold the same view regarding expected returns and non-diversifiable risks on all investment opportunities and,
(4) There is a dependence relation between value and expected return and non-diversifiable risk; there are no insolvency costs and no transaction costs.

The capital asset pricing model is very much dependent on the validity of the efficient market hypothesis. The efficient market theory stipulates that the price of a share in a stock exchange market is a true reflection of all the information about the company (whose share is quoted) known to investors in the market. In other words, any information about the company that is disclosed is reflected immediately in the price of the share. The efficient market theory therefore relies on perfect market conditions where investors are competent and have full knowledge of supply and demand conditions.

The efficient market hypothesis has been subjected to empirical testing by numerous researchers and the tests are classified into three categories: the weak-form, the semi-strong-form and the strong-form.

The weak-form tests essentially measure the serial correlation of price changes, that is, share price changes between successive intervals of time. The efficient market contention is strengthened if no dependence between successive prices is found. If the hypothesis is true, past prices cannot indicate what future prices will be; successive price changes are independent of past price movements and they behave randomly. This is sometimes known as the random-walk hypothesis.

Tests of the semi-strong-form hypothesis essentially involve measuring the impact of any new information (such as bonus-share issue) on the share price. The technique used consists of regressing the share price returns on market average returns or the industry returns and evaluating the residuals regarding their signs and magnitudes, the residuals being the differences between actual and expected returns and are supposed to measure the impact of any transaction affecting the share price. Thus if the semi-strong-form of the efficient market hypothesis is valid, any portfolio manager cannot perform better than the average market performance unless it is pure coincidence or he has insider information unavailable to other investors. This leads to a consideration of the strong-form hypothesis.

The strong-form hypothesis contends that the market price of a share reflects totally its true value as determined by the relevant information on that share whether or not any of the information is available to all investors. Tests of this hypothesis rely on ascertaining whether insiders or people who have insider information not available to others perform better than the latter. The answer to this question has policy implications for the regulatory mechanisms of stock exchanges.

The findings of some of these tests are described in some of the selected bibliography at the end of this chapter. The efficient market hypothesis, if it is valid, will have an impact on the kinds of accounting information made available to the public by companies. The kinds of accounting information which are immediately reflected in prices of shares may be given in more details, for instance. And those that are ignored by the market may be neglected. Whether accounting reports issued by companies should take the efficient market hypothesis into consideration in their disclosure policies is a very controversial issue. Perhaps more positive findings from empirical testing should be awaited, and the issue whether it is in the best interest and in accord with the objectives of stock exchanges that variability of share prices should decrease, should first be settled.

6.5.7. Estimating the Market Line

To arrive at the market line in practice, the estimator b in equation (6.5.4.2.) must be determined. A random sample of the returns on the market portfolio and that of the proposed investment project must be obtained. The availability of surrogates of returns on the proposed investment project poses a formidable problem though surrogates of returns on the market portfolio can be obtained from published sources.

Appendix B, Section 4.1, illustrates the least-squares method of arriving at the best linear unbiased estimator $\hat{b}$, from which the minimum acceptable rate of return is calculated.

Equation (6.5.4.2.) can be written as:

$$(R_Y - I) = a + b(R_X - I) + e \qquad (6.5.7.1.)$$

where e is a random disturbance term assumed to have zero mean and constant variance σ^2, and the e_i are uncorrelated.

This can be expressed as:

$$Y = a + bX + e \qquad (6.5.7.2.)$$

where

$$Y = (R_Y - I) \text{ and } X = (R_X - I) \qquad (6.5.7.3.)$$

With the data given in the first three columns of Table (6.5.7.) and equations (6.5.7.1.) and (6.5.7.2.) the estimated parameters are calculated as shown on pg. 80.

Equation (6.5.7.1.) can be expressed as:

$$R_{Yi} = I_i + a + b\,(R_{Xi} - I_i) + e_i \qquad (6.5.7.4.)$$

where $(i = 1, \ldots, n)$ is the number of observations.

Summing every term in equation (6.5.7.4.) and dividing by n gives the estimated minimum acceptable rate of return for investment project Y as:

$$\hat{R}_Y = \bar{I} + \hat{b}(\bar{R}_X - \bar{I}) \qquad (6.5.7.5.)$$

$$= .09 + .735\,(.06)$$

$$= 0.1341 \qquad (6.5.7.6.)$$

where $\hat{b} = \dfrac{\sum x_i y_i}{\sum x_i^2}$ [See Appendix B equation (55)] (6.5.7.7.)

Table 6.5.7.

I_i	R_{Yi}	R_{Xi}	$(R_{Yi}-I_i) = Y_i$	$(R_{Xi}-I_i) = X_i$	$(Y_i - Y) = y_i$	$(X_i - X) = x_i$	$x_i y_i$	x_i^2	y_i^2	$\hat{Y}_i$	$(Y_i - \hat{Y}_i)^2$
.05	.10	.08	.05	.03	−.06	−.03	.0018	.0009	.0036	.08794	.00144
.08	.20	.15	.12	.07	.01	.01	.0001	.0001	.0001	.11735	.00001
.10	.20	.15	.10	.05	−.01	−.01	.0001	.0001	.0001	.10265	.00001
.15	.25	.20	.10	.05	−.01	−.01	.0001	.0001	.0001	.10265	.00001
.10	.25	.20	.15	.10	.04	.04	.0016	.0016	.0016	.13941	.00011
.10	.25	.15	.15	.05	.04	−.01	−.0004	.0001	.0016	.10265	.00224
.07	.15	.15	.08	.08	−.03	.02	−.0006	.0004	.0009	.12471	.00200
.07	.20	.12	.13	.05	.02	−.01	−.0002	.0001	.0004	.10265	.00075
.72 $\bar{I} = .09$	1.60 $\bar{R}_Y = .20$	1.20 $\bar{R}_X = .15$	.88 $\bar{Y} = .11$	.48 $\bar{X} = .06$	0	0	.0025	.0034	.0084		.00657

Equation (61) of Appendix B gives the unbiased estimator of σ as:

$$S = \sqrt{\frac{1}{n-2}\sum (Y_i - \hat{Y}_i)^2} = 0.0331 \qquad (6.5.7.8.)$$

Equation (68) of Appendix B gives the 95% confidence interval for b as:

$$b = \hat{b} \pm t_{.025} \frac{S}{\sqrt{\sum x_i^2}}$$

$$= .735 \pm 1.389 \qquad (6.5.7.9.)$$

$$\hat{a} = \bar{Y} - \hat{b}\bar{X} \qquad \text{[See Appendix B equation (56)]}$$

$$= .11 - .735\ (.06)$$

$$= 0.0659 \qquad (6.5.7.10.)$$

The 95% confidence interval for $\bar{a}$ is:

$$\bar{a} = \hat{a} \pm t_{.025} \frac{S}{\sqrt{n}}$$

$$= .0659 \pm 0.0286 \qquad (6.5.7.11.)$$

Using the property that $E(a) = a$, $E(\hat{a}) = a$ [See Appendix B equation (60)] and that

$$\hat{R}_Y = \bar{R}_Y - \bar{a} \qquad (6.5.7.12.)$$

gives the 95% confidence interval for R_Y as:

$$0.1055 \leq R_Y \leq 0.1627 \qquad (6.5.7.13.)$$

Equation (6.5.8.3.) assumes that $\bar{R}_Y$ is the true mean of R_Y.

6.6. CERTAINTY EQUIVALENTS

Instead of using a risk-adjusted discount rate, the uncertain expected earnings streams may be converted into their certainty equivalents which are then discounted at the risk-free interest rate. The concept of certainty equivalents may be illustrated graphically:

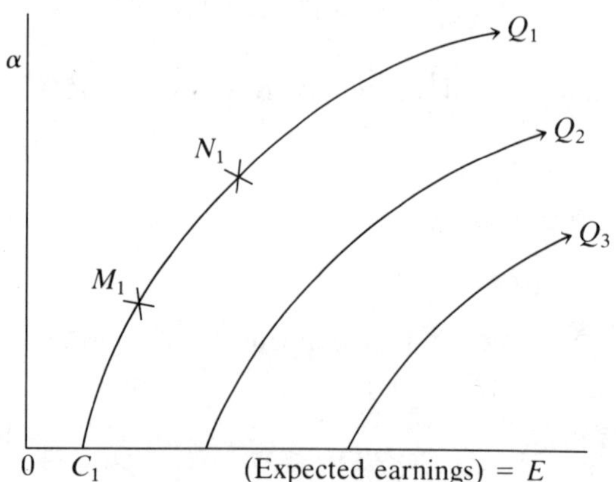

In the graph, we have three indifferent curves, Q_1, Q_2 and Q_3. Q_3 is preferred to Q_2 which is preferred to Q_1 since Q_3 gives the highest earnings levels. However, to an individual investor, the earnings at M_1, N_1 and C_1 are equivalent. At N_1, he gets more earnings than at M_1, but so will he incur greater risks. Each individual's indifferent curves will have different slopes depending on the degrees of his risk aversion. The slope of the indifferent curves measures the individual's subjective marginal rate of substitution between risks and earnings. C_1 is the certainty equivalent of M_1 and N_1. Thus instead of discounting the earnings associated with M_1 with the risk-adjusted discount rate, one can choose to discount the earnings associated with C_1 with the discounting rate r which is easily obtainable. But one must first convert M_1 into C_1 by the use of the individual's coefficients of certainty equivalents, q_t. An expected income streams E_t may be discounted to their present value by the following equation:

$$V_0 = \sum_{t=1}^{n} q_t E_t (1 + r)^{-t} \qquad (6.6.)$$

where V_0 is the certainty equivalent present value of the expected income streams, $0 \leq q_t \leq 1$, $(t = 1, 2, \ldots, n)$ give the individual's coefficients of certainty equivalents and r is the risk-free interest rate.

The use of a constant risk-adjusted discount rate as in the capital asset pricing model implies that risk in the forecasted cash flows increases at a constant rate. This contention of Robichek and Myers is now refuted by Beedles and Joy and others. Table 6.6.1. illustrates the Robichek and Myers contention and Table 6.6.2. illustrates the Beedles and Joy refutation.

Table 6.6.1.
Riskfree interest rate $(r) = 0.06$
Risky rate $(k) = 0.12$

	t_0	t_1	t_2	t_3	t_4
(1) Growth at $k = 0.12$	100	112	125.44	140.49	157.35
(2) Interest earned at $k = 0.12$	—	12	13.44	15.05	16.86
(3) Growth at $r = 0.06$	100	106	112.36	119.10	126.25
(4) Interest earned at $r = 0.06$	—	6	6.36	6.74	7.15
(5) Incremental interest earned due to risk bearing (2)–(4)	—	6	7.08	8.31	9.71
(6) Proportion of interest earned due to risk-bearing (5) ÷ (2)	—	0.50	0.53	0.55	0.58

Table 6.6.2.
Riskfree interest rate (r) = 0.06
Risky rate (k) = 0.12

	t_0	t_1	t_2	t_3	t_4
(1) Growth at $k = 0.12$	100	112	125.44	140.49	157.35
(2) Interest earned at $k = 0.12$	—	12	13.44	15.05	16.86
(3) Interest earned at $r = 0.06$		6	6.72	7.525	8.43
(4) Incremental interest earned due to risk bearing (2)–(3)		6	6.72	7.525	8.43
(5) Proportion of interest earned due to risk bearing (4) ÷ (2)		0.5	0.5	0.5	0.5

6.7. SELECTED BIBLIOGRAPHY

1. W.L. Beedles and O.M. Joy: Compounding Risk Over Time—A Note, *Journal of Business Finance and Accounting*, Autumn 1982.
2. H. Bierman, Jr. and J.E. Hass: Capital Budgeting Under Uncertainty—A Reformulation, Journal of Finance, March 1973.
3. M.E. Blume: Betas and their Regression Tendencies, Journal of Finance, June 1975.
4. E.J. Elton and M.J. Gruber: Modern Portfolio Theory and Investment Analysis.
5. Michael Firth: The Valuation of Shares and the Efficient Markets Theory.
6. Han Kang Hong: Cost and Management Accounting.
7. C.W. Haley and L.D. Schall: The Theory of Financial Decisions.
8. R.C. Klemkosky and J.D. Martin: The Adjustment of Beta Forecasts, Journal of Finance, September 1975.
9. A.A. Robichek: Interpreting the Results of Risk Analysis, Journal of Finance, December 1975.
10. A.A. Robichek and S.C. Myers: Conceptual Problems in the Use of Risk—Adjusted Discount Rates, Journal of Finance, December 1966.
11. A.A. Robichek and S.C. Myers: Optimal Financing Decisions.

12. W.F. Sharpe: A Theory of Market Equilibrium under Conditions of Risk, Journal of Finance, September 1964.
13. R.C. Stapleton: Portfolio Analysis, Stock Valuation and Capital Budgeting Uncertainty Decision Rules for Risky Projects, Journal of Finance, March 1971.
14. J.C. Van Horne: Financial Management and Policy.
15. J.F. Weston: Investment Decisions Using the Capital Asset Pricing Model, Financial Management, Spring 1973.
16. W.D. Whisler: Sensitivity Analysis of Rates of Return, Journal of Finance, March 1976.

CHAPTER 7

Other Investment Issues

7.1. ABANDONMENT VALUE AND CAPITAL BUDGETING

Whether an investment project should be abandoned before the end of its productive life depends on the abandonment value of the project at the end of each period as compared with its expected net present value at the end of that period calculated on the assumption of the continuity of the project. A project should be abandoned if the release of funds from its abandonment has an alternative use which offers a greater return than that expected from the project if it were continued. Many investment projects are flexible in the sense that they have alternative uses and therefore abandonment values. There are of course projects which are so specific in use that they have no abandonment values. Abandonment values should be incorporated into the capital budgeting model because its inclusion affects the expected net present value and standard deviation of the project's cash flows distribution. The illustration on page 87 will make this clear.

If there is no consideration of abandonment value, the following information is obtained:

The expected net present value of the net cash flows is:

$$NPV = \sum_{i=1}^{m} C_i p_i = \$4{,}539 \qquad (7.1.1.)$$

And the standard deviation is:

$$\sigma = \sqrt{\sum_{i=1}^{m} (C_i - NPV)^2 p_i} = \$7{,}006 \qquad (7.1.2.)$$

Suppose the abandonment value at the end of the first year is

Table 7.1.
Proposed Project
Forecasted Distribution of Net Cash Flows
Economic life: 2 years
Scrap value: nil
Minimum acceptable rate of return: 15%

Year 0			*Year 1*			*Year 2*				
C_{0i}	*Present Value of* C_{0i}	$P(C_{0i})$	C_{1i}	*Present Value of* C_{1i}	$P(C_{1i})$	C_{2i}	*Present Value of* C_{2i}	*Conditional Probability* $P(C_{2i}/C_{1i})$	*Total Present Value of each series* C_i	*Joint Probability* $P_i = P[C_{0i}, C_{1i}, C_{2i}]$
$	$		$	$		$	$		$	
−15,000	−15,000	1.0	10,000	8,696	0.6	6,000	4,537	0.7	−1,767	0.42
						9,000	6,805	0.3	501	0.18
			20,000	17,391	0.4	15,000	11,342	0.8	13,733	0.32
						10,000	7,561	0.2	9,952	0.08
										1.00

estimated as:

Amount	*Probability*	*Expected Value*
$ 8,000	0.4	$ 3,200
$12,000	0.6	$ 7,200
		$10,400

To decide whether the project should be abandoned at the end of the first year, it is necessary to calculate and compare the abandonment value at the end of the first year with the expected net present value of the subsequent cash flows from the end of that year. In this example we have two cases.

Case 1 The net cash flows of the project amount to $10,000 at the end of the first year.

Year 1	**Year 2** *Present value at end of Year 1*	*Joint Probability*	*Expected Present Value if project held to end of life*
$10,000	→ $5,217	0.7	$ 3,652
	→ $7,826	0.3	$ 2,348
			$ 6,000

The decision in Case 1 is to abandon the project since abandoning it results in a net cash inflow of $10,400 while holding it to the end of its economic life results in an expected net present value of $6,000.

Case 2 The net cash flows of the project amount to $20,000 at the year of the first year.

Year 1	**Year 2** *Present Value at end of Year 1* $	*Joint Probability*	*Expected Present Value if project held to end of life* $
$20,000	→ 13,043	0.8	10,434
	→ 8,696	0.2	1,739
			$12,173

The decision in Case 2 is to hold the project to the end of its life since the abandonment value is less than $12,173.

Table 7.2. illustrates how abandonment values are incorporated into the capital budgeting model.

$$NPV = \sum_{i=1}^{m} C_i p_i = \$6{,}834 \qquad (7.1.3.)$$

$$\sigma = \sqrt{\sum_{i=1}^{m} (C_i - NPV)^2 p_i} = \$5{,}106 \qquad (7.1.4.)$$

It can be seen that incorporating abandonment values into the model raises the expected net present value and lowers the standard deviation and thus makes the proposed project more desirable.

The abandonment value at the end of each year of the project's economic life must be estimated and a decision must be reached as to the year when the project can be most economically abandoned, if at all. The capital budgeting model incorporating abandonment values must then be applied to the new input information. The calculations involved will be phenomenal where the economic life of a project extends over many years and the number of series in the cash flows is large. For a practical solution, simulation techniques may have to be applied.[1]

7.2. MULTISTAGE DECISION TREE

The best way to understand a multistage decision model is through an example. Suppose a company is faced with the problem of deciding whether to invest initially in a small plant which may have to be expanded at the end of the second year of operations or to invest in a big plant at the very beginning, both plants being able to perform the assigned task equally well and both coming to the end of their economic lives at the end of the fourth year.

The big plant involves an initial outlay of \$2,000 while the small plant, of \$1,000. But the small plant may have to be expanded at the end of the second year, involving an additional outlay of \$1,000. The net cash flows and their associated probabilities for the four years are shown in Table 7.3.

1. See A.A. Robichek and J.C. Van Horne: Abandonment Value and Capital Budgeting, Journal of Finance, Dec. 1967.

Table 7.2.

Year 0			Year 1			Year 2				
C_{0i}	Present Value of C_{0i}	$P(C_{0i})$	C_{1i}	Present Value of C_{1i}	$P(C_{1i})$	C_{2i}	Present Value of C_{2i}	$P(C_{2i}/C_{1i})$	Total Present Value of each series C_i	Joint Probability $P_i = P[C_{0i}, C_{1i}, C_{2i}]$
$	$		$	$		$	$		$	
			20,400	17,739	0.6	0			2,739	0.60
−15,000	−15,000	1.0				15,000	11,342	0.8	13,733	0.32
			20,000	17,391	0.4	10,000	7,561	0.2	9,952	0.08
										1.00

Table 7.3.
Discounting Rate = 6%

Year 0		Year 1		Year 2		Year 3		Year 4		Joint Probability		NPV_i	
$P(C_{0i})$	C_{0i}	$P(C_{1i}/C_{0i})$	C_{1i}	$P[C_{2i}/C_{1i}]$	C_{2i}	$P[C_{3i}/C_{2i}]$	C_{3i}	$P[C_{4i}/C_{3i}]$	C_{4i}	$= p_i$	Total Present Value		i
	$		$		$		$		$		$		
1.0	−2,000	.6	800	1.0	500	1.0	4,000	1.0	2,000	.6	4,143	2,485.8	1
		.4	900	1.0	600	1.0	1,000	1.0	3,000	.4	2,599	1,039.6	2
												$ 3,525.4	
1.0	−1,000	.8	300	1.0	1,000	1.0	1,500	1.0	800	.80	2,066	$ 1,652.8	3
				.7	−400	1.0	2,000	1.0	3,000	.56	2,982	1,669.9	4
				.3	−400	1.0	3,000	1.0	5,000	.24	5,406	1,297.4	5
												$ 2,967.3	
		.2	243	1.0	600	1.0	600	1.0	300	.20	505	$ 101.0	6
				.5	−745	1.0	800	1.0	400	.10	−445	−44.5	7
				.5	−745	1.0	300	1.0	100	.10	−1,103	−110.3	8
												$ −154.8	

Big Plant Both Table 7.3 and Figure 7.1 explain that if the big plant is installed from the beginning, there is 0.6 probability that demand will be good and 0.4 probability that it will be poor. Their

Figure 7.1.

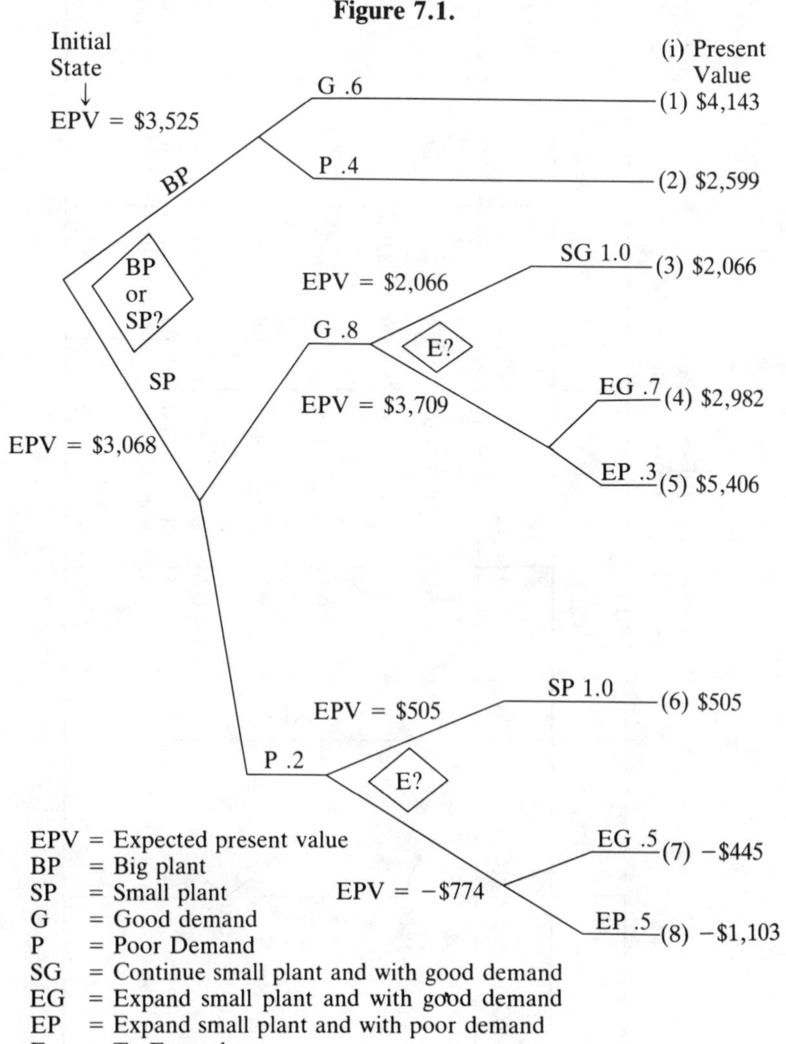

EPV = Expected present value
BP = Big plant
SP = Small plant
G = Good demand
P = Poor Demand
SG = Continue small plant and with good demand
EG = Expand small plant and with good demand
EP = Expand small plant and with poor demand
E = To Expand

total present values and expected net present values are shown in the last few columns of Table 7.3.

Small Plant Figure 7.1 shows that if a small plant is installed initially there is 0.8 probability that demand will be good and 0.2 probability that demand will be poor. If demand is good, the company can carry on with the small plant with a total present value of $2,066. If demand is good it can expand the small plant; in this case there is 0.7 probability that demand will be good after expansion resulting in a total present value of $2,982. On the other hand there is 0.3 probability that demand will be poor after expansion resulting in a total present value of $5,406.

Similarly, if the demand is poor with 0.2 probability, the company can carry on with the small plant resulting in a total present value of $505. If demand is poor and the company expands the small plant, this will result in negative present values of −$445 and −$1,103, as shown in Figure 7.1.

To solve the problem, the net present values of each branch of the decision tree must be first calculated. There are eight of them. Problems of this kind are solved recursively, starting from the last state and moving towards the initial state. Figure 7.1 shows that if demand is good with the small plant, expansion is preferable since the net expected present value is $3,709 compared with $2,066 without expansion. If demand is poor with the small plant, continuing with the small plant is better with a net expected present value of $505. Multiplying $3,709 and $505 by the probabilities 0.8 and 0.2 respectively gives the total expected net present value of the proposed investment project of $3,068 if the company starts with a small plant, and hence the branches or series i = 4, 5 and 6 are retained and the rest are discarded.

The total expected net present value of the proposed investment project is $3,525 if a big plant is installed initially, showing preference for the big plant.

7.3. MULTIPLE DISCOUNT RATES

If the investments of a firm are heterogeneous having different risks, a single risk-adjusted rate of discount may not be appropriate and multiple discount rates may have to be used. Proposed investment projects which are of equivalent risk class will be grouped together where a suitable risk-adjusted discount rate is applied. One example of such classification is as follows:

Risk Class	*Minimum Acceptable Rate of Return*
New product line	25%
Expansion and growth	15%
Replacement	12%
Staff Welfare facilities	Qualitative

Another way of solving this problem in a company having many divisions is to arrive at a minimum acceptable rate of return for each division. However, the practical problems of implementing this concept are difficult to overcome. Unless each division is a separate subsidiary company or is independent of the other divisions in operating activities, its cash flows and methods of finance cannot be easily segregated from those of other divisions. Sometimes the weighted average rate of return of firms dealing in the same line of business as the company's own division may be used as a surrogate if their risks are similar.

7.4. CONTRIBUTIONS TO EARNINGS PER SHARE

Both the internal rate of return and the net present value methods of evaluating investment projects ignore the effects on earnings per share. This is illustrated in Table 7.4.

Table 7.4.
Net Cash Flows

Project	*Year 0*	*Year 1*	*Year 2*	*Year 3*	*Net Present Value 15%*
	$	$	$	$	$
A	−1,000	1,200	1,400	1,600	2,154
B	−1,000	100	100	8,000	4,424

The net present value method indicates a preference for project *B*. But apparently project *A* contributes more to earnings per share in the first two years, though the position reverses in the third year.

If earnings per share has information value in the financial world this factor may have to be taken into account. One way of coping with this problem is the use of mathematical programming where the earnings per share may be included as a constraint. The zero-one programming model may be expressed as:

$$\text{Maximize} \quad \sum_{j=1}^{n} p_j x_j \qquad (7.4.)$$

$$\text{Subject to} \quad \sum_{j=1}^{n} e_{jt} x_j \geq \Delta E_t \qquad (t = 1, \ldots, m)$$

$$x_j = 0,\ 1$$

where p_j is the present value of proposed investment project x_j
e_{jt} is the earnings of proposed investment project x_j in year t, and
ΔE_t is the desired minimum increase in total earnings in year t.

7.5. INFLATION AND CAPITAL BUDGETING

In the capital budgeting models which make use of the techniques of discounting cash flows, the two important parameters that may or may not take into account the effects of inflation are the forecasted cash flows and the discount rates. In periods of inflation ignoring its effects may not lead to optimal decisions. The following symbols will be used for the various situations:

C_t = net cash flows in year t in terms of price level at year 0.
C_{It} = net cash flows in year t in terms of price level at year t
i = anual rate of inflation
k = minimum acceptable rate of return in terms of price level at year 0
k_I = minimum acceptable rate of return incorporating expected rate of inflation.

7.5.1. Both Estimates are in Terms of C_t and k

Since both the cash flows and the minimum acceptable rate of return are in terms of the present price level, no adjustments are required, and the expected net present value is calculated as:

$$\overline{NPV} = \sum_{t=0}^{n} C_t(1 + k)^{-t} \qquad (7.5.1.)$$

7.5.2. Both Estimates are in Terms of C_{It} and k_I

Since both the cash flows and the minimum acceptable rate of return take into account anticipated inflation when cash flows are expected to take place, no adjustments are required and the expected net present value is calculated as:

$$\overline{NPV} = \sum_{t=0}^{n} C_{It}(1 + k_I)^{-t} \qquad (7.5.2.)$$

7.5.3. Estimates are in Terms of C_{It} and k

Since the cash flows are in terms of the price levels in the years in which they take place and the minimum acceptable rate of return is in terms of the present price level, adjustments must be made to one or the other to render them comparable. If adjustments are made to the minimum acceptable rate of return, the calculations are as follows:

$$k_I = (1 + k)(1 + i) - 1 \qquad (7.5.3.)$$

$$\overline{NPV} = \sum_{t=0}^{n} C_{It}(1 + k_I)^{-t} \qquad (7.5.3.1.)$$

If adjustments are made to the annual cash flows, the calculations are as follows:

$$C_t = C_{It}(1 + i)^{-t},\ t = 1, \ldots, n \qquad (7.5.3.2.)$$

$$\overline{NPV} = \sum_{t=0}^{n} C_{It}(1 + i)^{-t}(1 + k)^{-t} \qquad (7.5.3.3.)$$

$$= \sum_{t=0}^{n} C_t(1 + k)^{-t} \qquad (7.5.3.4.)$$

7.5.4. Estimates are in Terms of C_t and k_I

In this case it is easy to convert C_t into C_{It} before calculating the expected net present value. The calculations are:

$$C_{It} = C_t(1 + i)^t,\ t = 1, \ldots, n \qquad (7.5.4.)$$

$$\overline{NPV} = \sum_{t=0}^{n} C_t(1 + i)^t(1 + k_I)^{-t} \qquad (7.5.4.1.)$$

$$= \sum_{t=0}^{n} C_{It}(1 + k_I)^{-t} \qquad (7.5.4.2.)$$

7.5.5. In Practice

In practice, observed market prices reflect inflation and hence observed market rates also reflect inflation. In other words the minimum acceptable rate of return obtained is in terms of anticipated inflation. Hence adjustments may have to be made to the C_t.

But in the world of subjective evaluation, investors may have their opinion that any proposed investment project will not be acceptable unless it yields a certain minimum acceptable rate of return in real terms which mean in terms of the present price level. Under such circumstances, forecasted future cash flows in terms of future price levels may be adjusted using equation (7.5.3.2.). Alternatively, k may be adjusted to k_I as in equation (7.5.3.)

7.5.6. A Numerical Example

Inflation Ltd invests $200,000 in a project at time t_0 which is expected to generate the cash flows as shown in Table 7.5 over the next four years after which the project will be scrapped with no salvage value. The same number of units of output will be produced each year. The selling price of the output is expected to increase by 8% per year and the input cash cost by 12%. Inflation is projected to be 10% per annum. The minimum acceptable rate of return of the company at time t_0 is 20%.

Table 7.5

Year	*Cash Sales Revenue*	*Cash Costs*	*Net Cash Flows in terms of C_{It}*
	\$'000	\$'000	\$'000
t_0	0	0	−200.000
t_1	518.400	392.000	126.400
t_2	559.872	439.040	120.832
t_3	604.662	491.725	112.937
t_4	653.035	550.732	102.303

The minimum acceptable rate of return k (0.20) is converted into k_I (incorporating the expected rate of inflation using equation 7.5.3.) as follows:

$$k_I = (1.20)(1.10) - 1 = 0.32$$

The net present value of the proposed project (using equation 7.5.3.1.) is as follows:

$$\begin{aligned}\overline{NPV} &= -200{,}000 + 126{,}400(1.32)^{-1} + 120{,}832(1.32)^{-2} \\ &\quad + 112{,}937(1.32)^{-3} + 102{,}303(1.32)^{-4} \\ &= \$47{,}907\end{aligned}$$

Since $\overline{NPV}$ is positive the proposed project is acceptable.

If adjustments are made to the annual net cash flows, the calculations (using equation 7.5.3.2. and 7.5.3.4.) are as follows:

$$C_1 = 126{,}400(1.1)^{-1} = 114{,}909 \quad C_2 = 120{,}832(1.1)^{-2} = 99{,}861$$
$$C_3 = 112{,}937(1.1)^{-3} = 84{,}851 \quad C_4 = 102{,}303(1.1)^{-4} = 69{,}874$$

$$\begin{aligned}\overline{NPV} &= -200{,}000 + 114{,}909(1.2)^{-1} + 99{,}861(1.2)^{-2} \\ &\quad + 84{,}851(1.2)^{-3} + 69{,}874(1.2)^{-4} = \$47{,}907\end{aligned}$$

The result is the same.

7.6. SELECTED BIBLIOGRAPHY

1. H. Bierman, Jr and S. Smidt: The Capital Budgeting Decision.
2. H. Bierman, Jr and W.H. Hausman: The Resolution of Investment Uncertainty through Time, Management Science, May 1972.
3. Han Kang Hong: Cost and Management Accounting.
4. R.F. Hespos and P.A. Strassmann: Stochastic Decision Trees for the Analysis of Investment Decisions, Management Science, August 1965.
5. A.G. Lockett and A.E. Gear: Multistage Capital Budgeting Under Uncertainty, Journal of Financial and Quantitative Analysis, March 1975.
6. J.F. Magee: How to Use Decision Trees in Capital Investment, Harvard Business Review, September–October 1964.
7. A.A. Robichek and J.C. Van Horne: Abandonment Value and Capital Budgeting, Journal of Finance, December 1967.
8. J.C. Van Horne: Capital Budgeting Decisions Involving Combinations of Risky Investments, Management Science, October 1966.
9. J.C. Van Horne: A Note on Biases in Capital Budgeting Introduced by Inflation, Journal of Financial and Quantitative Analysis, March 1971.

CHAPTER 8

Investment in Current Assets and Working Capital Management

8.1. SUB-OPTIMIZATION

It has been stated in Chapter 1 that an optimization model for the whole firm which will ensure concurrently an optimal portfolio of assets (both fixed and current) as well as an optimal mix of finance ought to be the objective of managerial finance in its function of maximizing the firm value. In this chapter, the sub-optimization of investment in current assets that is, stock, receivables and cash, will be discussed, so will the management of working capital.

8.2. INVESTMENT IN STOCK

Stock could mean one, some, or all of three things:

(1) raw materials,
(2) work-in-process,
(3) finished goods.

There are different types of stock in different industries. It is generally agreed that the quantity of stock is closely related to total assets and sales volume. What levels of stock are desirable, that is, what should be the maximum and minimum levels of stock? We shall now discuss briefly the determinants of work-in-process and finished goods.

Work-in-process consists of the cost of the raw materials which have gone into production but which have not been completed, the service charge so far collated such as direct labour, and the allocated overheads such as rent, heat and power. The amount of work-in-process is determined by the following:

(1) the length of the production cycle,
(2) the technical factors which determine (1) and which affect policies of management,
(3) the production flow (whether everything flows smoothly from process to process, or there are bottlenecks),
(4) the volume of production,
(5) prices of raw materials, labour and overheads, and
(6) the method of production employed, for instance, shift working. (Shift-working shortens the length of time during which money is tied up in work-in-process.)

Finished goods are in a state ready for sale. The following factors could determine the amount of finished goods carried:

(1) Producing for stock-piling or according to customers' orders. (The former tends to encourage heavy investment in stock, the latter minimizes stock.)
(2) Seasonal demand. (Here a balance must be struck between piling stock and stabilizing production, and minimizing stock and fluctuating level of production.)
(3) Degree of competition. (Marketing effectiveness becomes important. Stock may be stored at proximity to demand.)
(4) Relationship between forecasted demand and level of stock.

8.2.1. Optimal Decisions on Inventory Problems

The main purpose of inventory management is to minimize total inventory costs. The two types of inventory costs which are controllable and relevant are: (1) carrying costs, and (2) ordering costs. The objective is to decide when to order and how much to buy in each order so that the total costs of carrying and ordering are at a minimum. Ordering costs include all costs necessarily incurred in placing orders with suppliers and getting the goods into store. The following is an example illustrating how the cost of ordering one unit of stock is determined:

Total Variable Costs of Ordering for a Typical Period

		$
Salaries and wages		58,000
Stationery and postages		1,000
Sundry expenses		1,000
	Total ordering cost =	60,000
Total number of orders placed	=	30
Therefore ordering cost per order	=	$\frac{60,000}{30}$
	=	$2,000

Carrying costs include all costs necessarily incurred for holding stock in store. The following is an example illustrating how the cost of carrying stock is determined:

Variable Carrying Cost for One Typical Period

		$
Interest on capital tied up in average stock		17,600
Rent of stores		6,000
Store-keeping expenses		8,400
Insurance		1,000
	Total carrying cost =	$33,000

Therefore carrying cost as a percentage of average stock

$$= \frac{33,000 \times 100}{220,000} = 15\%$$

The average stock for a control period (which may be a year, a month or a week) is arrived at by adding the opening stock and the closing stock together and dividing the answer by 2. However, if the control period is a year, the more accurate average stock figure would be arrived at by adding the average stock figures of 12 months and dividing the answer by 12. The following example illustrates how the average inventory is determined:

Typical Periods	*Average Stock*
	$
1	200,000
2	240,000
3	220,000
4	260,000
5	220,000
6	200,000
7	180,000
8	240,000
9	260,000
10	200,000
11	220,000
12	200,000
Total =	$2,640,000

Therefore the average stock for the control period

$$= \frac{2,640,000}{12} = \$220,000$$

There are three ways by which the optimum number of orders per control period can be represented:

(1) By tabulating
(2) By graphic presentation
(3) By formula.

Of course, if we know the optimum number of orders to place per control period, we can arrive at the optimum number of units per order. Let us assume that the total number of units required during the control period is 12,000,000 which at a purchase price of $2 per unit amounts to $24,000,000.

By Tabulating

With the data given so far, the optimum number of orders is arrived at as shown in Table 8.2.1.

By Graphic Presentation

When the data of Table 8.2.1. are plotted on a graph, we produce Figure 8.2.1. Here, it can be clearly seen that the total

Table 8.2.1.

Number of Orders	*Total Ordering Cost (1)*	*Total Carrying Cost (2)*	*Sum of (1) and (2)*
	$	$	$
15	30,000	120,000	150,000
16	32,000	112,500	144,500
17	34,000	105,838	139,838
18	36,000	100,000	136,000
19	38,000	94,737	132,737
20	40,000	90,000	130,000
21	42,000	85,714	127,714
22	44,000	81,818	125,818
23	46,000	78,261	124,261
24	48,000	75,000	123,000
25	50,000	72,000	122,000
26	52,000	69,231	121,231
27	54,000	66,666	120,666
28	56,000	64,286	120,286
29	58,000	62,068	120,068
30	60,000	60,000	120,000
31	62,000	58,064	120,064
32	64,000	56,250	120,250
33	66,000	54,545	120,545
34	68,000	52,941	120,941
35	70,000	51,429	121,429
36	72,000	50,000	122,000
37	74,000	48,649	122,649
38	76,000	47,369	123,369
39	78,000	46,154	124,154
40	80,000	45,000	125,000

Optimum Number of Orders

Minimum total cost of ordering and carrying.

costs are at a minimum when the ordering cost is just equal to the carrying cost.

By Formula

Denoting total optimum number of orders as N and the ordering cost per order as C, we have

$$\text{Total ordering cost} = NC$$

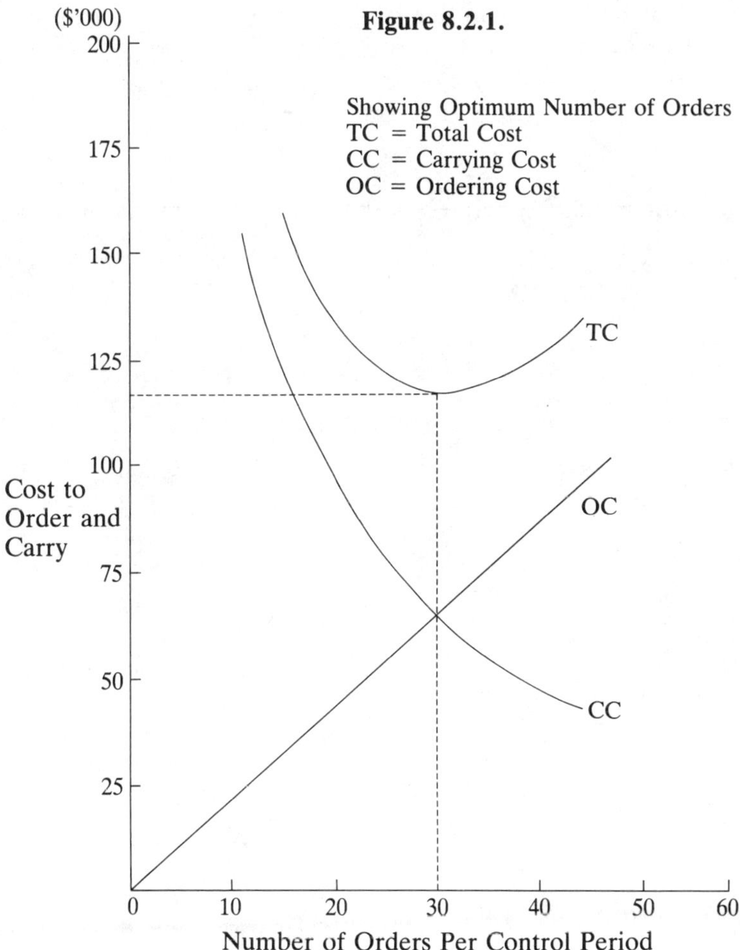

Figure 8.2.1.

Total carrying cost is expressed as a percentage of average stock in dollar value, or

$$\frac{V}{N} \times \frac{1}{2} \times P \quad \text{or} \quad \frac{VP}{2N}, \text{ where}$$

V = total dollar value of stock required in the control period,
P = carrying cost percentage.

Our objective is to minimize the sum of ordering cost and carrying cost.

$$Y = NC + \frac{VP}{2N}$$

Minimizing Y where $\frac{dY}{dN} = 0$, to arrive at a formula for N, we have

$$\begin{aligned} Y &= NC + \frac{VP}{2N} \\ &= NC + \left(\frac{VP}{2}\right)N^{-1} \end{aligned}$$

$$\frac{dY}{dN} = C - \frac{VP}{2N^2}$$

Therefore

$$\begin{aligned} C - \frac{VP}{2N^2} &= 0 \\ C &= \frac{VP}{2N^2} \\ 2N^2C &= VP \\ N^2 &= \frac{VP}{2C} \end{aligned}$$

Therefore

$$N^* = \sqrt{\frac{VP}{2C}} \qquad (8.2.1.)$$

Using the data given in the example, we can solve for N:

$$\begin{aligned} \sqrt{\frac{VP}{2C}} &= \sqrt{\frac{24{,}000{,}000 \times 0.15}{2 \times 2{,}000}} \\ &= 30 \text{ orders per control period.} \end{aligned}$$

Having obtained the optimum number of orders per control period, we can get the economic-order-quantity which is

$$\frac{\text{total quantity required in the control period}}{\text{optimum number of orders}}$$

$$= \$\,\frac{24{,}000{,}000}{30} = \$800{,}000$$

or 400,000 units per order.

Principles underlying the Economic-Order-Quantity Theory

It is necessary to understand the principles underlying the application of the economic-order-quantity theory so that one can decide whether it is applicable in any given practical situation and what conclusions can be drawn from its use. Some of the more significant variables to be considered are listed below:

(1) Purchase price: If there is an increase in the cost price of purchases, the optimum number of orders per control period increases. In other words the economic-order-quantity decreases as purchase price increases.
(2) The interest rate to be applied on the capital tied up in stock affects the economic-order-quantity. Hence, the interest rate chosen should be realistic.
(3) There may be practical difficulties in determining carrying and ordering costs. For instance, in the model illustrated, ordering cost is assumed to vary directly and proportionately with the number of orders placed. In other words, if we place one more order total ordering cost increases by $2,000 and we can save $2,000 by placing one order less. In practice, ordering cost may not behave in this manner because some of the components of ordering cost may be fixed such as the salaries of the staff in the Purchasing Department.
(4) The question of quantity discount may have to be considered since this affects the purchase price, and thus the economic-order-quantity.

8.2.2. Sensitivity Analysis

Alternatively, it can be shown that the optimal economic-order-quantity may be expressed as:

$$q^* = \sqrt{\frac{2DO}{H}} \qquad (8.2.2.1.)$$

where q^* is the optimal economic-order-quantity in units,
D is the number of units required in the control period,
O is the differential cost of placing an order, and
H is the differential cost of holding one unit of stock per control period.

The total relevant cost of inventory is:

$$y = \frac{qH}{2} + \frac{DO}{q} \qquad (8.2.2.2.)$$

where y is the total relevant inventory cost,

$\frac{qH}{2}$ is the total holding cost for the control period, and

$\frac{DO}{q}$ is the total ordering cost for the control period.

Hence, the minimum total relevant inventory cost is:

$$y^* = \frac{q^*H}{2} + \frac{DO}{q^*} \qquad (8.2.2.3.)$$

Substituting $\sqrt{\frac{2DO}{H}}$ for q^* in equation (8.2.2.3.) gives after some algebraic manipulation:

$$y^* = \sqrt{2DOH} \qquad (8.2.2.4.)$$

If the actual order quantity is q_a due to errors in the parameter estimates, D, O, or H, it can be expressed as:

$$q_a = dq^* = d\sqrt{\frac{2DO}{H}} \qquad (8.2.2.5.)$$

The actual total relevant inventory cost y_a is:

$$y_a = \frac{q_a H}{2} + \frac{DO}{q_a}$$

$$= \frac{\sqrt{2DOH}\,(d^2 + 1)}{2d} \qquad (8.2.2.6.)$$

(by substitution)
Hence,

$$\frac{y_a}{y^*} = \frac{\sqrt{2DOH}\,(d^2 + 1)}{2d}\left(\frac{1}{\sqrt{2DOH}}\right)$$

$$= \frac{1}{2}\left(d + \frac{1}{d}\right) \qquad (8.2.2.7.)$$

Therefore,

$$y_a = \left[\frac{1}{2}\left(d + \frac{1}{d}\right)\right]y^* \qquad (8.2.2.8.)$$

The following example illustrates the above analysis:

Quanlity Limited is a private company selling different brands of standard equipment. The following data for the next control period relate to one of its product lines, "Delun" and are considered reliable and accurate:

Differential cost of placing an order	. . . . . \$ 600
Differential cost of holding one unit per control period	. . . . . \$ 300
Purchase price of one unit	. . . . . \$10,000

The estimated demand for "Delun" in the next control period is 2,500 units. While forecasts of relevant inventory costs have been accurate and reliable, forecasted demand for "Delun" is subject to an error of about 10% either way.

The annual fixed costs relevant to inventory other than costs of stock (that is, the purchase price) amount to $7,000.

$$q_a = \sqrt{\frac{2 \times 2{,}500 \times 600}{300}} = 100 \text{ units}$$

The correct demand forecast is between 2,250 to 2,750 units.
(i) If correct demand is 2,750 units,

$$q_1^* = \sqrt{\frac{2 \times 2{,}750 \times 600}{300}} \cong 105 \text{ units}$$

$$y_1^* = \sqrt{2 \times 2{,}750 \times 600 \times 300} = \$31{,}464.27$$

and the difference in the total relevant inventory cost due to the error in q_a is:

$$\left[\frac{1}{2}\left(0.9523809 + \frac{1}{0.9523809}\right) - 1\right](31{,}464.27)$$

$$= \$37.46$$

(ii) If correct demand is 2,250 units,

$$q_2^* = \sqrt{\frac{2 \times 2{,}250 \times 600}{300}} \triangleq 95 \text{ units}$$

$$y_2^* = \sqrt{2 \times 2{,}250 \times 600 \times 300} \cong \$28{,}460.50$$

and the difference in total relevant inventory cost due to the error in q_a is:

$$\left[\frac{1}{2}\left(1.0526315 + \frac{1}{1.0526315}\right) - 1\right](28{,}460.50)$$

$$\cong \$37.45$$

8.2.3. Quantity Discount

In the example of Table 8.2.1., the economic-order-quantity is found to be 400,000 units at a cost of $2 per unit when the total requirement in the control period is 12,000,000 units. What would be the position should the supplier offer a discount of one cent per unit if the order quantity is 600,000 units? The simplest way of solving this type of problem is to compare the total costs of stock under the two alternatives. Presenting the data given, we have the following comparative positions:

Order Quantity	= 400,000 Units	600,000 Units
	= $2	$1.99
Total Quantity Required	= 12,000,000 units	12,000,000 units

Total Costs Per Control Period

Total Purchase Price	$24,000,000	$23,880,000
Total Carrying Cost	60,000	89,550
Total Ordering Cost	60,000	40,000
Total Cost of Stock	$24,120,000	$24,009,550

It is cheaper to buy 600,000 units per order and to have 20 orders per control period. If the answer is that it is cheaper to take advantage of the quantity discount, the question whether it will even be cheaper to increase further the order-quantity must be answered. There is a simple rule to apply in such a situation: If the carrying cost (with the discount taken into consideration) exceeds the ordering cost, the quantity at the discount level is the correct one; should the latter exceeds the former, a new economic-order-quantity must be computed at the discount price. A look at Figure 8.2.1. will enable one to see the logic of the rule.

8.2.4. The Reorder Point

So far we have assumed that the requirement of stock as well as the supply of stock is stable throughout the control period. This may not be so and supply may be delayed. In other words the lead time may not be constant. The lead time is the time interval between the placing of an order and the receipt of the goods ordered into store. Should there be a delay in the arrival of the goods ordered the firm would run out of stock. To minimize the probability of such an event, there must be some safety or buffer stock. Therefore, the reorder point, which is that level of stock at which an order must be placed with a supplier, is determined thus:

average daily requirement of stock × lead time (in days) + safety stock

How can one arrive at a safety stock level? Theoretically the cost of running out of stock must be balanced against the cost of carrying safety stock so that the sum of the two costs is at a minimum. To arrive at the total cost of running out of stock, we may get the aid of probability theory. Let us illustrate this with an example. The following table shows the probabilities of stock requirement during the lead time:

Requirement during the lead time	*Number of times this quantity is required*	*Requirement Probability*
100,000	5	0.05
150,000	8	0.08
200,000	70	0.70
250,000	11	0.11
300,000	4	0.04
350,000	2	0.02
	100 times	1.00

If the reorder point is 100,000 units, the firm is safe 5% of the time and will be out of stock 95% of the time. If the reorder point is 200,000 units the firm will be safe 83% of the time and out of stock 17% of the time.

The main difficulty involved in this kind of problem is to determine the cost of running out of stock per unit. This figure can only be arrived at by people who are fully conversant with the detailed business operations. It includes all the costs resulting from production delay.

Let us assume that the cost of running out of stock per unit is $0.50, the lead time is 5 days, daily average requirement is 40,000 units, the optimum number of orders for the control period is 20, and the cost of carrying one unit of stock is \$0.30.

The total annual cost of running out of stock is computed as shown in Table 8.2.4.1. The minimum cost of safety stock is shown in Table 8.2.4.2.

Hence, the reorder point

$$= \text{average daily stock requirement} \times \text{lead time} + \text{safety stock}$$
$$= 40{,}000 \times 5 + 100{,}000$$
$$= 300{,}000 \text{ units.}$$

8.2.5. Batch Costing

Where articles are manufactured in batches, it may be desirable to apply the economic-order-quantity theory to arrive at the optimum quantity to form an economic batch. It is necessary to arrive at the following variables:

(1) Setting up cost per batch (setting up the production lines on machines) = C
(2) Carrying costs as a percentage of finished goods = P
(3) The rate of demand per control period = V
(4) Optimum number of batches or lots per year = N

If the following particulars relate to Alowing Ltd. for a control period:

$$V = 350{,}000$$
$$P = 5\% \text{ per control period}$$
$$C = \$350$$

Then, $N = \sqrt{\dfrac{VP}{2C}} = \sqrt{\dfrac{350{,}000 \times 0.05}{2 \times 350}}$ = 5 batches or lots per control period.

Where a manufacturer produces a number of products which are inter-dependent in respect of productive processes, the economic-lot-size theory cannot be applied in its simple form. For

Table 8.2.4.1.

Safety Stock (a)	*Probability of Running Out of Stock (b)*	*Number of Units Out of Stock (c)*		*Total Cost of being Out of Stock*
Units	Units		$	$
0	0.11 when requirement = 250,000	50,000	50,000 × .11 × .5 × 20 = 55,000	
	0.04 -do- = 300,000	100,000	100,000 × .04 × .5 × 20 = 40,000	
	0.02 -do- = 350,000	150,000	150,000 × .02 × .5 × 20 = 30,000	125,000
50,000	0.04 -do- = 300,000	50,000	50,000 × .04 × .5 × 20 = 20,000	
	0.02 -do- = 350,000	100,000	100,000 × .02 × .5 × 20 = 20,000	40,000
100,000	0.02 -do- = 350,000	50,000	50,000 × .02 × .5 × 20 = 10,000	10,000
150,000	0 0	0	0	0

Table 8.2.4.2
Arriving at minimum cost of safety stock

	Safety Stock	*Cost of being Out of Stock (a)*	*Total Carrying Cost (b)*	*Sum of (a) and (b)*	
		$	$	$	
	0	125,000	0 × \$0.30 = 0	125,000	
	50,000	40,000	50,000 × \$0.30 = 15,000	55,000	
afety Stock →	100,000	10,000	100,000 × \$0.30 = 30,000	40,000	← Minimum Cost
	150,000	0	150,000 × \$0.30 = 45,000	45,000	

instance, the following particulars relate to a certain manufacturer:

Monthly Plant Capacity = 500 units

Products	*Demand*	*Economic-Lot-Size*
A	250	260
B	150	180
C	100	60
	500 units	500 units

If the economic-lot-size theory is applied in the simple form, at the end of the month there will be overstocking of Products *A* and *B* by 10 and 30 units respectively, while the stock on hand of Product *C* will be reduced by 40. The consequences would be disastrous if this were carried on in subsequent months.

Hence, simulation techniques or mathematical programming may be applied where all the constraints in the problem, such as the demand of each product, must be incorporated into the model.

8.2.6. Inventory Model and Steady Demand

Inventory policy and inventory control are two inter-related factors which can affect the profitability of business operations. Sometimes they are the principal determinants of the success or failure of business enterprises. In all manufacturing enterprises where raw material forms a major portion of the cost of production, stock policy and stock control are of vital importance to efficient management.

It is considered that the building of a model of an inventory policy, just as the building of models in engineering and architecture, will clarify and identify the main factors involved in problems so that their solutions are thereby facilitated. Tentatively the stock policy of any manufacturing enterprise can be reduced to either of two basic types: (1) as illustrated in Figure 8.2.6.1., and (2) as illustrated in Figure 8.2.6.2.

In the first type as illustrated by Figure 8.2.6.1., when the available quantity in store falls to or below the minimum level (m), a replenishment order is issued for a standard quantity ($M - m = q$). The quantity per order that will give the maximum advantage, or the minimum total annual cost can be calculated by the use of the economic-order-quantity theory.

In the second type as illustrated by Figure 8.2.6.2., at regular and equal intervals (i), a replenishment order is issued for a quantity sufficiently large to last until the next replenishment order. In the figure, the size of the first replenishment order is indicated by q_1; the second by q_2; and the third by q_3. The time-interval (i) between replenishment orders can be determined by economic-order-quantity computations.

In order that models can be built on the lines suggested, the main factors in the models must be determined, such as, maximum level of stock, minimum level, lead time and economic-order-quantity. The lead time (l) may be defined as the interval of time between the issue of a replenishment order and the receipt of inventory into store. The minimum level (m) is equal to the reasonable quantity (with a margin of safety) that must be issued from store for production during a lead time. All these factors can be established only if relevant data of the planned programme of production can be obtained. The quantity to be ordered and the time for issuing replenishment orders can then be determined.

The order quantity which will give the minimum total cost can also be illustrated graphically as shown in Figure 8.2.6.3.

Having stated in very brief outline how inventory models can be built, we could suggest how they may be used as tools of control. In the first type (Figure 8.2.6.1.), the quantity per replenishment order ($M - m$) is standard, that is, predetermined. The number of orders per control period (n) is

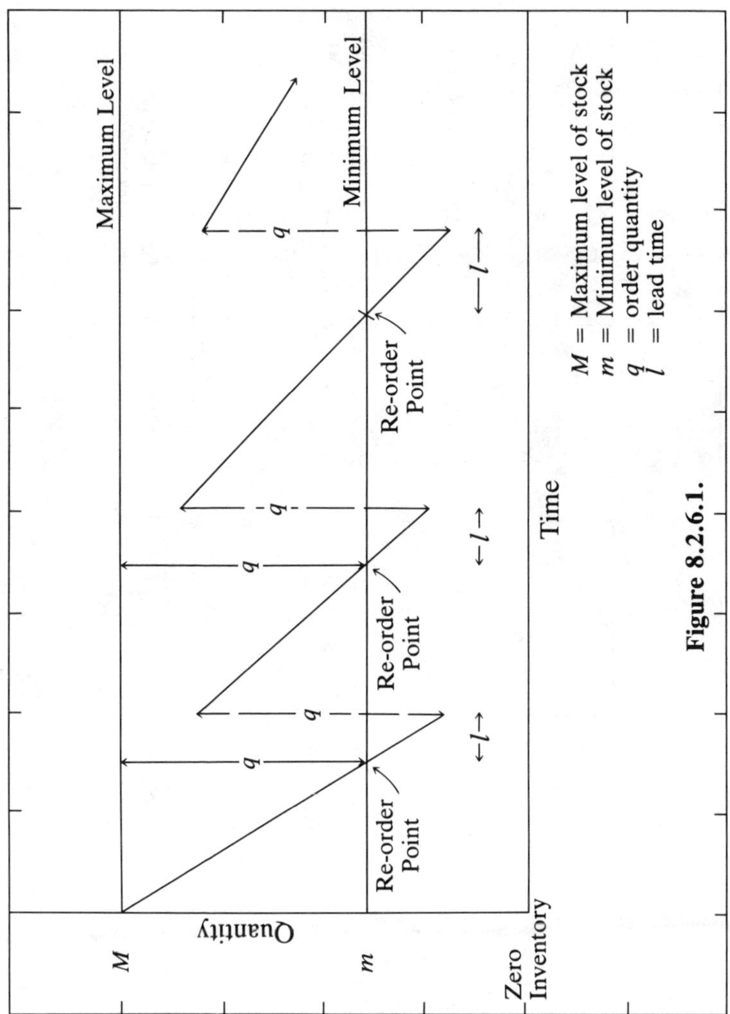

Figure 8.2.6.1.

controlled and recorded by the Purchasing Department or Accounting Department. The product of the order quantity and the number of orders per control period gives the total quantity ordered in the control period, or $n(M - m)$.

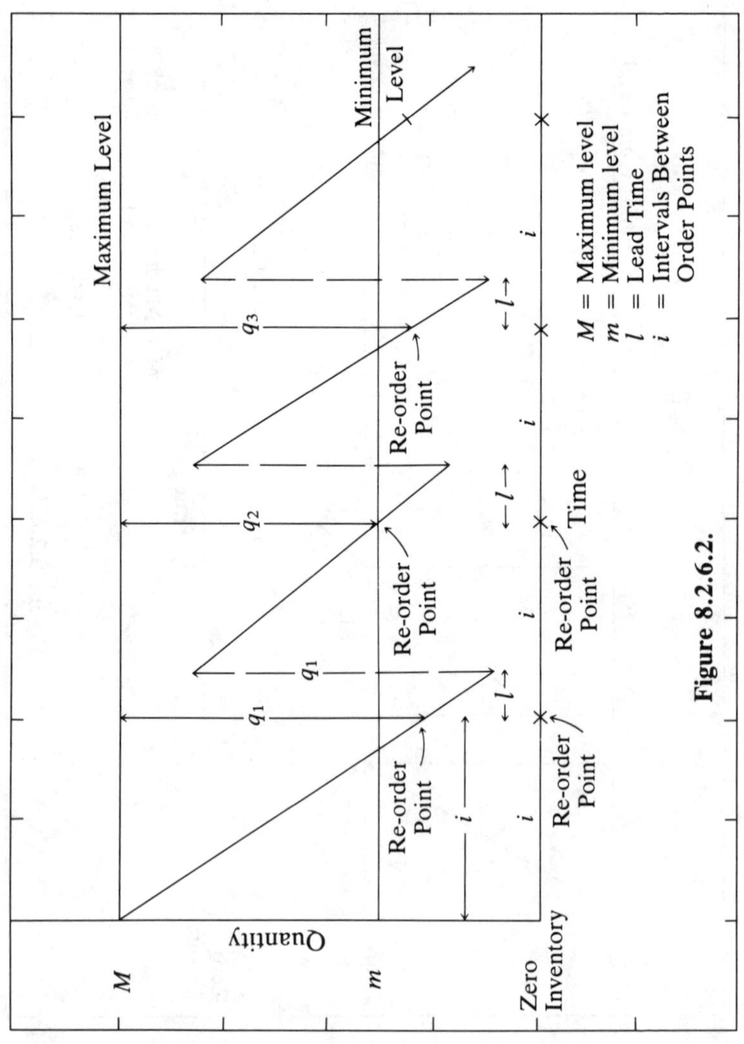

Figure 8.2.6.2.

In the second type, Figure 8.2.6.2., the number of replenishment orders per control period is pre-determined. The average quantity per order can be computed by statistical techniques. The

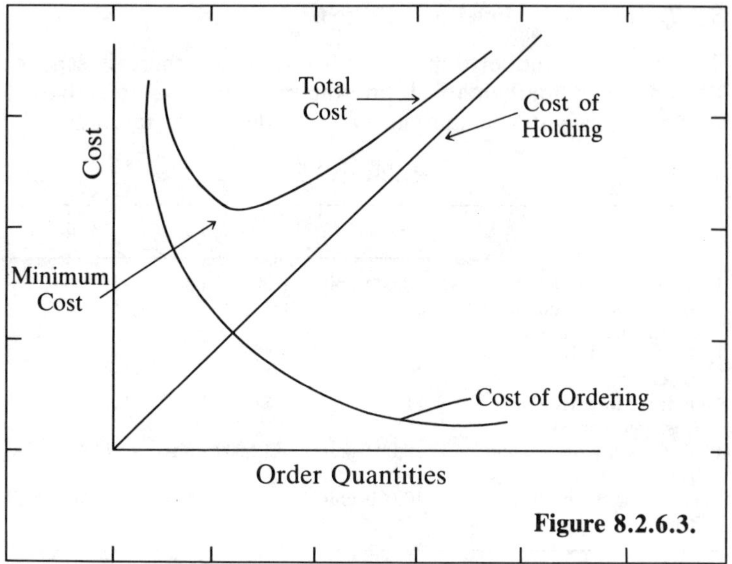

Figure 8.2.6.3.

product of the former and the latter gives the total quantity that should be ordered in thc control period.

The total quantity in the control period as determined by the model is compared with the total quantity as recorded by the Accounting Department according to usual accounting methods to reveal any variance. If the variance exceeds the calculated allowance of error, its cause or causes can be investigated.

The value of an inventory model as a tool of control lies in the fact that it tests the degree of effectiveness of the internal inventory control of an enterprise. The use of an inventory model pre-supposes the existence of an internal control system. The inventory model should be used to reveal any defects of the existing inventory control system which can then be rectified.

In enterprises where demand can be forecasted with reasonable accuracy so that production can be programmed over a control period, the use of an inventory model is practicable and should prove a valuable management tool. It is suitable for enterprises like public utilities undertakings, mass assembly lines, and enterprises producing goods for a wide and steady market.

8.2.7. Inventory Model and Seasonal Demand

The inventory model that is applicable where there is seasonal demand is a mathematical programming model. It is best to illustrate this with an example. With the data given in Table 8.2.7.

Table 8.2.7.

	Period 1	*Period 2*	*Period 3*
Demand	20,000 units	30,000 units	25,000 units
Unit Cost of Production on Regular Time	\$4	\$4	\$4
Unit Cost of Production on Overtime	\$7	\$7	\$7
Unit Inventory Holding Cost per Period	\$1	\$1	\$1
Plant Capacity on Regular Time	18,000 units	18,000 units	18,000 units
Plant Capacity on Over Time	10,000 units	10,000 units	10,000 units

the linear programming for the problem is:

$$\begin{aligned}\text{Minimize } Z = {} & 4x_{111} + 7x_{121} + 5x_{112} + 8x_{122} + 6x_{113} + 9x_{123} \\ & + 4x_{212} + 7x_{222} + 5x_{213} + 8x_{223} \\ & + 4x_{313} + 7x_{323}\end{aligned}$$

Subject to

$$\begin{aligned}
x_{111} + x_{121} &= 20{,}000 \\
x_{112} + x_{122} + x_{212} + x_{222} &= 30{,}000 \\
x_{113} + x_{123} + x_{213} + x_{223} + x_{313} + x_{323} &= 25{,}000 \\
x_{111} + x_{112} + x_{113} &\leqq 18{,}000 \\
x_{212} + x_{213} &\leqq 18{,}000 \\
x_{313} &\leqq 18{,}000 \\
x_{121} + x_{122} + x_{123} &\leqq 10{,}000 \\
x_{222} + x_{223} &\leqq 10{,}000 \\
x_{323} &\leqq 10{,}000
\end{aligned}$$

$$x_{ijk} \geqq 0$$

where x_{ijk} is the number of units produced in period i on shift j and sold in period k.

Other constraints may be introduced and the programme can be modified to meet the requirements of the particular problem. The optimal solutions are:

$$x^*_{111} = 16{,}000$$
$$x^*_{121} = 4{,}000$$
$$x^*_{112} = 2{,}000$$
$$x^*_{212} = 18{,}000$$
$$x^*_{222} = 10{,}000$$
$$x^*_{313} = 18{,}000$$
$$x^*_{323} = 7{,}000$$
$$Z^* = \$365{,}000$$

8.3. INVESTMENT IN RECEIVABLES

When goods are sold on credit, funds are tied up in trade debtors or bills receivable. Control over receivables is exercised in two ways: control over the granting of credit and supervising the collection of debts. In exercising this control, management may have to reconcile two conflicting objectives:

(1) Strict standards in evaluating credit-worthiness and stringent enforcement in the collection of debts.
(2) Maximizing sales volume and profitability.

The amount of receivables could be determined by the following:

(1) Terms of credit and cash discount granted,
(2) Standards adopted in evaluating credit-worthiness,
(3) Degree of stringency in the collection of debts,
(4) Paying habits of customers, and
(5) Volume of credit sales.

Since the first four determinants are relatively stable over short periods, the last one is usually the main cause of any short-term changes in receivables.

Let us use a simple example to illustrate how credit risks may be evaluated. *X* proposes to buy every month from *Y* Limited on credit goods worth $50,000. The credit allowed by *Y* Limited is 25 days, but *X* will take 60 days to pay. The profit margin is 10% on sales. Should *Y* Limited reject the order, there would be idle capacity, the cost of which is estimated to be $25,000 per month.

Assuming that *X* will buy from other suppliers if credit is refused, should *Y* Limited grant the credit?

The reasoning used to arrive at a decision may run something like this. If credit is not granted, the loss per month would be $25,000. If credit is granted, there will be savings of idle-capacity cost of $25,000 and a profit margin of $5,000, making a monthly effectual profit of $30,000 before income tax. If the credit allowed at any one time is limited to $100,000 (two months' orders), the total loss that can accrue to *Y* Limited is $100,000. The comparison to be used by management is, therefore, the risk of a bad debt of $100,000 against an annual revenue of $360,000. If the account can be expected to remain good for four months, the risk will be offset by profits.

The credit policy of a firm should be influenced by at least five factors:

(1) its likely impact on sales volume,
(2) its likely impact on the firm's profits,
(3) the cost of the funds tied up in the receivables,
(4) the cost of credit administration, and
(5) the cost of bad debts and, perhaps, of litigation involved in debt collection.

8.3.1. Granting Credit and the Customer's Paying Behaviour

Very often the firm has to decide whether to grant credit to a customer; such a decision may be based on the customer's paying behaviour. Suppose the customer's paying behaviour can be described as follows:

Payment in	*Probability*
1 month	0.10
2 months	0.45
3 months	0.25
4 months	0.18
Bad Debt	0.02
	1.00

The customer is expected to purchase $500,000 (25,000 units at $20 per unit) worth of goods per year. The marginal profit per unit is $2 and the minimum acceptable rate of return is 18% per annum before tax.

The investment criterion is:
Grant if the expected sales revenue exceeds the total expected cost of sales (8.3.1.)

Expected sales revenue = (.98)(500,000) = \$490,000.00
Expected cost of sales:

(i) Opportunity cost of investment in trade debtors
= [(.1)(.015) + (.45)(.03) + (.25)(.045)
+ (.18)(.06)](450,000)
= \$ 16,672.50
(ii) Cost of sales = (25000)(18) = \$450,000.00
\$466,672.50
Expected Profit = \$ 23,327.50

Since the expected sales revenue exceeds the total expected cost of sales, credit should be granted. It is to be noted that the time value of money is ignored in the above analysis. The assumption is made that no sales would result if credit was not granted.

8.3.2. Granting Credit Depending on the Class of Customers

Customers may be grouped into classes according to their paying behaviour and the degree of the firm's willingness to grant credit to an individual customer depends on the class to which he belongs. The investment criterion is:

Grant if the opportunity cost of not granting exceeds the cost of granting (8.3.2.1.)

The cost of granting credit to a customer consists of bad debt losses, the opportunity cost of investing in trade debtors and debt collection expenses and is calculated as follows:

Cost of granting credit
$= pbx + d + rbtx$ (8.3.2.2.)

The opportunity cost of not granting credit
$= (1 - p)(c)x$ (8.3.2.3.)

where p is the probability of bad debt,
b is the unit variable cost,
d is the debt collection expenses,
r is the minimum acceptable rate of return,
t is the inverse of debtors turnover,
x is the number of units of goods to be sold, and
c is the unit contribution.

The following example illustrates this.

Unit selling price	= \$20
Unit variable cost	= \$16
Minimum acceptable rate of return	= 20%

Customers' Grouping

Class	*Probability of Bad Debt*	*Collection Period*	*Collection Expenses*
		Days	\$
1	0.01	30	1
2	0.02	35	2
3	0.03	40	3
4	0.10	50	5
5	0.20	90	7

Using equations (8.3.2.2.) and (8.3.2.3.) give the solutions as shown in Table (8.3.2.)

Table 8.3.2.

Class of Customers	*Cost of Granting*	*Opportunity Cost of Not Granting*	*Break-even* x
	\$	\$	Units
1	$0.427x + 1$	$3.96x$	0.283
2	$0.631x + 2$	$3.92x$	0.608
3	$0.836x + 3$	$3.88x$	0.986
4	$2.044x + 5$	$3.6x$	3.213
5	$4x + 7$	$3.2x$	−8.750

From the analysis of Table 8.3.2., credit should be granted to customers of Classes 1, 2 and 3 but should not be granted to customers who belong to Class 5. Credit should be granted to a customer of Class 4 only if his demand exceeds 3 units.

In the above analysis total fixed costs are assumed constant. More relevant information relating to the problem may lead to better decision-making, but the costs of obtaining such information must be justified by the expected increase in benefits.

8.3.3. Changing Credit Terms Allowed

Credit terms given to customers may be changed if such changes bring about cost savings. One criterion often used is:

Change if the proposed change results in positive cost savings (8.3.3.)

The following example illustrates this.

Table 8.3.3.

	Present Position	*Proposed and Expected Position*
Credit terms	1/10, net 50	2/10, net 30
Average collection period	60 days	40 days
Discount taken on % of $ sales	40%	60%
Annual credit sales	$500,000	$500,000
Minimum acceptable rate of return before tax	20%	20%
Average amount of trade debtors	$500{,}000 \times \frac{60}{360}$ = $83,333	$500{,}000 \times \frac{40}{360}$ = $55,556

The reduction in the average amount of money tied up in trade debtors is $27,777.

Expected return on reduction of trade debtors = (.2)(27,777)	= $5,555
Expected cost of discount = (500,000)(.6)(.02)	= $6,000
Net expected cost of proposed change	= $ 445

Present cost of discount
= (500,000)(.4)(.01) = \$2,000
Hence, expected cost savings from proposed
change = \$(2,000 − 445) = \$1,555

Therefore, the credit terms should be changed. In the above analysis the assumption is made that sales volume will not be affected by the proposed change in credit terms.

8.3.4. Increase Credit Period to Increase Sales Volume

Sales volume can sometimes be increased if the credit period granted to customers is increased. One of the common criteria is:

Increase credit period if the profitability from the additional sales is greater than the opportunity cost of additional investment in trade debtors (8.3.4.)

The following example illustrates this.

Minimum acceptable rate of return before tax = 25%
Standard unit selling price. = \$2
Unit variable cost = \$1.50
Present annual total credit sales = \$200,000
Present collection period = 40 days

Table 8.3.4. gives the forecasted sales volume with increases in the collection periods.

Table 8.3.4.

Alternative Plan	*Expected Bad Debt Losses as % of \$ Sales*	*If Credit Period Inreased to*	*Total Annual Sales Increased to*
Present	0.5%		
1	1%	50 days	\$220,000
2	2%	60 days	\$230,000
3	3%	70 days	\$232,000

(See Solution on page 127 *infra*)

A comparison of (*k*) with (*g*) indicates that plans 1 and 2 are acceptable and plan 3 is not, though plan 2 is the best plan.

Solution

	Present Position	*Plan 1*	*Plan 2*	*Plan 3*
(*a*) Unit Sales	100,000	110,000	115,000	116,000
(*b*) Unit Profit before bad debt losses	\$0.50	\$0.50	\$0.50	\$0.50
(*c*) \$ Sales	\$200,000	\$220,000	\$230,000	\$232,000
(*d*) Average amount of trade debtors	$200,000 \times \frac{40}{360}$ = \$22,222	$220,000 \times \frac{50}{360}$ = \$30,555	$230,000 \times \frac{60}{360}$ = \$38,333	$232,000 \times \frac{70}{360}$ = \$45,111
(*e*) Average investment in trade debtors $\left[(d) \times \frac{1.5}{2}\right]$	\$16,667	\$22,916	\$28,750	\$33,833
(*f*) Opportunity Cost of investment in trade debtors [.25 × (*e*)]	\$ 4,167	\$ 5,729	\$ 7,188	\$ 8,458
(*g*) Increase of opportunity cost of investment in trade debtors over the present position		\$ 1,562	\$ 3,021	\$ 4,291
(*h*) Expected return on investment in trade debtors before bad debt losses [(*a*) × (*b*)]	\$50,000	\$55,000	\$57,500	\$58,000
(*i*) Bad debt losses of each plan	(.005)(200,000) = \$ 1,000	(.01)(220,000) \$ 2,200	(.02)(230,000) \$ 4,600	(.03)(232,000) \$ 6,960
(*j*) Expected return on investment in trade debtors after bad debt losses [(*h*) − (*i*)]	\$49,000	\$52,800	\$52,900	\$51,040
(*k*) Increase of expected return on investment in trade debtors of each plan over the present position		\$ 3,800	\$ 3,900	\$ 2,040

In the analysis, the assumptions are that the total fixed costs of the firm remain constant, that the expected results will hold true in the foreseeable future and that the other parameters such as unit selling price and variable cost will not change.

8.3.5. A Markov Chain Model

It is sometimes desirable to know whether an account will ultimately be settled or become bad, and how much can be expected to be collected from trade debtors every month and what is the likely size of the monthly bad debt. If a transition matrix can be obtained, such questions can be answered. Suppose we have the following transition matrix:

$$T = \begin{bmatrix} N & \emptyset \\ U & I \end{bmatrix} = \begin{array}{c} \\ C \\ M \\ S \\ B \end{array} \begin{array}{c} \begin{array}{cccc} C & M & S & B \end{array} \\ \begin{bmatrix} .3 & .3 & 0 & 0 \\ .1 & .4 & 0 & 0 \\ .6 & .2 & 1 & 0 \\ 0 & .1 & 0 & 1 \end{bmatrix} \end{array} \qquad (8.3.5.1.)$$

It is to be noted that all columns of the transition matrix add to one. In this example all accounts of the firm can belong to four states: current, one-month old, settled, or bad. Accounts of a firm can fall into more states than four of course.

Column one of the transition matrix means that an account that is at present current has a probability of 0.3 of remaining current, a probability of 0.1 of becoming one month old, a probability of 0.6 of being settled or paid, and 0 probability of becoming a bad debt. A current account remains a current account if it is paid and immediately becomes revived with a new purchase.

Column two of the transition matrix explains that an account that is at present one month old has a probability of 0.3 of becoming current, a probability of 0.4 of remaining one month old, a probability of 0.2 of being settled and a probability of 0.1 of becoming bad. A one-month old account becomes current if the amount owing is paid at the same time as a new purchase is made. It remains one month old if part of the amount owing is paid so that it is still one month old. It is settled if at the end of the period the amount owing is completely paid. It is assumed here that if the one-month old account is not settled at the end of the month, the amount owing is written off as bad debt. The third column means that an account that is settled remains settled and the fourth column means that an account that becomes bad remains bad.

The following calculated matrices provide useful information:

$$P = (I - N)^{-1} = \begin{bmatrix} .7 & -.3 \\ -.1 & .6 \end{bmatrix}^{-1}$$

$$= \begin{bmatrix} 20/13 & 10/13 \\ 10/39 & 70/39 \end{bmatrix} \quad (8.3.5.2.)$$

$$UP = \begin{bmatrix} .6 & .2 \\ 0 & .1 \end{bmatrix} \begin{bmatrix} 20/13 & 10/13 \\ 10/39 & 70/39 \end{bmatrix} = \begin{array}{c} \\ S \\ B \end{array} \begin{array}{c} \begin{array}{cc} C & M \end{array} \\ \begin{bmatrix} .974 & .821 \\ .026 & .179 \end{bmatrix} \end{array} \quad (8.3.5.3.)$$

The matrix UP in (8.3.5.3.) explains that a current account has a probability of 0.974 of ultimately being settled and a probability of 0.026 of becoming bad. A one-month old account has a probability of 0.821 of ultimately being paid and a probability of 0.179 of becoming bad.

Suppose there is a sales campaign where 1,000 accounts are opened per period. The following matrix will provide useful information:

$$A = PL = \begin{bmatrix} 20/13 & 10/13 \\ 10/39 & 70/39 \end{bmatrix} \begin{bmatrix} 1{,}000 \\ 0 \end{bmatrix}$$

$$= \begin{array}{c} C \\ M \end{array} \begin{bmatrix} 1{,}538 \\ 256 \end{bmatrix} \quad (8.3.5.4.)$$

The matrix A in (8.3.5.4.) explains that ultimately when the sales campaign settled, 1538 accounts will be current and 256 will be one month old.

If the average size of an account is \$50, the following matrix can be calculated:

$$M = ZA = [50 \quad 50] \begin{bmatrix} 1538 \\ 256 \end{bmatrix}$$

$$= 76{,}900 + 12{,}800$$

$$= \$89{,}700 \quad (8.3.5.5.)$$

Matrix M in (8.3.5.5.) explains that ultimately when the sales campaign settled down, outstanding trade debtors will amount to \$89,700, of which \$76,900 will be current and \$12,800 will be one month old.

The following matrix provides useful information:

$$R = \begin{bmatrix} .6 & .2 \\ 0 & .1 \end{bmatrix} \begin{bmatrix} 76{,}900 \\ 12{,}800 \end{bmatrix} = \begin{bmatrix} 48{,}700 \\ 1{,}280 \end{bmatrix} \qquad (8.3.5.6.)$$

The matrix R in (8.3.5.6.) means that every month \$48,700 will be collected from the outstanding trade debtors and \$1,280 will be written off as irrecoverable.

8.4. INVESTMENT IN CASH RESOURCES

Cash resources include cash in hand, cash at bank and readily marketable securities like treasury bills, which can be sold at any time without substantial loss. The aim of cash management is to ensure that there are no idle cash resources which are not required in operating the business efficiently because idle cash reduces the overall return on investment.

Investment in cash resources is determined, inter alia, by the following factors:

(1) the quantity and timing of inflows of cash from sales of goods and other sources,
(2) normal requirements of business operations, such as cash outflows in meeting purchases of goods, payment of wages and other services, etc.,
(3) capital expenditures requiring cash outlays as programmed,
(4) cash resources for seizing investment opportunities,
(5) meeting contingent cash requirements.

The only way by which cash management can be effective is through cash budgeting and control. Long-term and short-term cash budgets must be prepared. Long-term could mean two to five years or more, and short-term could mean one week or one month to a year. In cash budgeting the total amounts of inflows and outflows for a period are shown. But the critical thing in cash budgeting should be the timing of such flows. In this way, the times when cash shortages or cash surpluses are likely to occur should be known so that timely productive measures are planned in advance, for instance, overdraft facilities may be arranged well in advance if the shortages are going to be temporary. And if cash surpluses are temporary, ways and means of using them productively may be planned. If the cash generated by profits is insufficient to meet planned cash requirements in capital expenditures, capital contributions or long-term loans must be arranged long before the actual needs arise. Contingent cash requirements should not be just what is felt to be necessary; the contingencies envisaged must be specified and capable of being identified and their probabilities of occurrence quantified so that a reasonable and rational amount can be arrived at. All this means that cash forecasting must be more accurate and reliable, and ways of minimizing investment in cash resources explored.

8.4.1. The Cash Flow Cycle

The normal cash flow cycle cycle can be depicted diagrammatically as shown in Figure 8.4.1.

In the cash flow cycle shown, the flows depicted by dark print indicate the normal operating cycle of the business which must be thoroughly studied so that investment in current assets is optimal. The optimal levels of stock, receivables and cash can then be determined.

8.4.2. An Inventory Model Approach to Cash Management

The inventory model described in Section 8.2.1. may sometimes be useful as a tool for cash management. In this model it is assumed that the firm can borrow or withdraw cash from any source at a cost at any time and that holding cash involves an opportunity cost in the sense that the cash so held involves a sacrifice of forgoing the return it can earn if invested elsewhere.

There are three motives for holding cash: precautionary, speculative and transactions. The first motive results in holding cash to meet contingencies or unforeseen cash requirements and

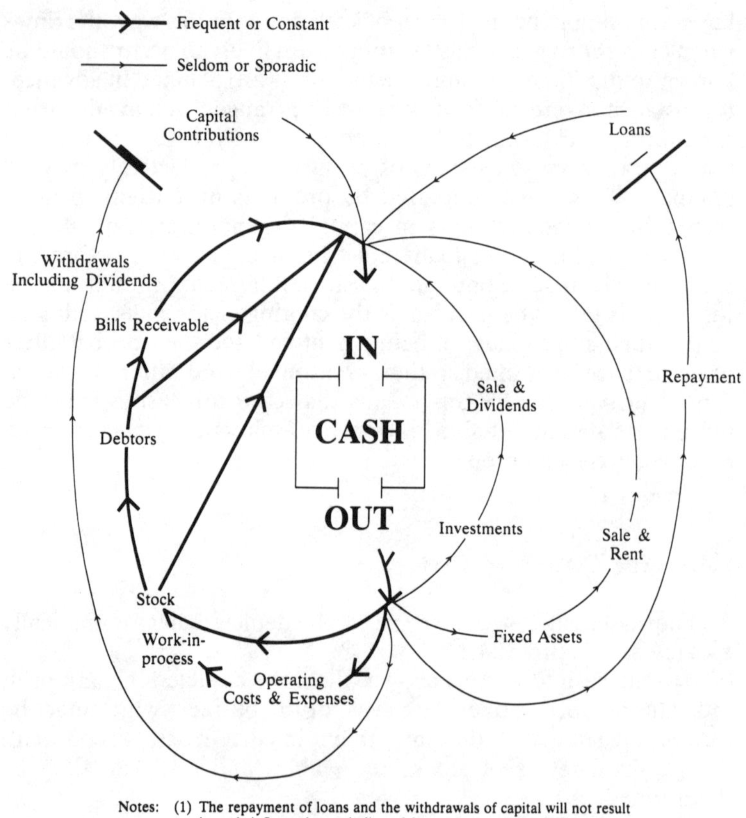

Notes: (1) The repayment of loans and the withdrawals of capital will not result in cash inflows, hence indicated by ▬▬ and ▬▬

Figure 8.4.1.

the second may result in holding cash to take advantage of unexpected investment opportunities. Holding cash under the first two motives may not always be sound policy of cash management. It may be much cheaper to have open to the company at any time a line of credit which can be utilized for such purposes. A good example of such line of credit is bank overdraft facilities. Temporary cash surpluses can of course be invested in short-term securities like treasury bills. The economies of the different approaches should be worked out to ascertain the optimal approach.

The inventory model approach to cash management is mainly concerned with the transactions motive for holding cash. Equation (8.2.2.1.) is repeated here:

$$q^* = \sqrt{\frac{2DO}{H}} \qquad (8.4.2.)$$

where q^* is the optimal economic transactions demand for cash,
D is the total budgeted cash requirement for the period,
O is the differential cost of each borrowing or withdrawal, and
H is the opportunity cost of holding cash (the company's opportunity interest rate)

Using the data in Table 8.4.2., we arrive at the following relevant information for decision-making:

Table 8.4.2.

Budgeted total cash outlays	= \$2 (million)
The company's opportunity interest rate	= 0.08
Differential cost of each borrowing or withdrawal	= \$50

$$q^* = \sqrt{\frac{2 \times 50 \times 2{,}000{,}000}{.08}} = \$50{,}000$$

y^* = total optimal relevant cost for the use of cash needed for transactions.

$$= \sqrt{2DOH}$$

$$= \sqrt{2 \times 2{,}000{,}000 \times 50 \times 0.08} = \$4{,}000$$

$$\frac{q^*}{2} = \text{average cash balance}$$

$$= \frac{50{,}000}{2} = \$25{,}000$$

Velocity or cash cycle

$$= \frac{2,000,000}{50,000} = 40 \text{ times a year}$$

or 9 days

The above model is suitable for enterprises whose transactions demand for cash is steady and not seasonal. The availability of bank overdraft facilities may reduce the operational advantage of the inventory model for cash management.

8.5. WORKING CAPITAL MANAGEMENT

The term working capital refers to the mix of current assets (such as stock, receivables and cash) and current liabilities (such as trade creditors, dividends and income tax payable, bank overdrafts and short-term bank loans). And working capital management refers to decision-making and control regarding optimal levels of current assets and optimal sources and mix of finance.

Patterns of working capital requirements and their magnitudes depend on the nature of the business activities of the firm and its management style as well as their risk attitude. Nevertheless, the trade-off between risk and cost is often evaluated and short-term sources of finance are resorted to when short-term needs arise. Short-term finance is discussed in Chapter 10. Since working capital requirement usually fluctuates as a whole, a distinction is often drawn between the permanent base and the fluctuating portion of working capital. The permanent base is supposed to be the stable amount that must be maintained all the time to support the normal level of business activities. The distinction is purported to facilitate the evaluation of the risk-cost trade-off in determining the optimal mix of short-term and long-term finance.

However, the inter-relationships and inter-dependence between short-term and long-term finance and current and fixed assets must never be lost sight of and a consideration of one without the other may not lead to the long-term interest of the firm. These inter-relationships are clearly depicted in the firm's cash flow cycle in Figure 8.4.1.

Some accounting ratios (such as the working capital and liquid ratios) are often calculated at different points of time to gauge the efficiency of working capital management. Accounting ratios are discussed in Chapter 15. Working capital management in such circumstances often consists of resolving the conflicting objectives of maintaining a high degree of liquidity and a high level of profitability. Holding high levels of liquid assets entails high opportunity costs while ensuring wide safety margins for meeting immediate commitments that involve cash outflows. On the other hand, running down investments in current assets releases cash for other profitable uses at the same time increasing the risk of insolvency. Efficient working capital management involves finding the appropriate equilibrium and this necessitates accurate forecasting of working capital requirements.

8.6. SELECTED BIBLIOGRAPHY

1. W.J. Baumol: The Transactions Demand for Cash (An Inventory Theoretic Approach), Quarterly Journal of Economics, November 1952.
2. E.S. Buffa: Models for Production and Operations Management.
3. M. Budin and R.J. Van Handel: A Rule-of-Thumb Theory of Cash Holdings by Firms, Journal of Financial and Quantitative Analysis, March 1975.
4. Michael Firth: Management of Working Capital.
5. C.C. Greer: The Optimal Credit Acceptance Policy, Journal of Financial and Quantitative Analysis, December 1967.
6. C.W. Haley and R.C. Higgins: Inventory Control Theory and Trade Credit Financing, Management Science, December 1973.
7. Han Kang Hong: Cost and Management Accounting.
8. S. Lane: Submarginal Credit Risk Classification, Journal of Financial and Quantitative Analysis, January 1972.
9. J.C.T. Mao: Controlling Risk in Assets Receivable Management, Journal of Business Finance and Accounting, Autumn 1974.
10. G.L. Marrah: Managing Receivables, Financial Executive, July 1970.
11. D. Melta: The Formulation of Credit Policy Models, Management Science, October 1968.
12. W.L. Reed, Jr: Cash—The Hidden Asset, Financial Executive, November 1970.

CHAPTER 9

The Cost of Capital and Capital Structure

9.1. WHAT IS THE MINIMUM ACCEPTABLE RATE OF RETURN?

In maximizing the firm value, in evaluating investment projects or capital budgeting, in fact, in all managerial finance problems involving discounting cash flows, a rate of discount called the minimum acceptable rate of return is used. But what is the minimum acceptable rate of return?

9.2. WORLD OF CERTAINTY

When the cash flows are devoid of risks, such as cash flows which take place in the world of certainty, the risk-free rate of discount is used. A good surrogate of risk-free discount rate is the interest rate of a government stock of appropriate maturity. A risk-free rate of discount is used, for instance, in Chapter 4 and in discounting the certainty equivalents of cash flows in Section 6.6. of Chapter 6. The risk-free discount rate is also used for discounting cash flows if the expected net present value of such cash flows can only be analysed if it does not embody any risk element, as in Section 6.4. of Chapter 6.

9.3. WORLD OF UNCERTAINTY AND PERFECT MARKET

Under perfect market conditions in the world of uncertainty, the risks associated with forecasted cash flows are categorised into diversifiable and non-diversifiable risks as explained in Chapter 6. The minimum acceptable rate of return is considered to be a risk-adjusted discount rate as explained by the capital asset pricing model in Section 6.5. of Chapter 6. Under the net present value method of capital expenditure analysis, the forecasted net cash flows are discounted by this risk-adjusted discount rate. In symbols,

$$\overline{NPV} = \sum_{t=0}^{n} C_t(1 + k)^{-t} \qquad (9.3.1.)$$

where $\overline{NPV}$ is the expected net present value of the forecasted cash flows,
C_t is the net cash flows after tax in period t, and
k is the risk-adjusted discount rate.

And the decision rule is:

Invest if $\overline{NPV} > 0$ (9.3.2.)

Under the internal rate of return method, the cash inflows and cash outflows are discounted by trial and error with a discount rate so that the sum of their net present values is zero. In symbols,

$$\sum_{t=0}^{n} C_t(1 + i)^{-t} = 0 \qquad (9.3.3.)$$

where C_t is the algebraic sum of the cash inflow and cash outflow after tax of period t, and
i is the internal rate of return which is obtained by trial and error in order to achieve the equation in (9.3.3.)

And the decision rule is:

Invest if $k \leq i$ (9.3.4.)

where k is the risk-adjusted discount rate called the minimum acceptable rate of return.

9.4 WORLD OF UNCERTAINTY AND IMPERFECT MARKET

In the capital asset pricing model, from which the risk-adjusted discount rate is computed, the firm value can be maximized without recourse to the risk attitudes of individual shareholders. The capital market for securities is efficient in the sense that their prices adjust smoothly and promptly to new information and hence price fluctuations are random. Diversifying the portfolio of securities held, securities that are not positively correlated, can therefore reduce risk.

Though the market line is theoretically justified, it is not widely used because of the difficulties of obtaining the non-diversifiable risk of individual investment projects. Under imperfect market conditions risks of insolvency cannot be ruled out and bankruptcy and transactions costs cannot be ignored. If the assumption is made that the company's investments are broadly homogeneous and that the proposed investment projects do not differ significantly from the company's existing portfolio of assets in their non-diversifiable risk, there is justification for the use of the weighted average cost of capital as a criterion for evaluating average-risk investment projects. The use of the cost of capital is also justified on the grounds that using it will enhance the market price of the company's shares if the necessary incremental finance does not alter perceptibly the capital structure of the firm.

The cost of capital is important for another reason. It is desirable to know whether, and in what ways, the cost of capital is affected by the capital structure of the company, that is, by the ratio of debt to equity capital, whether there is an optimal capital structure at which the firm value is at a maximum. This will facilitate a choice of finance where different sources of finance are available.

9.5. THE COST OF A SPECIFIC SOURCE OF FINANCE

The explicit cost c of a specific source of finance, S, is determined by achieving the following equality:

$$\sum_{t=0}^{n} I_t(1 + c)^{-t} = \sum_{t=0}^{n} 0_t(1 + c)^{-t} \qquad (9.5.1.)$$

where I_t is the net cash received by the company from the source of finance, S at time t, and 0_t is the cash outflows (interest or dividend and principal repayment) at time t. If the cash inflow is received all at time $t = 0$, we have

$$I_0 = \sum_{t=0}^{n} 0_t(1 + c)^{-t} \tag{9.5.2.}$$

9.6. THE COST OF DEBT CAPITAL

Interest being deductible for income tax purposes, the after-tax cost of debt is k_i:

$$k_i = c(1 - T) \tag{9.6.1.}$$

where c is obtained as in (9.5.1.) or (9.5.2.) and T is the tax rate. If it is assumed that the debt will be continuously replaced by a new one when it matures and the interest rate on the debt remains constant, then the streams of cash outflows will be a perpetual stream of interest payments, and k_i is obtained by solving the following equation for k_i:

$$I_0 = \sum_{t=1}^{\infty} (1 - T)A(1 + k_i)^{-t}$$

$$= \frac{(1 - T)A}{k_i}$$

Therefore $$k_i = \frac{(1 - T)A}{I_0} = \frac{B_0}{I_0} \tag{9.6.2.}$$

where A is the annual fixed interest payment before tax and B_0 is the annual fixed interest payment after tax.

9.7. THE COST OF PREFERENCE SHARES

Like debt preference shares carry a fixed rate of dividend irrespective of the profits of the company, but unlike debt preference dividend is not tax deductible. If it is assumed that the preference shares are non-participating and irredeemable, their cost is k_p:

$$k_p = \frac{D_p}{I_p} \tag{9.7.}$$

where D_p is the fixed annual preference dividend and I_p is the net cash inflow resulting from the issue of the preference shares at time $t = 0$

9.8. THE COST OF EQUITY CAPITAL

The cost of equity capital is much more difficult to determine. There are many models to choose from and each can be used only with caution bearing in mind the relevant underlying assumptions. A simple model is to arrive at the cost of equity capital, k_e, by achieving the following equality:

$$P_0 = \sum_{t=1}^{n} D_t(1 + k_e)^{-t} \tag{9.8.1.}$$

where P_0 is the market price of the issued shares and D_t is the dividend expected to be received in time t including the liquidating dividend which is the net proceeds from the sale of the shares or from liquidating the company.

If the annual dividend is expected to grow at the rate e per annum, we have:

$$P_0 = \sum_{t=1}^{n} D_1(1 + e)^{t-1}(1 + k_e)^{-t} \tag{9.8.2.}$$

where $D_1 = D_0(1 + e)$, that is D_1 is the dividend at the end of the first year.

If it is assumed that a constant amount of dividend D will be received annually during the perpetual life of the company, equation (9.8.1.) becomes:

$$P_0 = \sum_{t=1}^{\infty} D(1 + k_e)^{-t} = \frac{D}{k_e} \qquad (9.8.3.)$$

Therefore
$$k_e = \frac{D}{P_0} \qquad (9.8.4.)$$

And if D in equation (9.8.3.) grows at the rate e annually, we have

$$\begin{aligned} P_0 &= \sum_{t=1}^{\infty} D_1(1 + e)^{t-1}(1 + k_e)^{-t} \\ &= \frac{D_1}{k_e - e} \qquad (9.8.5.) \end{aligned}$$

Therefore
$$k_e = \frac{D_1}{P_0} + e \qquad (9.8.6.)$$

Formula (9.8.5.) becomes unrealistic if k_e is smaller than e since P_0 will become infinitely large.

The assumption of a constant growth rate is also sometimes not very realistic, and equation (9.8.5.) is replaced by:

$$P_0 = \left\{ \sum_{t=1}^{n} D_0 \prod_{i=1}^{t} (1 + e_i)(1 + k_e)^{-t} \right\} \qquad (9.8.7.)$$

where the growth rates e_i may be different.

If the assumption is made that D grows at the rate e annually from year $t = 0$ to year $t = n$, and then at the rate f annually to $t = m$, and finally at the rate g annually forever, we have:

$$\begin{aligned} P_0 = &\sum_{t=1}^{n} D_1(1 + e)^{t-1}(1 + k_e)^{-t} \\ &+ \sum_{t=n+1}^{m} D_{n+1}(1 + f)^{t-(n+1)}(1 + k_e)^{-t} \\ &+ \sum_{t=m+1}^{\infty} D_{m+1}(1 + g)^{t-(m+1)}(1 + k_e)^{-t} \end{aligned}$$

$$P_0 = \sum_{t=1}^{n} D_1(1 + e)^{t-1}(1 + k_e)^{-t} + \sum_{t=n+1}^{m} D_{n+1}(1 + f)^{t-(n+1)}(1 + k_e)^{-t} + \frac{D_{m+1}}{(k_e - g)}(1 + k_e)^{-m} \qquad (9.8.8.)$$

9.9. THE COST OF RETAINED EARNINGS

It can be argued that since retained earnings can be distributed to the ordinary shareholders, the cost of retained earnings is the same as the cost of equity capital. Another way of measuring the cost of retained earnings is to use the opportunity cost concept. That is, it is the return which an alternative equivalent risk investment could offer if the retained earnings were invested in the alternative project.

9.10. WEIGHTED AVERAGE COST OF CAPITAL

As explained in Section 9.4. it is necessary to know the weighted average cost of capital. In practice, the source of finance of a firm for most purposes is a mix finance. From equation (9.6.2.) the cost of debt is:

$$k_i = \frac{B_0}{I_0}$$

From equation (9.8.4.) the cost of equity is:

$$k_e = \frac{D}{P_0}$$

And from equation (9.7.1.) the cost of preference shares is:

$$k_p = \frac{D_p}{I_p}$$

Therefore the weighted average cost of capital is k:

$$k = \frac{k_i I_0 + k_e P_0 + k_p I_p}{I_0 + P_0 + I_p} \tag{9.10.}$$

where $(I_0 + P_0 + I_p)$ is the value of the firm.

9.11. RISK ELEMENTS IN THE COST OF CAPITAL

Sometimes the cost of capital is derived by taking the elements of risk specifically into account. For instance,

$$k = r + \alpha \tag{9.11.1.}$$

where r is the risk-free interest rate and α measures the degree of risk in the expected income streams. And α is very often assumed to be the variance of the distribution of expected earnings streams. It can be seen that the higher the risk the higher k will be.

Sometimes the risk element is subdivided into two components, business risk and financial risk, and the formula becomes:

$$k = r + B + f \tag{9.11.2.}$$

where B, the business risk is measured by the variance of the probability distribution of future earnings, and f, the financial risk includes the risk of liquidation of the company and the uncertainty of the availability in the earnings to ordinary shareholders. Hence, while B is primarily determined by the investment decisions of the company, f is brought about by its financing decisions and is therefore related to the leverage in its capital structure.

9.12. OPPORTUNITY COST OF CAPITAL

Conceptually the opportunity cost concept is most tenable, since unless the proposed project can give a return that is at least equal to the best available alternative of the same equivalent risk, the proposed project should not be undertaken. One would then rather invest in the alternative. In practice, however, the opportunity cost is not easily obtainable because different alternative investment opportunities carry different degrees of risk and the adjustments for risk are subjective. It is suggested that if the company has been successful and the conditions explained in Section 9.4. hold to a large degree, its weighted average cost of capital should be a good approximation of the opportunity cost, and can therefore be used for most practical purposes.

9.13. COST OF CAPITAL AND CAPITAL STRUCTURE

It is often argued that as the ratio of debt to ordinary share capital increases, the risk of failure to meet debt obligations increases. As a consequence, the market value of the debt falls, and the cost of debt increases; the risk of return to ordinary shareholders also increases resulting in an increase in the expected rate of return of equity capital. Some contend that an increase in the debt-equity ratio increases the value of the firm so long as the firm does not increase its leverage to an extreme point, while others maintain that in a perfect market the debt-equity ratio has no effect on the firm value. The issue is an important one because if an optimal capital structure can be determined management ought to strive for this optimum in its financial decision-making.

9.14. THE MODIGLIANI-MILLER PROPOSITION (A Perfect Market Model)

According to Modigliani and Miller, in a perfect market the weighted average cost of capital of a company is not affected by its debt-equity ratio. Assume that two companies belong to the same risk class, that is, they have identical income distributions. But company d is indebted while company n is debt-free. The market value of company d is

$$V_d = P_d + I_d$$

while that of company n is

$$V_n = P_n$$

where P_d is the market value of the equity capital and I_d is the market value of the debt of company d, and P_n is the market value of the equity capital of company n.

Let the annual income of the two companies be y. Then the debt holders of company d receive the total interest income of rI_d. If an investor holds p part of the share capital of company n, he is entitled to py of the total income of company n with an investment outlay of $pP_n = pV_n$.

It can be demonstrated that by engaging in an arbitrage process, the investor can obtain the same income with a reduced investment outlay, if $V_n > V_d$. Selling his shares in company n, he can buy $pP_d = p(V_d - I_d)$ of the share capital of company d as well as pI_d of its debt, involving a total investment outlay of pV_d and receiving a total income of $\{p(y - rI_d) + prI_d\} = py$. Thus his income is the same as before but he makes a gain of $(pV_n - pV_d) = p(V_n - V_d)$ since it is assumed that $V_n > V_d$. All investors of company n will carry out similar processes driving the share price of company d up and that of company n down until the equilibrium is reached where $V_n = V_d$.

The case of $V_n < V_d$ can be similarly illustrated. A holder of p part of the share capital of company d receives an income of $p(y - rI_d)$ with an investment outlay of $pP_d = p(V_d - I_d)$. He can sell his shares in company d and buys shares of company n worth $pP_n = pV_n$ by personally borrowing an amount of pI_d at the same rate of interest r as the corporation d where r is the risk-free interest rate. (Debt is assumed to be risk-free). And the ordinary shareholders of company d receive $y - rI_d$. His income will be $(py - rpI_d) = p(y - rI_d)$ and his investment outlay, $p(V_n - I_d)$. Thus his income remains the same but he makes a gain of $p(V_d - I_d) - p(V_n - I_d) = p(V_d - V_n)$ in investment outlay, since $V_d > V_n$ by assumption. Other shareholders of company d will perform the same switching operations until the equilibrium is reached where $V_d = V_n$. Hence, at the equilibrium, the weighted average cost of capital of a company is unaffected by its debt-equity ratio.

The underlying assumptions of the model should be noted to evaluate the proximity of the model to conditions of the real world. First, there must be conditions of a perfect market so that the arbitrage process can take place smoothly, and transaction costs are not significant. Secondly, companies can be divided into equivalent classes having identical income distributions. Thirdly, personal leverage can be substituted for corporate leverage. And finally, tax advantages of indebtedness are not taken into account.

Taxation can be introduced into the analysis. Assume that $V_d > (V_n + TI_d)$, the before-tax income of the two companies is $\bar{y}$ and the tax rate, T. A shareholder holding p part of the share capital of company d receives an income of $p(1 - T)(\bar{y} - rI_d) = p(1 - T)\bar{y} - p(1 - T)rI_d$, with an investment outlay of pP_d. He can sell his shares in company d and buys $pP_n = pV_n$ of the shares of company n by personally borrowing $p(1 - T)I_d$ at the same rate of interest as company d. This will give him an income of $[p(1 - T)\bar{y} - p(1 - T)rI_d] = p(1 - T)(\bar{y} - rI_d)$, with an investment outlay of $[pV_n - p(1 - T)I_d)] = p[V_n - (1 - T)I_d)]$. Thus his income remains the same, but he makes *aa* gain in investment outlay of

$$pP_d - p[V_n - (1 - T)I_d] = p[V_d - (V_n + TI_d)]$$

since it is assumed that $V_d > (V_n + TI_d)$. Other shareholders of company d will perform similar switching operations until $V_d = (V_n + TI_d)$. The case of $V_d < (V_n + TI_d)$ can be similarly illustrated. Hence, at the equilibrium, with tax advantages of indebtedness taken into account, $V_d = V_n + TI_d$, that is, the value of the indebted company exceeds that of the debt-free company by TI_d; the weighted average cost of capital of the indebted company is therefore lower.

9.14.1. False Ltd and Lie Ltd

The following information relates to two hypothetical companies:

		False Ltd	*Lie Ltd*
		$	$
Net operating income	(a)	100,000	100,000
Interest on debt	(b)	—	20,000
Earnings to ordinary shareholders	(c)	100,000	80,000
Cost of equity (k_e)	(c/d)	.125	.14
Market value of shares	(d)	800,000	571,000
Market value of debt	(e)	—	333,000
Total value of firm	(f)	800,000	904,000
Average cost of capital (k)	(a/f)	.125	.11
Debt/equity ratio	(e/d)	0	.5832
Cost of debt k_i (20,000/333,000)			.06

False Ltd and Lie Ltd belong to a single equivalent-risk class. While False Ltd is entirely dependent on equity financing, Lie Ltd has 8% \$250,000 debentures outstanding.

REQUIRED:

Show how an investor owning \$57,100 worth of shares in Lie Ltd could reduce his capital outlay through arbitrage.

(a) The shareholder of Lie Ltd receives an income of (using the explanations of Section 9.14.):

$$p(y - rI_d) = (.1)(100{,}000 - .06 \times 333{,}000) = \$8{,}000$$

His investment outlay:

$$pP_d = p(V_d - I_d) = (.1)(904{,}000 - 333{,}000) = \$57{,}100$$

(b) By engaging in arbitrage, he sells his shares in Lie Ltd and buys $pP_n = pV_n$ of the shares in False Ltd by borrowing an amount pI_d. That is, he buys (.1)(800,000) = \$80,000 of False shares and borrows (.1)(333,000) = \$33,300 of debt at the interest of 0.06.

(c) His income after the arbitrage is:

$$(py - rpI_d) = p(y - rI_d) = (.1)(100{,}000 - .06 \times 333{,}000) = \$8{,}000$$

His investment outlay is now:

$$p(V_n - I_d) = (.1)(800{,}000 - 333{,}000) = \$46{,}700$$

(d) Comparing (a) with (c) reveals that after the arbitrage, his income remains the same, but he makes a saving in outlay of \$(57,100 − 46,700) = \$10,400.

9.15. IMPERFECT MARKET MODELS

The analysis under imperfect market conditions is much less certain than under perfect market conditions, and the number of

Figure 9.15.1.

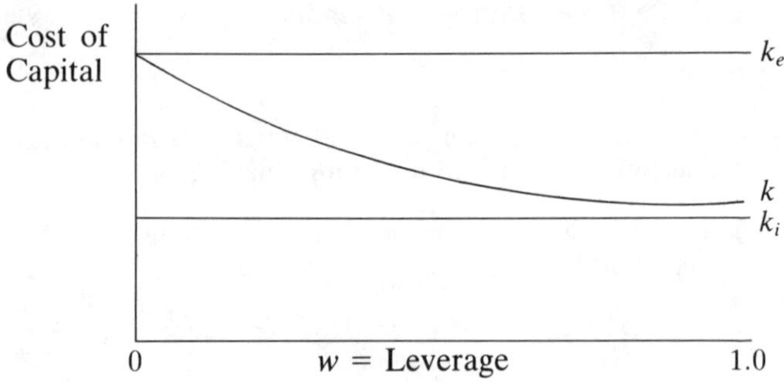

models becomes very large. One model explains that the weighted average cost of capital, k, decreases as the debt-equity ratio of a company increases. And the value of the firm increases as more debt is substituted for equity capital, while the cost of equity capital, k_e, as well as the cost of debt, k_i, remains constant within the relevant range of leverage. See Figure 9.15.1. Another model explains that as the debt-equity ratio increases, the advantages of indebtedness are exactly offset by an increase in the cost of equity capital, k_e, as investors feel that the company is becoming more risky. The weighted average cost of capital therefore remains constant so long as the cost of debt remains constant. Under this model there is no optimal capital structure, and k_e is a linear function of the debt-equity ratio. See Figure 9.15.2.

The traditional model suggests that there is a minimum k. As the debt-equity ratio rises, there is a rise in k_e. However, this rise in k_e is more than offset by the advantages of the use of more debt-finance. As a result, the weighted average cost of capital declines until the minimum point is reached. After that any further increase in the debt-equity ratio will cause an increase in k_e which more than offsets the advantages of further debt-finance, thus raising k, whose rise will be accelerated by an increase in k_i.

Under the perfect market conditions model, one is encouraged to use one hundred per cent debt-finance since this will maximize the value of the company. However, market imperfections render this impossible. Denoting the ratio of market debt value to market firm value by w, we are likely to find the optimum

Figure 9.15.2.

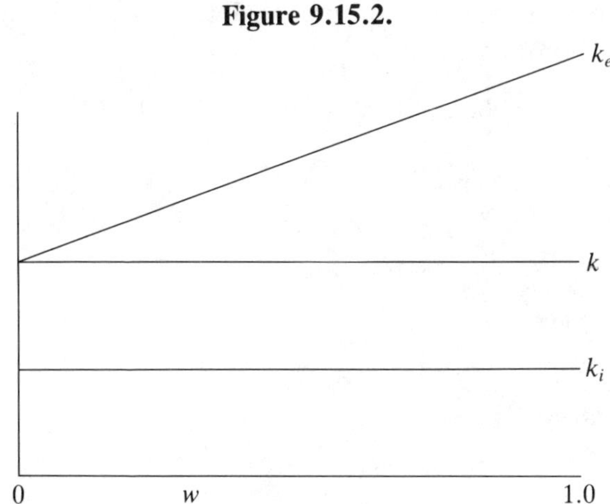

Figure 9.15.3.

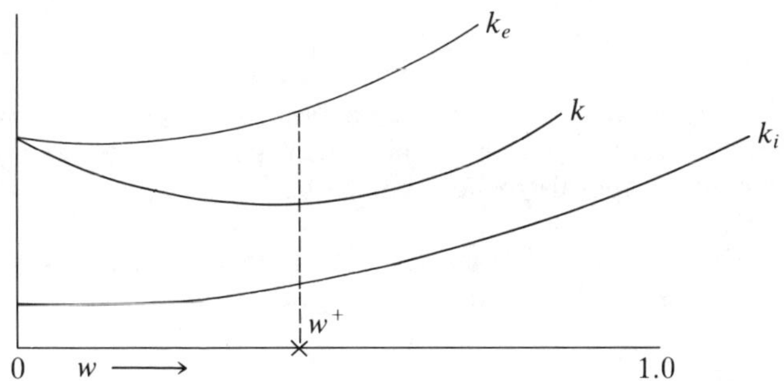

$w+$ in the range $0 < w+ < 1$. Graphically, this may be represented by Figure 9.15.3.

It should be noted that at the optimal value of the firm, k is also optimal.

9.15.1. Narcissus Limited

Narcissus Limited is an established and successful company operating in Singapore. At the request of its board of directors, the company's accountant has prepared the latest information as shown below:

Balance Sheet as at 31st March 1975

	($'000)
Issued and Paid-up Capital	2,000
($1 fully paid shares)	
Profit and Loss Appropriation	2,000
	4,000
10% $100 Debentures	5,000
Trade Creditors	1,000
	$10,000
Fixed Assets	6,000
Current Assets	4,000
	$10,000

Year ended 31st March	Earnings per Share
1972	$0.550
1973	0.605
1974	0.666
1975	0.733

The board of directors inform you that they want a minimum acceptable rate of return which can be used for evaluating investment proposals to be financed by both long-term debt and equity.

You have ascertained that the current market price of the company's share is $5 and that of its debenture is $80.

REQUIRED:

What is the company's weighted average cost of capital? The average annual growth rate of the earnings per share (by the geometric mean) is:

$$e = \sqrt[3]{\frac{0.733}{0.550}} - 1 = 0.10$$

The cost of equity of Narcissus Ltd (using equation 9.8.6.) is:

$$k_e = \frac{(.733)(1.1)}{5} + 0.1 = 0.261$$

The cost of debt (using equation 9.6.2.) is:

$$k_i = \frac{(1 - .4)(0.10)(5{,}000{,}000)}{(80)(50{,}000)} = 0.075$$

The weighted average cost of capital (using equation 9.10.1.) is:

$$k = \frac{(0.075)(4{,}000{,}000) + (0.261)(10{,}000{,}000)}{(4{,}000{,}000) + (10{,}000{,}000)} = 0.208$$

9.15.2. Tanjong Ltd

The following is the balance sheet of Tanjong Ltd:

Tanjong Ltd
Balance Sheet as at 31st December 1979

	Historical Cost	*Current Market Value*		*Historical Cost*	*Current Market Value*
Equity Capital	$100 m	$200 m	Fixed Assets	$70 m	$190 m
Debt Capital	$ 50 m	$ 75 m	Current Assets	$80 m	$ 85 m
	$150 m	$275 m		$150 m	$275 m

The company is proposing to invest in a project which requires a cash outlay of $100 m and which will generate an annual net cash inflow of $25 m before interest and tax in perpetuity. The company's existing cost of equity is 15% and cost of debt is 10% before tax. Income tax rate is 40%.

REQUIRED:

(a) Calculate the company's weighted average cost of capital.
(b) Calculate the rate of return before interest and tax on the proposed investment.
(c) Calculate the effect on the company's cost of equity capital if the proposed project is financed
 (i) entirely from debt,
 (ii) entirely from equity, and
 (iii) in the debt/equity ratio of $\frac{3}{8}$.

(a) The weighted average cost of capital:

$$k = \frac{(0.06)(75) + (0.15)(200)}{75 + 200} = 0.1255$$

(b) The rate of return before interest and tax on the proposed investment:

$$R = \frac{25}{100} = 0.25$$

(c)

	(i) *Entirely from Debt* (\$'000)	(ii) *Entirely from Equity* (\$'000)	(iii) *Debt/Equity* $\frac{3}{8}$ (\$'000)
Earnings before interest and tax	82.5	82.5	82.50
Interest	17.5	7.5	11.25
Earnings before tax	65.0	75.0	71.25
Less Income tax	26.0	30.0	28.50
Earnings after tax	\$39.0	\$45.0	\$42.75

Cost of equity:

$$k_e = \frac{39}{200} \qquad \frac{45}{300} \qquad \frac{42.75}{262.5}$$

$$= 0.195 \qquad = 0.15 \qquad = 0.1629$$

The above case illustrates that as the company becomes more indebted equity shareholders expect a higher rate of return as they sense that the company's financial risk has increased. Resorting to debt finance increases the cost of equity in the normal case where the cost of equity is higher than the cost of debt.

9.16. SELECTED BIBLIOGRAPHY

1. F.D. Arditti: The Weighted Average Cost of Capital—Some Questions on the Definition, Interpretation and Use, Journal of Finance, September 1970, Comments on Arditti's Article, June 1973.
2. W. Baumol and G.M. Burton: The Firm's Optimal Debt-Equity Combination and the Cost of Capital, Quarterly Journal of Economics, November 1967.
3. G.M. Burton: The Debt-Equity Combination of the Firm and the Cost of Capital (Introductory Analysis).
4. W.G. Lewellen: The Cost of Capital.
5. F. Modigliani and M.M. Miller: The Cost of Capital, Corporation Finance, and the Theory of Investment, American Economic Review, June 1958—Taxes and the Cost of Capital: A Correction, American Economic Review, June 1963.
6. M.F. Rubinstein: A Mean-variance Synthesis of Corporate Financial Theory, *The Journal of Finance*, March 1973.
7. E. Solomon: Leverage and the Cost of Capital, Journal of Finance, May 1963.
8. D. Vickers: The Cost of Capital and the Structure of the Firm, Journal of Finance, March 1970.

CHAPTER 10

Financing Problems of a Firm

10.1. BALANCE SHEET EXPLAINED

If we look at a balance sheet of a limited company (see Exhibit 10.1.) we find that it has two major aspects: the items on the left which are called equities, and the items on the right which are called assets.

The division of all balance sheet items into assets and equities which must always be equal, arises from the fundamental accounting equation. This fundamental equation (Equities = Assets) is the tenet of double-entry bookkeeping. The business unit around which accounting entries are made is a separate and distinct entity from the proprietor or proprietors of that business. The business thus becomes an accounting entity. From this point of view, the assets are what the business owns and the equities what it owes. The accounting entity can be compared to a slave. A slave can own no property; what he possesses belongs to his master or others. Hence, the assets of a company usually belong partly to the shareholders and partly to the creditors of the company.

10.2. SOURCES OF FUNDS

We can also look at a balance sheet from another point of view. A company needs funds to carry on its business operations. The equities show the sources of its funds, and the assets, the investments of such funds. Funds are defined as means of making payments. Hence they are more comprehensive than the term cash, which consists only of coins, currency notes and bank deposits. If an entrepreneur commences business with an initial capital contribution of $100,000, made up of a building valued at $80,000 and office equipment valued at $20,000, the total funds obtained by the business amount to $100,000 which are invested in

EXHIBIT 10.1.

A LTD
Balance Sheet as at 31st December 19x1

(Authorised Capital: 1,000,000 shares of $1 each = $1,000,000)

EQUITIES

(1) SHAREHOLDERS' FUNDS			
Issued and paid-up capital			
500,000 $1 shares fully paid		$500,000	
Capital Reserves			
Share premium	$100,000		
		100,000	
Revenue Reserves			
Profit and loss appropriation		200,000	
			$ 800,000
(2) LONG-TERM LIABILITIES			
8% Debentures (redeemable 19x7)			700,000
(3) CURRENT LIABILITIES			
Trade creditors		$150,000	
Bills payable		50,000	
Provision for income tax		80,000	
Provision for dividend		50,000	
			330,000
			$1,830,000

ASSETS

(1) FIXED ASSETS			
Land and building			
at cost	$900,000		
Less Provision for depreciation	250,000		
		$650,000	
Office equipment			
at cost	$300,000		
Less Provision for depreciation	100,000		
		200,000	
			$ 850,000
(2) INVESTMENTS			
6% Government Stock 19x7/19x8 at cost			400,000
(3) CURRENT ASSETS			
Stock		$100,000	
Debtors		230,000	
Prepaid insurance		50,000	
Cash at bank		199,000	
Cash on hand		1,000	
			580,000
			$1,830,000

a building and some office equipment. The balance sheet of the business at this point of time would appear below:

Balance Sheet as at . . . .

EQUITIES		ASSETS	
Capital	$100,000	Building	$ 80,000
		Office Equipment	20,000
	$100,000		$100,000

Funds may also be derived from profits earned which are not distributed as dividends. The aggregate of capital contributions from shareholders and retained earnings is termed shareholders' funds, which are regarded as an internal source of funds.

Some of the assets of a company may be financed from borrowing, for instance, it may obtain its merchandise or raw materials on credit, or it may finance the construction of its building by a long-term debt. These sources of funds are referred to as liabilities. Liabilities are regarded as an external source of funds. The classification of equities into shareholders' funds and liabilities is a useful one because it indicates the financing policy of the enterprise, for instance, whether its expansion is financed by additional capital or by ploughing back profits or by borrowing from external sources.

Liabilities are traditionally sub-divided into two classes on the basis of their maturity: long-term and current. Long-term liabilities are obligations which must be met after a long period of time, say, more than one year, such as mortgage on land maturing in three years, or debentures redeemable in two years' time. Current liabilities are defined as liabilities that will be paid in the ordinary course of business within a short period of time, say, one year. Examples are trade creditors, bills payable, dividend payable and income tax payable. Debt-financing can, therefore, be long-term or short-term.

10.3. INVESTMENT OF FUNDS

We explained that the assets in a balance sheet can be considered as the investments of a company's funds. These investments can be classified, however, on the basis of their liquidity, in other words, on the basis of their readiness of conversion into cash. All assets are first of all divided into two broad groups: current and non-current. Current assets consist of cash and other assets which will be turned into cash in the ordinary course of business within a short period of time, say, one year. Examples are trade debtors, stock, bills receivable and prepaid expenses. All other assets are non-current. The non-current assets may be sub-divided into three divisions: Fixed, Investment and Intangible. Fixed assets can then be defined as the internal investment of the company's funds in tangible properties for the purpose of using them productively in the business for a long period of time, usually several years. Land and buildings, plant and machinery, office furniture and equipment, and delivery vehicles—these may be examples. The purpose is to use them for a long period of time. Occasionally a fixed asset is sold if it is found to be unsuitable or no more productive.

Investments are the external investment of the enterprise's funds in securities or shares of other entities for the purpose of holding them for a long period of time to earn income. Hence, temporary investments of surplus funds which will be sold within a year should be classified as current assets. The distinction between fixed assets and investments is an internal or an external investment of the company's funds. The usefulness of this distinction lies in the fact that management would like to know which investment is more rewarding, since this will help them in making decisions, such as those in respect of expansion policies and dividend policies.

Intangible assets can include all non-current assets other than fixed assets and investments. Under this heading will be goodwill, trade marks, and preliminary expenses. Sometimes, another class of assets known as deferred assets, is used to include loans to directors and other loans which are not income-yielding.

Not all companies in practice follow exactly the same methods of classification as explained by us. However, it is put forward here as an essential criterion upon which any company may base its logic of classification, and that is,

"The division of a class should be mutually exclusive and, together exhaustive of the class." (Classification in Accounting by A.A. Fitzgerald and L.A. Schumer)

The classification of the balance sheet adopted by us can be summarized diagrammatically as below:

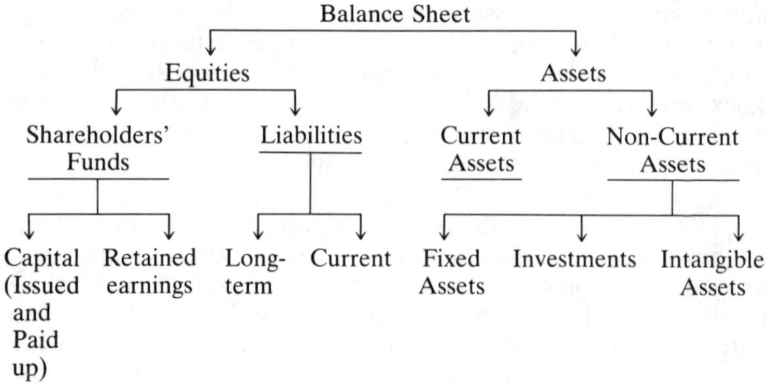

10.4. CAPITAL CONTRIBUTIONS

The capital contributions of the shareholders are an internal source of finance. In the case of a limited company this is obtained by the issue of shares. There are two broad classes of shares: ordinary and preference, and within each class there may be variations which confer different rights on the holders.

Ordinary shares normally form the main risk-bearing capital of the company. Each ordinary share has a norminal or face value which is fixed by the company's Memorandum of Association and which can be changed only if the Memorandum of Association is altered. Ordinary shares may be issued:

(i) at par, that is, at the nominal value,
(ii) at a premium, or at above par value, and
(iii) at a discount, that is, below the nominal value.

The Articles of Association of the company as well as statutory provisions govern the issue of shares and these must be consulted before the company makes an issue. The nominal value of shares, even if they are fully paid, often does not coincide with their market value which is determined by the forces of supply and demand.

Ordinary shares usually carry voting rights, which are exercised at meetings of members of the company. Theoretically, therefore, ordinary shareholders control the operations of the company since they can as a body alter the constitution and appoint the directors of the company. In practice, their right of control is not always exercised. Being the greater risk-bearers, ordinary shareholders are entitled to share the surplus of the trading profits after all fixed interest charges (including preference dividend) have been paid and a prudent amount has been set aside to reserves. The rate of dividend to ordinary shares is usually higher than the fixed rate of dividend to preference shares. Anyway this has to be so if the chance of success in raising ordinary capital is to be enhanced. In the event of the liquidation of the company, the ordinary shareholders are normally entitled to share in the surplus, after the proceeds from the realization of the assets have been utilized to discharge all liabilities and return of paid-up share capital. But they will be the last among all the claims to the company's assets to get back their paid-up capital.

Preference shares are sometimes issued by a company in addition to its ordinary shares. They normally carry a fixed rate of dividend which must be paid (if profits are made) before other classes of shares get their dividend. Unless otherwise stated, they are cumulative, that is, should they fail to receive any dividend in any year, arrears of such dividends would be carried forward which must be paid out of future years' profits in priority to other dividends. If provided for in the Articles of Association, they enjoy priority in the return of capital should the company liquidate. Preference shares may also be participating. For instance, they may get 7% dividend on their nominal value, and after the ordinary shares have received a dividend of up to, say 12%, they will share an additional 1% dividend for every additional 3% paid to the ordinary shareholders.

Preference shares do not usually carry voting rights, but the Articles of Association may sometimes confer on them the power to vote in specific circumstances, for instance, when their dividends are more than three years in arrears, or when there is a scheme of capital reduction.

Redeemable preference shares are sometimes issued if authorised by the company's Articles. This may be resorted to if the fixed rate of dividend is high and the company thinks that the general rate of interest will fall in the future. Before the redeemable preference shares are redeemed, certain statutory provisions must be observed:

(1) The redeemable preference shares must be fully paid.
(2) They may be redeemed either out of the proceeds of a fresh issue of shares or out of profits which would otherwise be available for distribution as cash dividend.
(3) If redeemed out of profits, a sum required out of profits equal to the nominal value of the shares so redeemed must be transferred to a Capital Redemption Reserve. This Reserve must be treated as if it were the paid-up capital of the company, and can be used to issue bonus shares.

In all published accounts before redemption, the balance sheet of the company must indicate the amount of redeemable preference shares and the date of their redemption. Very often redeemable preference shares are issued with a right to the holders to convert them into ordinary shares on redemption. This right of conversion acts as an inducement to investors. However, it may be considered by some people as an indication of the financial weakness of the company since it must offer inducement to obtain funds.

Non-voting ordinary shares are issued sometimes where the existing ordinary shareholders do not wish to lose control of the company. These non-voting ordinary shares share the same risks and income as the other ordinary shares, but they have no voting power, and hence have no control. The issue of non-voting shares is justified by the claim that the payment of death duties through the sale of non-voting shares does not dilute the original control, that the market of the company's shares is given variety, and that additional funds can be obtained without the risk of a take-over bid. It is considered, however, that the issue of non-voting shares is morally unjustified. While bearing equal risks, they can exercise no control, and the existence of non-voting shares makes it feasible for minority shareholders to gain complete control at the expense of the majority.[1]

Workers' shares are sometimes issued to workers as an encouragement to increased effort. Most of these shares are not freely transferable and merely represent an entitlement to share in the company's profits. There are companies, however, like Im-

1. Under Section 55 of The Companies Act, a public company having a share capital and its subsidiaries can no longer have non-voting ordinary shares.

perial Chemical Industries, which issue bonus shares to workers, who become full shareholders with full voting rights. The workers may sell these shares, and the purpose of getting workers to participate in the control and ownership of the company may be defeated.

When shares are fully paid they may be converted into stock; stock cannot be issued directly. Stock is not numbered like shares, and hence saves clerical work in transfer procedures. Shares are always transferable in whole units, whereas stock may be transferred in fractions.

Shares of no par value are not permissible in Singapore or Malaysia though they are common in the United States and Canada. If a company has 100,000 shares, a holder of one share is entitled to receive one 100,000th share of the profits, and of the surplus after all claims have been met in the event of liquidation. The balance sheet will show the amount paid-up as the capital comprising of so many shares. The advantages claimed for shares of no par value are:

(1) Avoidance of confusion in the minds of the uninformed in respect of nominal value, uncalled-capital, called-up or paid-up capital and the market price. Some may think that the market price has a direct connection with the nominal value or paid-up capital.

(2) In shares of par value, dividends are often declared as a percentage of nominal value, which is not a true return on the investment. In shares of no par value, dividends are simply paid as a stated amount of cash per share.

10.5. METHODS OF OBTAINING CAPITAL CONTRIBUTIONS

In raising additional finance from capital contributions, a company can issue shares directly to the public or through an issuing house. An issuing house (or a broker who performs this function in Singapore and Malaysia) is an organization whose function is to obtain share capital or long-term debentures for companies.[2] It acts as a link between the companies who need funds and the

2. Merchant bankers also provide advice on the issue of shares in addition to their other services.

investors. Besides this main function, the issuing house offers various other services to its clients:

(1) It gives advice on the best capital structure a company should have, the type of share or debenture to issue, the price at which the share is to be offered, and the rate of dividend or interest which is appropriate.
(2) It may undertake to advertise the issue and to ensure that all legal requirements are complied with.
(3) It gives advice on all financial matters, such as the best form of reconstruction or merger, and how to convert a private company into a public one.

The following are the main methods of raising share capital:

(1) Stock Exchange Introduction
(2) Stock Exchange Placing
(3) Offer for Sale
(4) Public Issue by Prospectus
(5) Rights Issue
(6) Issue by Tender

10.5.1. Stock Exchange Introduction

When a company desires to have its shares quoted on the Stock Exchange, it will instruct its broker to lodge with the Council of the Stock Exchange a formal letter of application to have a quotation. The company must comply with the requirements of the Exchange and make available to the jobbers shares for dealings on the Exchange. Sometimes shares are made available by existing shareholders and in this case there is no "public issue of shares". Very often, however, an application for quotation is made so as to have a public issue. If this is the case, the method becomes a placing or an offer for sale.

10.5.2. Stock Exchange Placing

When the amount of capital to be raised is relatively small, the company may wish to have a Stock Exchange placing. The broker or the issuing house "places" the shares with interested investors, mainly investment institutions such as insurance companies and investment trusts. The broker or the issuing house purchases the shares from the company and then sells them to these institutional investors. Alternatively, they may just act as middlemen. But in most cases, there is a contract between the company and the issuing house or broker to buy the shares. There is no such contract in an introduction.

The advantages of this method are the comparatively small expenses of issue and the avoidance of underwriting. As soon as the placing is arranged, application for quotation is lodged. The Stock Exchange normally allows a private placing only if the circumstances of the case warrant it, such as the smaller cost involved, because a placing does not have any publicity and the benefit of any appreciation in price, after quotation has been obtained, is limited to the few participants.

10.5.3. Offer for Sale

This method is very similar to a Stock Exchange placing in that in both cases, the issuing house or the broker purchases the shares from the company and then resells them to investors. In the case of an offer for sale, however, the resale is to the public at large and not a few chosen clients. The price paid by the issuing house or broker will be found in the contracts included in the advertisement. The difference between the two prices is to cover its expenses and a disclosed margin of profit.

The offer for sale must observe the regulations of the Stock Exchange, and a copy must be filed with the Registrar of Companies. The information which must be provided by the company in a prospectus is, in the case of an offer for sale, contained in a "Chairman's" letter addressed to the issuers. Liability for the accuracy of the information is attached to the directors of the issuing company.

10.5.4. Public Issue by Prospectus

This method is much more elaborate than previously-mentioned ones, because the issue is comparatively large and it is essential to be able to sell to the public the whole issue on a single day. An organization must be set up to deal with the necessary advertising and the large number of applications. Most public issues are, therefore, made with the help of an issuing house or a broker. The first step is to have the company's shares quoted on the Stock Exchange if this is not already the case. While the issuing house or the broker is able to give a host of advice regarding the issue, including the size and form of the issue, the exact rights to be given to the future shareholders such as voting, dividends and repayment of capital, the company's directors may have their own views on these matters. The help of accountants and auditors as well as professional valuers and solicitors will be enlisted to draw up all the necessary information about the company which will be published in a prospectus. Statutory provisions require many items of information to be included in a prospectus, Stock Exchange regulations also specify certain information to be disclosed. The following is a summary, inter alia, of what is required of a prospectus[3]:

(1) The prospectus must be filed with the Registrar of Companies before it is issued. It must be signed by the chairman and any two directors, and by an expert who gives opinions on it. A copy of any material contract, such as purchase of property, must be attached to the prospectus.
(2) Every prospectus must be dated and must contain words to the effect that a copy has been registered with the Registrar of Companies.
(3) Every prospectus must contain, inter alia, the following particulars:
    (i) Information about the directors, such as qualification shares, remuneration, any interest in the promotion of the company or any property acquired by the company.
    (ii) Promoters' profits or commissions, and preliminary expenses.
    (iii) Details of capital required, including the amount that must be paid in cash.
    (iv) Voting rights and rights in respect of dividends and capital repayments of the different classes of shares, including details of the rights of deferred shares, if any.

3. Section 39 of The Companies Act specifies the legal requirements regarding prospectuses.

(v) The minimum subscription which is necessary for the acquiring of property, the payment of preliminary expenses and commissions and the provision of working capital.
(vi) The time of opening of the subscription lists, and the amount to be payable on application and on allotment where the shares are to be paid for by instalments.
(vii) Reports to be included:
   (a) Auditors' report on the profits and losses of the company for the past five years as well as the rates of dividends declared, and on the assets and liabilities of the company at the last date on which the accounts were made up.
   (b) Report on any business intended to be purchased out of the proceeds of the issue.
   (c) Report on acquisition of shares of another company, whose control is to be taken over by the purchase of its shares out of the proceeds of the issue.

For shares offered to the public a prospectus is always required. A rights issue or an issue of bonus shares, which is not a public issue, does not require a prospectus. In order that the shares will be fully subscribed, and the financial plans of the company will not be frustrated through lack of funds, the company almost always arranges with the issuing house or broker to have the issue underwritten. Underwriting is a form of insurance where a commission is paid in return for an undertaking to buy up any shares which the public has not taken up. Usually the issuing house or broker underwrites the issue and then gets other financial institutions (that is, other issuing houses or brokers, or insurance companies) to undertake part or all of the insurance. If the issuing house merely arranges for the issue to be underwritten by other financial institutions, he gets a commission known as overriding commission.

10.5.5. Rights Issue

A rights issue is one where rights to purchase the shares are offered to existing shareholders in the proportions of their existing holdings.[4] For instance, shareholders may be offered two shares for every five shares they hold. A shareholder holding five hundred shares is given the right to buy two hundred shares of the new issue. In order to ensure that the issue will be a success the price of a rights issue is lower than the market price of the existing shares. A shareholder can sell the "rights", if he wishes, by signing a letter of renunciation, and may make a profit out of the deal.

A rights issue is a simple and inexpensive way of raising additional funds from capital contributions. It is often the method adopted if the intention is to preserve the control of the existing shareholders.

10.5.6. Issue by Tender

Under this method the public are invited to tender for the new issue of shares. The applicants with the highest bids will be issued with the shares. All the shares must be issued at one price, and this will be the highest price at which all the shares can be sold. For instance, if 500,000 shares are to be issued and the tender bids are:

300,000 shares at $1.50
400,000 shares at $1.40
500,000 shares at $1.35
500,000 shares at $1.30

the price at which the shares will be issued is $1.40. If the shares are under-subscribed, the minimum price as advertised by the company is applied to issue the shares.

The object of issuing shares by tender is to prevent "stagging." Stagging is a term which refers to the activities of "stags". A stag is one who applies for shares in any new issue, and when successful, he sells them at a profit. His intention is not to hold the shares and he can make profits whenever the demand for the shares exceeds the supply.

10.6. DIFFICULTIES OF OBTAINING CAPITAL CONTRIBUTIONS

The difficulties of obtaining capital contributions or long-term debts in the form of debentures are encountered mostly by small

4. Official approval must be obtained by a company before it effects a rights issue.

companies or other companies whose prospects are regarded as unsound. The difficulties may be grouped under two main headings: (1) the cost of issue, and (2) the illiquidity of the securities.

Most of the expenses incurred in an issue of shares are fixed irrespective of the size of the issue. Since small companies usually make new issues of shares of comparatively small magnitude, that is the number of shares issued is small, the cost of issue per dollar unit of security is often exhorbitant. Hence, a public issue by prospectus is not a very feasible method. Private placings or rights issue are sometimes resorted to. The other difficulty is the illiquidity of the securities. Most investors are prepared to invest their money in shares provided they can sell them easily without too great a risk of any loss of capital. In other words, there must be a ready market for the securities. There should always be demand and supply of the securities. The small number of shares of a small company means that this characteristic of the market may not be present. Hence, a holder of its shares may not be able to dispose of them easily without much loss of capital at a time when he needs cash. A new issue by a small company may not, therefore, always be successful.

10.7. THE PUBLIC LIMITED COMPANY

It would be noticed that all the methods of raising capital contributions except the rights issue, can be employed only by a public limited company. A private limited company is prohibited from having its shares freely transferable and from making an issue of shares to the public. Hence, if additional finance is required by using the methods mentioned which involve issue to the public, it is necessary to convert a private company into a public one. Though a private company enjoys certain privileges, such as, privacy in the management of its affairs and little danger of losing control of the company to other people, it cannot reap the advantages of a public company. A public company can raise additional finance by issuing shares or debentures to the public. Its shares and debentures can be quoted on the Stock Exchange. Besides making the securities marketable, quotation may give beneficial publication to the company's activities. There are other advantages but these are the main ones pertaining to finance.

10.8. FINANCIAL INSTITUTIONS

In most countries of the world, special financial institutions are established with backing from the governments to give financial support to new or old companies which may otherwise be unable to commence or expand business operations. Very often financial support is given in the form of long-term loans or by buying the shares of the companies, but they are very selective in granting financial support. The companies must be engaged in business activities which are within the ambit of the government's economic development or industrialization programmes, and they must comply with the requirements of these institutions. In Singapore, the Economic Development Board and the Development Bank of Singapore sometimes participate in the financing of firms in addition to its many other functions.

10.9. RETAINED EARNINGS (OR AUTO-FINANCING) AND DEBT FINANCE

Retained earnings is an internal source of funds; instead of distributing the earnings to the shareholders, the company re-invests them in the business.

If we make the assumption that virtually all the shares of a company are owned by a single individual we can analyse the tax advantages of debt, as against retained earnings, as a source of finance. The following symbols will be used:

y = net profit before interest and tax of the company
T = income tax rate of the company
t = income tax rate of the shareholder
p = proportion of net distributable profit paid to the shareholder
I = amount of interest payment

There are two cases which will be discussed: (a) where the company does the borrowing, and (b) where the shareholder does the borrowing.

Under case (a), the net profit after interest is $\$(y - I)$, the amount of tax paid by the company is $T(y - I)$, and the net profit after interest and tax is therefore $\$[(y - I) - T(y - I)]$. The shareholder receives in dividend.

$$\$p[(y - I) - T(y - I)] \quad \ldots\ldots \quad (1)$$

The taxation liability of the shareholder is derived as follows. The taxation liability on the grossed-up dividend is $\$[tp(y - I)]$. The tax rebate (being the income tax paid at source by the company on the dividend declared) amounts to $\$[pT(y - I)]$. Hence, the net taxation liability of the shareholder is $\$[tp(y - I)] - [pT(y - I)] =$

$$\$[p(y - I)(t - T)] \quad \ldots\ldots \quad (2)$$

And the net income Y_d received by the shareholder is:

$$\begin{aligned} Y_d &= \$\{p[(y - I) - T(y - I)] - [p(y - I)(t - T)]\} \\ &= p(y - I)(1 - T) - p(y - I)(t - T) \\ &= \$p(y - I)(1 - t) \\ &= py - pyt + pI(t - 1) \quad \ldots\ldots \quad (3) \end{aligned}$$

Assuming that the company's and the shareholder's borrowing rates are the same, case (b) can now be presented. The net profit after interest and tax is $(y - Ty) = \$y(1 - \mathrm{T})$. And the shareholder receives in dividend

$$\$py(1 - T) \quad \ldots\ldots \quad (4)$$

The taxation liability of the shareholder on the grossed-up dividend is $\$(tpy)$. The tax rebate now consists of two parts: the income tax paid at source by the company on the dividend declared which amounts to $\$pTy$, and the deductible tax allowance on interest which is tI. Hence, the net taxation liability of the shareholder is:

$$\$(tpy - pTy - tI) \quad \ldots\ldots \quad (5)$$

And the net income received by the shareholder becomes:

$$\begin{aligned} Y_s &= py(1 - T) - (tpy - pTy - tI) - \mathrm{I} \\ &= py - pyt + I(t - 1) \quad \ldots\ldots \quad (6) \end{aligned}$$

Comparing equation (3) with equation (6) indicates that

$$Y_s \leq Y_d, \text{ since } 0 \leq p \leq 1 \qquad (7)$$

And $Y_s = Y_d$ if $p = 1$, that is, if the company distributes all its net distributable profit as dividend. Other things being equal, the difference, $(Y_d - Y_s)$ increases as p decreases. Hence, it can be concluded that where interest is a deductible allowance and personal leverage can be substituted for corporate leverage, debt finance by the company is preferable to debt finance by the shareholder. This conclusion remains valid if the shareholder cannot claim the interest paid by him as a deductible allowance since equation (6) now becomes:

$$\$(py - pyt - I) \qquad (8)$$

10.10. LONG-TERM DEBT-FINANCING

A long-term debt is one which is repayable after at least one year, usually after several years. In the commercial world it is known as a Debenture. A debenture could be either secured or unsecured. An unsecured debenture is sometimes referred to as a naked debenture. A debenture is secured by a fixed charge or a floating charge or by both. A debenture holder is a creditor of the company that borrows the money from him. He would like some form of protection from loss of his money should the company fail and some means of enforcing the contractual obligations of the company in the payment of interest and the return of principal. This protection is obtained by entering into an agreement with the company, very often in the form of a debenture trust deed. By the agreement some specific property of the company, such as a piece of land or some buildings, is mortgaged to the debenture holder or holders. This is known as a fixed charge. The agreement often provides that should the company fail to pay the interest accrued when due or to return the principal either by instalments or in a lump sum as agreed the debenture holder has the right to enforce the agreement, and the proceeds from the sale of the charged properties must be used first to repay the debentures secured on them. A fixed charge attaches to some specific pieces of property, and the company cannot freely dispose of those properties without getting the consent of the debenture holders.

A floating charge, on the other hand, does not attach to any specific property; it is a charge on all the assets of the company as a going concern, and it ranks after a fixed charge. The assets used as security in a floating charge such as, cash, stock, debtors, and other current assets, are freely disposable by a company in the ordinary course of its business. But a floating charge becomes crystallized and attaches to the assets when the company commits a breach of the debenture agreement. A receiver may than be appointed as in the case of a breach by the company in a fixed charge.

Since security is perhaps uppermost in the mind of the debenture holder when he decides to put his money in this type of investment, it is pertinent to ascertain how real his security is in a fixed or floating charge. The properties used as security in a fixed charge may be specific or non-specific. If they are non-specific and capable of being used for other purposes, they usually possess good realisable value when sold. But if they are specific in use they may not possess any realisable value and the cost that must be incurred to convert them to other uses may be too high to warrant their conversion.

When a company is very prosperous and reaping good profits, debenture holders get no extra benefits except that their security is greater. In fact the high profits make the ordinary shares of the company more attractive, thereby lowering the market price of debentures. In lean years, the reverse is true and the price of debentures rises. However, in times of business slump, even good debentures may find no buyers at all. In a very bad economic depression, only companies with good management, enjoying monopolistic power and producing necessities or goods that are always in demand, may be able to meet their interest payments.

The debenture agreement almost always provides that the debenture holders cannot interfere with the administration and operation of the company so long as it observes the contractual obligations. So when the company is in financial difficulties but is still able to meet its interest payments, we may find the debenture holders waiting patiently while the directors of the company try to salvage the company or allow its resources to be gradually eroded. When the company finally does go into liquidation, we may find that its assets are worth very little, if any. The question is often asked as to whether clauses should be inserted in the debenture agreement whereby the debenture holders are entitled to interfere in the management of the company even before it commits any breach of the agreement. The degree of competition among lenders of funds as well as the bargaining powers of the parties concerned and the wider social issue may all contribute to an acceptable solution. The real security offered to a debenture holder is the company's profitability.

Provisions for the repayment of long-term indebtedness are often made by the sinking fund method. By this method an annual fixed sum is set aside from profits and invested outside the business at a fixed rate of interest. Annually the interest earned is re-invested with the annual fixed sum. In this way, the principal of the loan can be repaid on maturity out of the proceeds of the investment which will be realised. Incidentally, it may be mentioned that while the interest paid on the loan annually is a charge against revenue and, therefore, an operating cost, the annual fixed instalments are provided from profits and constitute repayments of loan and cannot be considered as operating costs.

10.11. CONVERTIBLES

Convertible preference shares are shares which carry a fixed rate of dividend and are similar to preference shares except that they can be converted into ordinary shares usually at the option of the holders after a lapse of time from the date of issue. Convertible debentures like convertible preference shares can be converted into ordinary shares; the terms of conversion are laid down at the time of issue.

If a company issues convertible debentures one of which can be converted to three ordinary shares at any time, and if the market price of an ordinary share is $10, then one convertible debenture is worth at least $30. If the market price of ordinary shares rises to $15, the price of the convertible debentures will rise to at least $45. On the other hand, should ordinary shares fall in price, the convertible debentures might not fall in price; they might not at any rate fall in price to the same extent since they are still paid the fixed rate of interest. The market price of the convertible debentures should then follow the price trend of similar fixed-interest obligations.

If the convertible debentures are issued at the par value of $30 and each is exchangeable for three ordinary shares whose market price is $9, then the equivalent share value of each debenture is $27. The premium of $3 is paid by investors for the greater safety of debentures as compared with ordinary shares as well as the expected capital gain following any share price increase. The above analysis suggests that issuing convertibles enables the company to obtain long-term finance at lower cost than ordinary long-term loans. But the effect of convertibles on the earnings per share ratio may have informative value on the market price of the ordinary shares and this must not be lost sight of.

10.12. SHORT-TERM DEBT-FINANCING

A short-term debt is defined as one that must be discharged within a year, and the following may be considered as common forms of short-term debt financing:

(1) Trade credit
(2) Accrued expenses
(3) Income tax payable
(4) Bills Payable
(5) Bank overdrafts and bank loans
(6) Advances from finance companies.

10.12.1. Trade Credit

In the business operations of an enterprise, it often obtains merchandise or raw materials in advance of payment. This is trade credit. Financially healthy business concerns do not normally encounter any difficulty in obtaining credit. Some types of business concerns depend very heavily on trade credit, especially those in the wholesale and retail business. Trade credit is more important to small firms than to big ones as a source of finance, because the former may find it more difficult to obtain loans or bank overdrafts.

The practice of suppliers of goods of offering cash discount to debtors as an inducement for prompt payment arises from the scarcity of finance. A discount term of 3/10, net 46 means that if the buyer pays in 10 days, he gets a discount of 3%, otherwise he has to pay within 46 days. If he buys $100 worth of goods, and he does not take advantage of the discount offered, he will make use of $97 for 36 days at a cost of $3. This amounts to an interest of about 31% per annum, which is very high. Even if the supplier allows him an additional 36 days to pay, making a total of 72 days in which he can make use of $97, the interest rate per annum is still high, 15.5% approximately. Generally trade credit is a very costly source of funds. Taking advantage of cash discount whenever possible can be recommended as a good business policy. Besides the cost advantage derived from other means of finance, prompt payment of debts will earn for the firm a good reputation which may enable it to get supplies even in times of scarcity.

The average amount of funds obtained from trade credit of an individual company is determined by:

(1) the payment policy of the company,
(2) the discount terms offered, and
(3) the volume of purchases.

Usually the first two factors remain relatively stable while the third factor may change over short periods of time.

10.12.2. Accrued Expenses

Many of the services used by a company are not immediately paid, such as wages and salaries, contributions to the central provident fund, and rent. The amount is determined mainly by the level of business operations. The amount outstanding on a balance sheet date, however, depends on the date of the balance sheet in relation to the usual dates of making such payments.

10.12.3. Income Tax Payable

A company is liable to pay to the Inland Revenue Department 40% of its current year's net profit as income tax. But as a matter of practice, the tax is usually paid later. In the meantime, the amount due is being used by the company. Hence, so long as profits are earned year by year, the income tax provision is a source of funds. But what happens if the company ceases to make profits as previously, the spontaneous inflow of funds from net profit stops flowing and at the same time the liability of income tax payable on last year's net profit must be paid. This may cause a strain on the company's financial resources, and is something which the financial management must not lose sight of.

10.12.4. Bills Payable

A bill of exchange is no more widely used as a financial device in internal trade, but is still very important in foreign trade, where bank bills are popular. In a bank bill the bank's name is used as a sort of guarantee for payment. A draft is drawn on a bank requiring the bank to pay on a certain date a specified sum of money to a person named therein. The bank expresses its consent to pay by writing its name and the word "accepted" across the face of the draft. When this has been done, the draft becomes a bank bill.

If an importer, A Limited, wishes to import goods from B Limited, he may arrange to open a letter of credit with his bank in favour of the exporter, B Limited. B Limited will draw on A Limited's bank in accordance with the detailed terms of the letter of credit and the bank will accept the draft. Once the draft has been accepted by A Limited's bank, B Limited can discount it with his own bank to get an advance of cash on the goods exported by him. A Limited on his part need not pay for the goods until after a lapse of a few months, normally three to six months.

Credit instruments used for the finance of international trade are complicated and diverse and we have to recommend the reader to consult specialized books on the subject if he wishes to pursue it further.

10.12.5. Bank Overdrafts and Bank Loans

A bank overdraft is different from a bank loan. When a bank overdraft facility is granted, no accounting entry is made in the customer's account in the bank's ledger. His account is debited when and as the customer draws cheques on the bank. Any paying-in of cash by the customer into his account will be credited to his account to reduce the overdraft balance. And the interest charged is calculated on the daily balance standing to the debit of his account, and not on the full amount of the overdraft facility as agreed. This is the main difference between a bank overdraft and a bank loan, because in the latter, once the loan agreement is signed for a fixed sum of money repayable after a specified period of time, the whole amount is placed to the customer's account and interest is charged on this total amount for the full period of the loan. Advances by way of overdraft are, therefore, more attractive than loans if the interest rate per annum is the same in both cases.

But a bank overdraft is legally repayable on demand, and is the source of finance resorted to for three main purposes:

(1) to finance seasonal needs of funds where the business of the firm is seasonal,
(2) to finance the working capital requirements of the firm, and
(3) to meet capital expenditure which will be permanently financed by long-term debt or capital contributions very shortly later so that the overdraft is repaid within a short time.

A commercial bank relies mainly on depositors' money for its funds and does not as a matter of prudence normally grant loans for the finance of fixed assets. Nevertheless, some banks do grant fixed loans though they usually form a very small proportion of their total lending.

A bank overdraft may be unsecured, in which case it is known as a clean overdraft. It is commonly secured by a fixed or floating charge over the property of the borrower, or on the personal guarantee of some credit-worthy people. Trade credit, on the other hand, is almost always unsecured. A bank overdraft can be used for a wide range of purposes whereas a trade credit is granted only for the purchase of goods. The cost of borrowing is usually higher in a trade credit than in a bank overdraft.

10.12.6. Advances From Finance Companies

By finance companies we mean firms engaged in lending money other than banks, insurance companies and investment trusts. These finance companies obtain their sources of funds mainly from equity capital, deposit money of depositors, long-term debts and loans from banks. Many of them are subsidiaries of banks. The types of financing activities they engage in may include:

(1) Financing instalment purchases, and
(2) Financing hire purchases.
(3) Granting advances to wholesalers and retailers, and
(4) Granting loans to small companies.
(5) Factoring.

In financing instalment purchases, they advance the cash price of the purchase to the vendor and may undertake to collect the debt by a stated number of instalments (including the interest charged) from the buyer. This is similar to the arrangement in a hire purchase transaction except that in an instalment purchase, the property and possession of the goods bought pass to the buyer when the agreement is signed, whereas in a hire-purchase transaction the possession of the goods passes to the buyer at the time of signing the agreement, but the legal ownership usually passes to the buyer only when the final instalment is paid.

Since financing companies normally undertake greater risks in that most of their lending does not have good security, the interest rates charged by them are relatively higher than those charged by banks.

Receivables especially trade debtors are sometimes sold to a factor and in this way finance is obtained. If advances are obtained in this manner before the maturity of the debts the factor charges interest on the advances besides the usual fees for their servicсs. Some factors assume losses from bad debts as well as litigation expenses, others do not. An advantage of factoring is the savings that result from obviating the setting up of a debt collection department. Its disadvantage is its high cost and the dislike of factoring by the firm's customers.

10.13. LONG-TERM *v*. SHORT-TERM DEBT FINANCING

The provider of finance always expects to receive in the future a sum greater than what he lends at present. The excess is an inducement for him to do this, and is the compensation for his forgoing the present enjoyment of his money as well as for the risks he undertakes in such a venture. The risks are:

(1) failure to recover his money should the borrower default,
(2) a rise in the interest rate in the future, (he loses because

had he not lent then, he could lend at the higher rate), and

(3) a fall in the purchasing power of money.

Generally the longer the term of the loan, the greater the risks will be, hence the interest on a short-term loan tends to be lower than that on a long-term one. The borrower is willing to pay a higher interest rate for a long-term loan, because he may be faced with two types of risk in a short-term indebtedness:

(1) inability to repay the loan in a short time, (in a long-term loan, it is easier for him to make provisions for repayment), and
(2) likelihood of having to pay a higher rate of interest should he renew the loan. (The interest rate, in fact, may fall at the time when he renews the loan. The general interest rate is more a matter of governmental monetary policy).

The above conclusions are generalizations, and the reverse state of affairs may prevail under special circumstances. Because of the greater risks to a borrower in short-term financing, we find that business prudence prefers to use short-term indebtedness to finance current assets, and long-term indebtedness to finance fixed assets or capital expenditures.

10.14. CAPITAL CONTRIBUTIONS *v*. LONG-TERM LOANS

The relationship between capital contributions and long-term loans is often referred to as capital gearing or leverage. The question that is asked of most companies contemplating an expansion of business operations is: Should the expansion be financed from a loan or an issue of shares? The question can also be put in a different way: What should be the correct leverage for a particular company? One would expect that there are as many viewpoints as there are groups of people who have an interest in the company: shareholders, prospective shareholders, creditors, and management. It is considered that the viewpoint of equity shareholders is the relevant one since it is they who should represent the company's ownership with power of control and bearing a greater proportion of the risks that the company may face. The viewpoint of management must reflect the interest of the shareholders because they are agents of the company, and as such, they provide trusteeship over the resources of the business. This does not mean that management should ignore their social and moral obligations to other interested parties, but they should not forget that their primary responsibility is to the shareholders. On the assumption that the viewpoint of management coincides with that of the equity shareholders, we can attempt to answer the question posed earlier from the following aspects:

(1) Control of existing equity shareholders
(2) Risks involved
(3) Nature of the business
(4) Phase of the trade cycle
(5) Earnings of ordinary shares or equity.

Unless the existing shareholders are able to subscribe fully to a fresh issue of ordinary shares, control of the company becomes diluted; the existing shareholders may even lose control to another substantial group of shareholders. This factor may greatly influence the decision-making process in this type of problem. On the other hand, any increase in indebtedness increases the risks to equity shareholders. Creditors and often preference shareholders have prior claims on the company's assets should it go into liquidation, and interest on debentures and preference dividend must be paid first out of profits before any ordinary dividend can be declared. The ratio of indebtedness to equity, or leverage, may also affect the overall cost of capital against which decisions on new investments may be measured.

Where a business is speculative and its prospective earnings are uncertain, too much dependence on debt-financing makes the business more risky; if the forecast of earnings is too optimistic the business may find itself unable to meet the contractual obligations of indebtedness. On the other hand, where a business enjoys stability in the demand for its products and thus profits, debt-financing increases the earnings yield (or return) on equity. The phase of the business cycle at the time when new finance is required affects the prospective earnings of the business as well as the interest rates at which funds can be acquired, and hence, this factor must be taken into account. Where interest rates are high because funds are scarce, redeemable preference shares or redeemable debentures may become attractive because they can be exchanged with cheaper sources of funds when interest rates have fallen.

Perhaps the more interesting aspect to be considered is how the alternative methods of financing can affect the earnings of ordinary shares. Let us take the following as an example. The company is considering business expansion which needs a funds requirement of $100,000. It could either issue 75,000 ordinary shares of $1 each which at the market price of $1.33 1/3 per share will bring in $100,000, or issue $100,000 7% Debentures at par. This investment is expected to increase earnings before interest and income tax by $12,000. The tabulated figures below show the positions of the alternative proposals:

Hopeful Limited

	Present Position	*Proposed Positions*	
		Debenture	*Ordinary Share*
	$	$	$
Earnings before interest and income tax	75,000	87,000	87,000
Interest on debenture	21,000	28,000	21,000
	54,000	59,000	66,000
Less Income Tax payable (40%)	21,600	23,600	26,400
Earnings of ordinary shares	32,400	35,400	39,600
Number of ordinary shares	300,000	300,000	375,000
Earnings per share	$ 0.108	$ 0.118	$ 0.1056

Existing Balance Sheet as at ....

Issued Capital ($1) shares fully paid)	$ 300,000	Land and buildings	$ 500,000
Revenue Reserves	88,400	Stock	450,000
7% Debentures	300,000	Sundry debtors	240,000
Sundry creditors	700,000	Bank	120,000
Income tax payable	21,600	Other	100,000
	$1,410,000		$1,410,000

From the tabulated figures, it is apparent that from the aspect of earnings per share, the issue of debenture is more attractive. But the table fails to indicate what the position will be should earnings be different from those predicted. To overcome the defect, a range-of-earnings chart can be constructed as shown below:

Chart Showing Range of Earnings before Interest and Income Tax—the Attractiveness of Debenture versus Ordinary shares as indicated by Earnings per share.

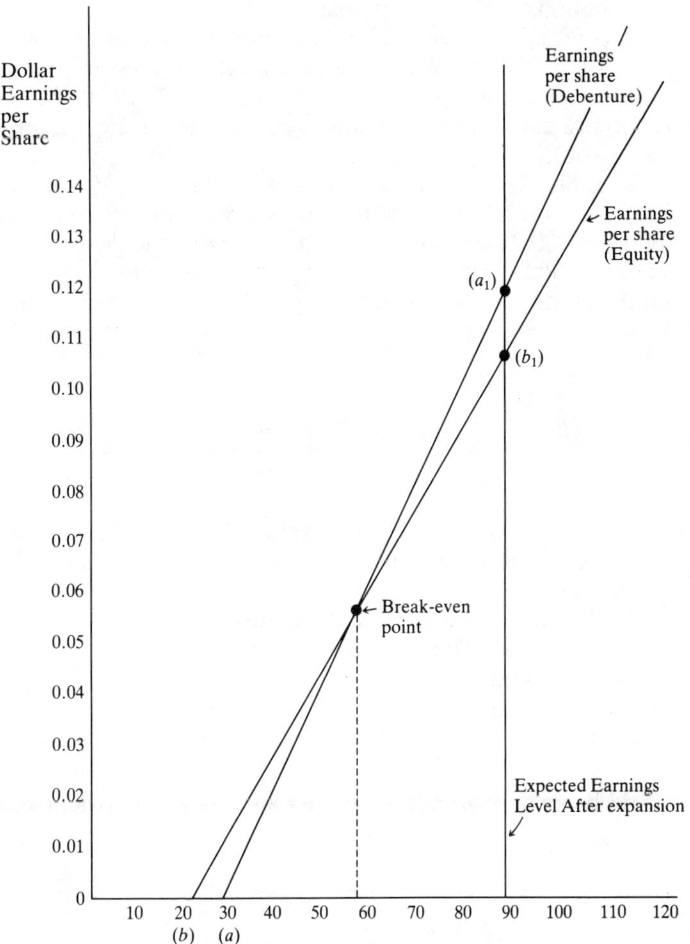

The chart is constructed by drawing two straight lines:

(1) the line showing earnings per share (Debenture), and
(2) the line showing earnings per share (Equity).

To construct the first line, two points must be taken, (a) and (a_1). (a_1) indicate the earnings per share, \$0.118, where total earnings are equal to \$87,000, and (a) indicates the total earnings of \$28,000 which is just sufficient to pay the fixed interest charges, leaving nothing for ordinary shares.

To construct the second line, two points must be determined, (b) and (b_1). (b_1) is the point where total earnings are equal to \$87,000 and the earnings per share amount to \$0.1056. (b) is the point where total earnings amount to \$21,000 and earnings per share are nil.

From the chart it can be read that if total earnings are below \$56,000, it is more attractive to issue shares. But if total earnings exceed \$56,000, it becomes more attractive to issue debenture. At \$56,000 of total earnings the earnings per share are the same for both alternatives. The break-even point of total earnings before income tax and interest can also obtained from the following formula:

$$\frac{(B - I)(1 - T)}{S_1} = \frac{(B - I_2)(1 - T)}{S_2}, \text{ where}$$

B = break-even point of total earnings before income tax and interest where earnings per share are the same for both alternatives.
I = total interest before new debenture issue.
I_2 = total interest after new debenture issue.
T = rate of income tax.
S_1 = number of shares including new issue of shares.
S_2 = number of existing shares excluding new share issue.

Applying the formula to the data given in the example, we have

$$\frac{(B - 21{,}000)(1 - .40)}{375{,}000} = \frac{(B - 28{,}000)(1 - .40)}{300{,}000}$$

Solving the equation, we get

$$\underline{\underline{B = \$56{,}000}}$$

Although the earnings per share increase as a result of an issue of debenture rather than shares, the issue of debenture may also increase the risk of the ordinary shareholders in two ways. First, the profits may not materialize as expected and the contractual commitments in interest payment and principal repayment cannot be met. This breach of contract may force the company into liquidation or to borrow at excessive cost from other sources. Some loan agreements may even provide clauses for the debenture holders to take over control of the company should it default. And secondly, if expected profits are very much over-estimated the earnings per share may in fact decrease. It is very desirable, therefore, to measure the risk involved, and to compare the attractiveness of debentures as an alternative to shares in the light of such measurement. One way of doing this is as shown in the table below:

Hopeful Limited

		Proposed Position	
	Existing Position	*Debenture*	*Ordinary Shares*
	$	$	$
Net earnings of ordinary shares	32,400	35,400	39,600
Less Sinking Fund requirements annually	6,500	9,500	6,500
Net earnings on ordinary shares .... available for distribution (Distributable Earnings)	25,900	25,900	33,100
Number of ordinary shares	300,000	300,000	375,000
Distributable earnings per share	$0.08633	$0.08633	$0.08826

The annual sinking fund requirements are funds generated from profits which must be set aside for the repayment of the debentures on maturity. After the sinking fund requirements are deducted from net earnings of ordinary shares we arrive at net distributable earnings, from which the distributable earnings per share are obtained. This is the amount available to the ordinary shareholders after the contractual commitments are met. From the table above, one can read that an issue of ordinary shares is in this instance more attractive when one accepts safety as a criterion, since the issue of shares leaves a wider margin of surplus after debt obligations are met. The position can also be depicted on a chart as follows:

Range-of-Earnings Chart showing the attractiveness of Debenture V. Equity as depicted by DEPS.

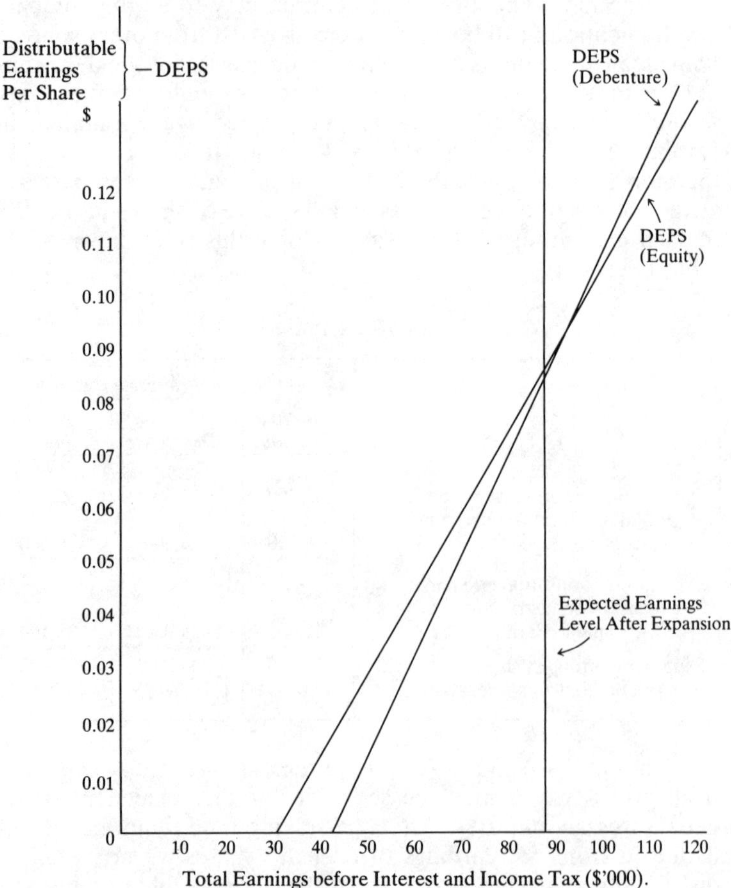

The break-even point, B is:

$$\frac{(B - 21{,}000)(1 - .40) - 6{,}500}{375} = \frac{(B - 28{,}000)(1 - .40) - 9{,}500}{300}$$

$$B = \$91{,}833$$

From the chart it can be seen that from the viewpoint of safety the issue of shares is more attractive than the issue of debenture within the range of earnings anticipated. However, if total earnings before income tax and interest were to exceed, say, $92,000, the issue of debenture becomes more attractive from the viewpoint of safety.

There are ratios which are often used to measure a firm's ability to meet its debt commitments. It is important to repeat here that the considerations of paramount importance in deciding the appropriate capital gearing of an individual company must be determined on the special circumstances of the case, and may include the questions of control, income and risk.

In using the EPS/EBIT chart as a tool of financial analysis, one must bear in mind the assumptions implicit in the model. One of the assumptions often overlooked is that the new equity is issued at the true market value. Should the proposed issue of ordinary shares be made at a price much below the market value, such as a rights issue, an adjustment to the denominator (the number of shares) should be effected. The following example illustrates this point. E. Ltd. requires $2 million additional funds for plant expansion. Specific proposals are: (a) Make a rights issue of ordinary shares at $50 per share, or (b) Issue 8% Debentures at par. The shares of E. Ltd. are presently quoted at $400 per share. The expected earnings per year on completion of the expansion programme are $1 million before charging interest and tax. The income tax rate is 40%. The company's existing capital structure comprises 100,000 ordinary shares and $1 million 5% Debentures. The profit and loss statement below may be prepared:

Although 40,000 additional ordinary shares are issued (40,000 × 50 = $2 million), these are equivalent to 5,000 of the

	Ordinary Share	*Debenture*
	$	$
Earnings before interest & income tax	1,000.000	1,000,000
Less interest on debentures	50,000	210,000
	950,000	790,000
Less income tax (40%)	380,000	316,000
Earnings of ordinary shares	570,000	474,000
Number of ordinary share equivalents	105,000	100,000
Earnings per share (EPS)	$5.43	$4.74

existing shares ($\frac{50}{400} \times 40{,}000 = 5{,}000$). This adjustment is necessary so that the EPS under the ordinary shares is comparable to that under the debenture alternative. If no adjustment was made, the EPS under the ordinary shares alternative would be \$4.07 (570,000/140,000). This figure of \$4.07 does not form a valid basis for comparing with \$4.74 since the latter is the earnings of shares worth \$400 each while the former is the earnings of shares worth only \$300 ((400 × 100,000 + 50 × 40,000)/140,000) the theoretical after-rights-issue price.

10.15. A MATHEMATICAL PROGRAMMING APPROACH

The relationship between capital contributions and long-term loans, often referred to as capital gearing or leverage, has been a subject of discussion in many articles. The issue is an important one since the ratio of indebtedness to equity, or leverage, may affect the overall cost of capital against which decisions on new investments may be measured.

It is often argued that as the ratio of debt to ordinary share capital increases, the risk of failure to meet debt obligations increases. As a consequence, the market value of the debt falls, and the cost of debt increases; the risk of return to ordinary shareholders also increases resulting in an increase in the expected rate of return of equity capital. Some contend that an increase in the debt-equity ratio increases the value of the firm so long as the firm does not increase its leverage to an extreme point, while others maintain that in a perfect market the debt-equity ratio has no effect on the firm value.

The issue is an important one because if an optimal capital structure can be determined management ought to strive for the optimum in its financial decision-making. It has been well established, however, following the Modigliani-Miller article that for the perfect market case the weighted average cost of capital of a company is unaffected by its capital structure, and that the cost of equity is a linear function of leverage. This independence hypothesis has been demonstrated by the capital asset pricing model which does not rely on the existence of equivalent risk classes of firms. Thus where the capital market is perfect and efficient leverage cannot be used as a tool for increasing the value of the firm. Nevertheless, it does matter in practice whether a firm raises its additional finance from equity or debt since the implicit cost of finance such as bankruptcy costs, and tax advantages of debt are relevant factors for consideration.

This section illustrates the technique that is very often used in practice in financial decision-making where a choice has to be made between the issue of long-term debt and equity, and explains why this technique has serious drawbacks. It then suggests alternative approaches to the problem of arriving at a satisfactory mix of finance.

The practical model often used in decision-making involving the financial leverage of the firm evaluates the effect of a particular source of finance on the earnings per equity share. Though the model has greater utilitarian value than many theoretical concepts, it suffers the defect of ignoring the implicit costs of debt finance.

The model also implies that the different incremental sources of finance are mutually exclusive and that the firm operates without financial constraints. These drawbacks can be overcome by a linear programming approach where the objectives and constraints can be formulated and modified.

Suppose a proposed investment project requiring an outlay of $500,000 will yield a rate of return before tax of 20%. The existing position before the proposed project is shown in Exhibits 10.15.1. and 10.15.2.

Exhibit 10.15.1.
Mix of Finance at Market Prices

Ordinary share capital ($1 shares)	$500,000
7% Preference shares ($1 shares)	300,000
8% Debentures	200,000
	$1,000,000

Exhibit 10.15.2.

Earnings before interest and tax	$140,000
Less Interest on Debentures	16,000
Net profit before tax	$124,000
Less Income Tax (40%)	49,600
Net profit after tax	$ 74,400
Less Preference dividend	21,000
Net profit of ordinary shareholders	53,400
Earnings per share $= \frac{53,400}{500,000} =$	$0.1068

In the example the proposed investment project will yield an after-tax return of 12% while the after-tax returns of the existing sources of finance are:

$$\text{Ordinary shares} \quad \ldots \quad \frac{53{,}400}{500{,}000} = 10.68\%$$

$$\text{Preference shares} \quad \ldots \quad \frac{21{,}000}{300{,}000} = 7\%$$

$$\text{Debentures} \quad \ldots \quad \frac{(.6)(16{,}000)}{200{,}000} = 4.8\%$$

The incremental rates of return of the different sources of finance are therefore:

Ordinary shares	. . .	(0.12 − 0.1068) = 0.0132
Preference shares	. . .	(0.12 − 0.07) = 0.05
Debentures	. . .	(0.12 − 0.048) = 0.072

The following linear programming problem, where X_1 represents the amount of ordinary shares, X_2 the preference shares and X_3 the debentures, can be formulated:

Maximise $\quad 0.0132X_1 + 0.05X_2 + 0.072X_3$

Subject to

(1) $$X_1 + X_2 + X_3 = 1{,}500{,}000$$

(2) $$\frac{.6(240{,}000 - 0.08X_3) - 0.07X_2}{X_1} \geqq 0.1068$$

(3) $$\frac{144{,}000}{X_1 + X_2 + X_3} \geqq 0.084$$

(4) $$\frac{X_3}{X_1 + X_2 + X_3} \leq 0.2$$

(5) $$\frac{X_2 + X_3}{X_1 + X_2 + X_3} \leq 0.6$$

(6) $X_1 \geqq 500{,}000$

(7) $X_2 \geqq 300{,}000$

(8) $X_3 \geqq 200{,}000$

(9) $X_1,\ X_2\ X_3 \geqq 0$

In the above linear programming problem, the objective is to maximise the sum of the incremental returns of the different methods of finance. The first constraint indicates that the total finance of the firm must equal \$1.5 million. The second constraint is to ensure that the existing earnings per share of \$0.1068 will not decrease and the third constraint makes sure that the present weighted average return of 8.4% of the firm will at least be maintained. The financial risk of debt finance is incorporated in the fourth and fifth constraints, the fourth indicating that debentures will not exceed 20% of the total finance and the fifth that the sum of debentures and preference shares will comprise not more than 60% of the total finance. Here financial risks are assumed to be a function of capital gearing (leverage), other things being equal. Legal or other restrictions that do not permit any reduction of the existing sources of finance are indicated by the 6th, 7th and 8th constraints. The optimal solutions of the programme are

$$X_1^* = \$1{,}000{,}000,\ X_2^* = \$300{,}000 \text{ and } X_3^* = \$200{,}000.$$

The above linear programming model, as well as the other single-objective mathematical programming models, cannot cope with the increasing complexities of modern organizations with conflicting multiple goals.

In the LP model all the constraints in the program must be absolutely satisfied before a solution is feasible. In other words, all constraints cannot be violated. Very often however, these constraints are viewed as desirable goals in the same way as the objective function. Of course, some may be absolute goals while others may have lower priority. Here, management policies may be one of satisficing rather than maximizing. If this is the case, multiple goal programming will be a useful model.

Exhibit 10.15.3.
Existing Mix of Finance at Market Prices

Ordinary share capital ($1 shares)	$600,000
10% Debentures	400,000
	$1,000,000
Earnings before interest and tax	$ 150,000
Less Interest on debentures	40,000
Net profit before tax	110,000
Income tax	44,000
Net profit after tax	$ 66,000
Earnings per share	$ 66,000 / 600,000 = $0.11

Exhibit 10.15.3. shows the existing capital structure as well as the earnings per equity share of a company. Suppose a proposed project requires an additional $1 million of finance, giving a marginal rate of return of 15% per annum before tax. The problem of finding a satisfactory mix of finance may be solved by the following multiple-goal program: Find (X_1, X_2) so as to minimize

$$Z = [(Y_{-1} + Y_{+1}), (Y_{+2}), (Y_{-3}), (Y_{-4} + Y_{+5})]$$

Goal (1) $X_1 + X_2 + Y_{-1} - Y_{+1} = 2{,}000{,}000$

Goal (2) $0.11X_1 + 0.06X_2 - Y_{-2} + Y_{+2} = 180{,}000$

Goal (3) $X_1 + Y_{-3} - Y_{+3} = 600{,}000$

Goal (4) $X_2 + Y_{-4} - Y_{+4} = 1{,}000{,}000$

Goal (5) $X_2 + Y_{-5} - Y_{+5} = 1{,}400{,}000$

(6) $X_1, X_2 \geqq 0$

(7) $Y_{-i} \geqq 0, i = 1, 2 \ldots, 5$

$Y_{+i} \geqq 0, i = 1, 2 \ldots, 5$

The above multiple-goal program shows that the first goal is an absolute objective and must be satisfied and hence is on priority level 1. Here, the sum of the two sources of finance, X_1 and X_2, that is, equity and debentures, must be equal to \$2 million.

One of the models, very often used in share valuation is:

$$P_0 = \sum_{t=0}^{\infty} D_t(1 + k_e)^{-t}$$

where P_0 is the price of the company's share,
D_t is the dividend at the end of the year, and
k_e is the cost of equity.

Apparently, P_0 increases as k_e decreases, other things being equal. This being the case, the company's management may choose the second goal which is at priority level two as one of achieving the objective of making $k_e \leq 0.11$. The third goal which is at priority three is to have an equity capital of not less than \$600,000. The fourth and fifth goals are of equal importance and have priority four. This is to attain a leverage ratio of between 0.5 and 0.7.

The optimal solutions of this goal programming problem are:

$$X_1^* = \$1.2 \text{ million}$$
$$X_2^* = \$800{,}000$$
$$Z^* = [0, 0, 0, 200{,}000]$$

Z^* shows that the fourth and fifth goals are not fully obtained.

Sensitivity analysis is possible with multiple goal programming. For instance, if the priority of the second goal is changed into an absolute objective at priority level one, the optimal solutions remain optimal.

Other parameters in the program may be changed and their effects, if any, on the optimal solutions evaluated. The most outstanding advantage of the multiple goal programming approach is that not all goals need be of equal importance or absolutely achieved. If a certain goal has priority over another, it is placed on a higher priority level.

Solving the finance mix problem of goal programming entails that standards or goals for acceptable financial risks and rates of return are known to management. These may be subjective but they do not render the goal programming approach less pragmatic. The interdependence of the investment and financing decisions is an area requiring much effort from research workers. It is suggested that mathematical programming provides the most promising approach.

10.16. EARNINGS PER SHARE

In recent years earnings per share have been widely used as a tool of analysis, very often in conjunction with price earnings ratio. Its usefulness as an indication of earning capacity should be considered in the light of its inherent limitation and the price earnings ratio should not be the sole criterion for evaluating share prices. We shall explain some calculations which are necessary for arriving at earnings per share under different definitions. The following profit and loss accounts and balance sheets will be used for illustrations:

Exhibit 10.16.

Profit and Loss Statement for the Year Ended 31st December

		19x1 ($'000)		19x2 ($'000)
Sales		200		250
Less Cost of Sales		120		150
Gross Profit		80		100
Less Operating Expense		48		65
Net Operating Profit before tax		32		35
Less Income tax thereon		13		14
Net Operating Profit after tax		19		21
Add Non-Operating Income	$ 20		$ 25	
Less Income tax thereon	8		10	
		12		15
Net Profit after tax		$31		$36

Balance Sheet as at 31st December

	19x1 ($'000)	19x2 ($'000)
Shareholders' funds		
Paid-up capital ($1 fully paid shares)	50	50
Profit and loss balance	40	76
	$ 90	$ 126
Long-term liabilities		
10% Debentures	20	20
Current Liabilities	80	113
	$ 190	$ 259
Sundry assets	$ 190	$ 259

In this simple example, two EPS (earnings per share) figures may be obtained:

	19x1	19x2
Basic EPS before extraordinary items:	$\frac{19}{50}$ = $0.38	$\frac{21}{50}$ = 0.42

EPS for the two years show clearly that there is an increase in earnings in 19x2. However, this does not tantamount to an increase in profitability or in the rate of return on shareholders funds. The amount of shareholders' funds has increased from $90,000 in 19x1 to $126,000 in 19x2 as a result of ploughing back all the net profit in 19x2. On the average the amount of shareholders' funds utilized in the year is approximately $((90,000 + 126,000) ÷ 2) = $108,000. The returns on shareholders' funds (RSF) are:

	19x1	19x2
RSF before extraordinary items:	$\frac{19}{90}$ = $0.211	$\frac{21}{108}$ = $0.194
RSF after extraordinary items:	$\frac{31}{90}$ = $0.344	$\frac{36}{108}$ = $0.333

The above RSF indicate clearly that a dollar of shareholders' funds is less profitable in 19x2 compared with 19x1. Hence, whilst EPS is useful as an aid to potential investors in deciding whether to buy shares of a company, it is less useful to existing shareholders as an indication of the profitability of their funds already invested in the company. Anyway, share prices should be evaluated with more than one criterion. Growth factors, dividends, management of the company, economic trends and others are factors that cannot be ignored.

10.16.1. Bonus Issue

If we assume that there has been a bonus share issue of one for two at the beginning of 19x2, the Shareholders' Funds of the company now appear as:

	19x1 ($'000)	19x2 ($'000)
Shareholders' funds		
Paid-up capital ($1 fully paid shares)	50	75
Profit and loss balance	40	51
	$90	$126

Assuming that all the other things are exactly as before, we can calculate the EPS:

	19x1	19x2
EPS before extraordinary items:	$\frac{19}{50}$ = $0.38	$\frac{21}{75}$ = $0.28
EPS after extraordinary items:	$\frac{31}{50}$ = $0.62	$\frac{36}{75}$ = $0.48

Thus while the RSF remain the same as before and are not affected by the bonus issue, EPS become distorted by the bonus issue. To have meaningful EPS entails an adjustment for the bonus issue so that the denominators for the two years are comparable.

Similarly, the denominators must be adjusted to make them comparable should there be a rights issue at a price that is very much below the market price.

10.16.2. Convertibles

The calculations for EPS may have to take into account convertibles and options to purchase ordinary shares. Suppose the 10% Debentures shown in our balance sheet are convertible into ordinary shares within the next ten years. The profit and loss accounts, after adjusting for the interest on debentures which are no more payable, now appear as follows:

Profit and Loss Statement
for the Year Ended 31st December

		19x1 ($'000)		19x2 ($'000)
Net Operating Profit before tax		34		37
Less Income tax (say)		14		15
Net Operating Profit after tax		20		22
Add Non-Operating income	$20		$25	
Less Income tax	8		10	
		12		15
Net Profit after tax		$32		$37

The number of ordinary share equivalents is:

19x1	19x2
70	70

And the fully diluted earnings per share are:

Fully diluted EPS before extraordinary items: $\frac{20}{70} \simeq \$0.286$ (19x1); $\frac{22}{70} \simeq \$0.314$ (19x2)

Fully diluted EPS after extraordinary items: $\frac{32}{70} \simeq \$0.457$ (19x1); $\frac{37}{70} \simeq \$0.529$ (19x2)

10.16.3. Options to Purchase Shares

If there is an option to purchase 30,000 ordinary shares of the company at a price of $2 per share, then if we take this into account in calculating EPS, the number of shares will increase from 50,000 to 80,000 (See Exhibit 10.16.) and the company's cash position will improve by $60,000. This $60,000 will be assumed to earn an extra revenue. If the after-tax rate of return on this $60,000 is 5%, the Profit and Loss Statement now becomes:

		19x1 ($'000)		19x2 ($'000)
Net Operating Profit after tax		22		24
Add Non-Operating income	$20		$25	
Less Income Tax	8		10	
		12		15
		$34		$39

And the fully diluted earnings per share are:

	19x1	19x2
Fully diluted EPS before extraordinary items:	$\frac{22}{80}$ = \$0.275	$\frac{24}{80}$ = \$0.30
Fully diluted EPS after extraordinary items:	$\frac{34}{80}$ = \$0.425	$\frac{39}{80}$ = \$0.488

It should be noted that the various major professional bodies have issued their own recommendations regarding the use and methods of computing EPS, and they all have their variations: the conditions under which fully diluted EPS should be calculated, the methods of calculating ordinary share equivalents, and the imputed rates of return on the additional cash resources resulting from a consideration of outstanding options to purchase ordinary shares.

The methods illustrated above are simple and easy to apply and comply with the basic requirements of the major professional bodies in legal environments similar to ours.

In the United States, the "Treasury Stock Method" may be used to calculate ordinary share equivalents where there are options to purchase ordinary shares. Using Exhibit 10.16., and assuming there is an outstanding option to purchase 30,000 ordinary shares at $2 per share when the average market price is $10, the Treasury Stock Method is applied as follows:

Existing number of ordinary shares	50,000
Additional ordinary shares if option is exercised	30,000
Total number of ordinary shares	80,000
Number of ordinary shares that can be purchased back with the additional cash (60,000 ÷ 10)	6,000
Number of Ordinary share equivalents	74,000

	19x2
Fully diluted EPS before extraordinary items:	$\frac{21}{74}$
	≏ $0.284
Fully diluted EPS after extraordinary items:	$\frac{36}{74}$
	≏ $0.486

The Treasury Stock Method may not be suitable in our legal environment since under Section 67 of the Companies Act a company cannot purchase its own shares.

10.16.4. Illustration

The following profit and loss statement and balance sheet are extracted from Urningspershare Limited:

Profit and Loss
Statement for the year ended 31st December 19X7

		($'000)
Trading profit before tax		2,000
Less Income tax payable		800
Net Operating profit after tax		1,200
Add Non-operating income	$500,000	
Less Income tax	200,000	300
Net profit available for appropriation		$1,500

Balance Sheet as at 31st December 19X7

	($'000)		($'000)
Authorised Capital			
5,000,000 shares of $1 each		**Fixed Assets**	$2,100
Issued and Paid-Up Capital		**Current Assets**	4,900
1,000,000 shares of $1 each fully paid	$1,000		
Capital reserve	2,000		
Revenue reserve	2,000		
6% Convertible Debentures	1,000		
Current Liabilities	1,000		
	$7,000		$7,000

The following additional information is obtained:

(i) The ordinary share capital issued and outstanding as at 1st January, 19X7 is made up of 500,000 shares of $1 each fully paid.

(ii) On 31st March, 19X7 500,000 ordinary shares of $1 each fully paid were issued at $2 per share.

(iii) For the year ended 31st December 19X7 6% convertible debentures (convertible at par) at the nominal value of $1,000,000 were outstanding and due for redemption in three years. The bank prime rate was 10% when the debentures were issued.

(iv) There is an option to purchase 300,000 shares of Urningspershare Limited at a price of $2 per share. It is considered that the funds made available by the exercise of option can earn an after-tax rate of return of 5%.

The calculations of basic earnings per share and fully diluted earnings per share are shown below:

	Ordinary share equivalents
Ordinary shares as at 1st January	500,000
Ordinary shares issued on 31st March: (9/12)(500,000)	375,000
Basic ordinary share equivalents =	875,000
6% Convertible debentures	1,000,000
Option to purchase 300,000 ordinary shares	300,000
Fully diluted ordinary share equivalents	2,175,000

Basic EPS before extraordinary items

$$= \frac{\$1{,}200{,}000}{875{,}000} = \$1.37$$

Basic EPS after extraordinary items

$$= \frac{\$1{,}500{,}000}{875{,}000} = \$1.71$$

Fully diluted EPS before extraordinary items

$$= \$\,\frac{1{,}200{,}000 + (.6)(.06)(1{,}000{,}000) + (.05)(600{,}000)}{2{,}175{,}000}$$

$$= \$\,\frac{1{,}266{,}000}{2{,}175{,}000} = \$0.58$$

Fully diluted EPS after extraordinary items

$$= \$\,\frac{1{,}266{,}000 + 300{,}000}{2{,}175{,}000} = \$0.72$$

10.17. FINANCING IN KIND

There are at least two main ways by which fixed assets can be used for business operations without owning them: (1) hiring, and (2) leasing. We distinguish these two methods by the length of duration in, and the degree of formality in the arrangement for, their use. Usually things are hired for use for short periods of time and properties are leased for many years. In hiring there is normally a simple contract in the form of a standard document which the hirer must sign. In leasing the legal contract is usually under seal.

Things which are suitable for hire must possess two characteristics. They must be durable and capable of being used efficiently by different people in different locations. They are usually standard goods, like vehicles, certain types of machines, and air-conditioners. Management may be faced at times with the alternatives of buying or hiring a fixed asset. Some of the factors that must be considered in making the choice may include the following:

(1) If the need is a permanent one, it is perhaps more secure to own it. And if it is temporary, one must ascertain whether it is cheaper to hire, or to buy and sell it a short time later.
(2) The tax advantages of hiring must be compared with those of owning in arriving at comparative cost figures.
(3) The terms of the hire agreement must be scrutinized to see if repairs and maintenance are to be the responsibility of the hirer or the hiring company. Such costs must be imputed to arrive at a valid comparison.
(4) If the fixed asset were purchased, the cost and availability of funds must be taken into account.
(5) Sometimes purchase of a fixed asset is delayed if a fall in its price is anticipated or if a more efficient and cheaper model is expected to come into the market. In the meantime one is hired for temporary use.

10.18. MORE ILLUSTRATIONS

Example 1

The board of directors of Long Limited has decided to invest in a long-term project requiring an outlay of $4 million which is expected to increase trading profit before tax and interest by a constant amount of $600,000 per year for three years over and above the company's present normal operations.

The chief financial officer was asked to supply information regarding the alternative sources of finance available to the company. The following information supplied is considered reliable:

(*a*) The major supplier of raw materials to the company offers cash discount on terms of 2/10, net 60.
(*b*) Long Limited can factor its trade debtors. The charges are 3% of the total gross amount of trade debtors plus an interest charge of 10% per annum. Customers usually take about 90 days to settle their debts.
(*c*) Bank overdraft facilities may be obtained by mortgaging the company's land and buildings. Interest is charged at 12.5% per annum.
(*d*) 9% naked debentures may be issued at par.

(*e*) A rights issue of ordinary shares may be offered at a premium of $1 per share. The current quoted market price on 1.1.19x3 per share is $10.

The board has approached you for advice. On further inquiry, you have obtained the following financial statements which, you have been assured by the company's auditor, are reliable and reasonably accurate:

Long Limited

Profit and Loss Statement for the year ended 31st December

	19x1 ($'000)	19x2 ($'000)	19x3 ($'000)
Trading profit before tax and interest	2,000	2,200	2,420

Balance Sheet as at 31st December, 19X2

	($'000)
Fixed assets (net)	19,000
Current assets	4,000
	23,000
Issued and paid-up capital ($1 fully paid shares)	20,000
Retained earnings	1,000
Current liabilities	2,000
	$23,000

The profit trend is expected to continue in the next few years. The proposed project has an expected economic life of 3 years. The authorised capital of the company is $50 million and the income tax rate is 40%.

The bank overdraft is legally repayable on demand while the debentures are redeemable at par three years from the date of issue. The debentures also carry a contractual obligation of creating a sinking fund to be accumulated in an investment giving an interest of 11% per annum.

REQUIRED:
Advise the board of Long Limited. Support your advice with statements, calculations and reasons.

(*a*) The effective cost is:

$$\frac{2}{98} \times \frac{365}{50} \cong 0.149$$

(*b*) The effective cost is:

$$\left(\frac{3}{100} \times \frac{365}{90}\right) + \left(\frac{10}{97}\right) \cong 0.225$$

(*c*) The effective cost is 0.125
(*d*) The effective cost is 0.09

$$R = \frac{(.11)(4{,}000{,}000)}{(1.11)^3 - 1} = \frac{440{,}000}{0.367631} = 1{,}196{,}850$$

(using equation 11 of Appendix A)

Equivalent number of New Shares Issued
$= (\frac{2}{10})(2{,}000{,}000) = 400{,}000$

EPS break-even point: $$\frac{(B)(1 - T)}{20{,}400} = \frac{(B - 360)(1 - T)}{20{,}000}$$

$20{,}000\ (.6B) = 20{,}400\ (.6B - 216)$
EBIT at break-even $= B^* = \$18.360$ million
EPS at break-even $= \$.54$

DEPS break even point:

$$\frac{(B)(1 - T)}{20{,}400} = \frac{(B - 360)(1 - T) - 1{,}196.85}{20{,}000}$$

EBIT* = \$120,092.25 million
DEPS* = \$3.532125

Long Limited
Profit and Loss Statement for the year ended 31st December

	19x3		*19x4*		*19x5*	
	Shares ($'000)	*Debentures* ($'000)	*Shares* ($'000)	*Debentures* ($'000)	*Shares* ($'000)	*Debentures* ($'000)
EBIT without project	2,420,00	2,420,00	2,662.00	2,662.00	2,928.20	2,928.20
EBIT of project	600.00	600.00	600.00	600.00	600.00	600.00
Total EBIT	3,020.00	3,020.00	3,262.00	3,262.00	3,528.20	3,528.20
Less Interest	—	360.00	—	360.00	—	360.00
EBT	3,020.00	2,660.00	3,262.00	2,902.00	3,528.20	3168.20
Less Income tax	1,208.00	1,064.00	1,304.80	1,160.80	1,411.28	1267.28
Net profit after tax	1,812.00	1,596.00	1,957.20	1.741.20	2,116.92	1900.92
Less R	—	1,196.85	—	1,196.85	—	1196.85
Net distributable *profit*	1,812.00	399.15	1,957.20	544.35	2,116.92	704.07
No. of equity shares	20,400.00	20,000.00	20,400.00	20,000.00	20,400.00	20,000.00
EPS =	0.08824	0.0798	0.09594	0.08706	0.10377	.09505
DEPS =	0.08824	0.01996	0.09594	0.02722	0.10377	0.03520

Non-quantifiable factors must of course be taken into consideration. For example: Should long-term requirements be financed by short-term debts with risk implications? Will mortgage of the company's land and buildings reduce the company's operational flexibility? What are the likely future share prices and interest rates? These issues have been discussed and are not repeated here.

Example 2
Redeemp Ltd purchased on 1st July, 1981 $8\frac{1}{2}\%$ $100,000 Government Stock for $80,000 cum dividend and paid $3,500 transaction costs. Interest is payable on 1st January every year. The maturity date of the Government Stock is 30th June, 1988. Redeemp Ltd. intends to hold the stock to the date of maturity.

REQUIRED:
Calculate the effective interest rate to the date of maturity (the redemption yield).

Total cash paid	= 80,000 + 3,500	= $83,500
Less Accrued Interest		
	$= \frac{1}{2} \times 0.085 \times 100{,}000$	= 4,250
Net price paid for stock		= $79,250

Using equation 5 (modified for signs) of Appendix A results in:

$$P_n = \left(P_0 - \frac{R}{i}\right)(1 + i)^n + \frac{R}{i}$$

$$100{,}000 = \left(79{,}250 - \frac{8{,}500}{i}\right)(1 + i)^7 + \frac{8{,}500}{i}$$

$$i \simeq 0.13225$$

Effective Interest Rate $\simeq 13.2\%$

10.19. SELECTED BIBLIOGRAPHY

1. Krish Bhasker: A Multiple Objective Approach to Capital Budgeting, *Accounting and Business Research*, Winter 1979.

2. E. F. Brigham: Analysis of Convertible Debentures (Theory and Some Empirical Evidence), Journal of Finance, March 1966.
3. G. Donaldson: In Defence of Preferred Stock, Harvard Business Review, July/August 1962.
4. H. E. Dougall: Capital Markets and Institutions.
5. Han Kang Hong: Finance Mix and Capital Structure, *Journal of Business Finance and Accounting*, April 1981.
6. Han Kang Hong: Earnings Per Share *The Singapore Stock Exchange Journal*, January 1975.
7. J. C. Van Horne: Financial Management and Policy.
8. James P. Ignizio: Goal Programming and Extension.
9. Yuri Ijiri: Management Goals and Accounting for Control.
10. Sang, M. Lee: Goal Programming for Decision Analysis.
11. W. G. Lewellen: Convertible Debt-Financing, Journal of Financial and Quantitative Analysis, December 1973.
12. A. A. Robichek, D. Teichroew, and J. M. Jones: Optimal Short-term Financing Decision, Management Science, September 1965.
13. M. F. Rubinstein: A Mean-variance synthesis of Corporate Financial Theory, *The Journal of France*, March 1973.
14. U. K. Accounting Standards Steering Committee: SSAP 3.
15. J. F. Weston and E. F. Brigham: Managerial Finance.

CHAPTER 11

Lease Disclosure and Financing

11.1. SCOPE

In this chapter leases are confined to those which are either non-cancellable or the costs of repudiation are so high that cancellation is not economical. Two topics will be discussed. The first considers the disclosure of leases in the annual published accounts of the lessee and the second considers the financing of the fixed assets under consideration.

11.2. DISCLOSURE OF LEASES IN THE PUBLISHED ACCOUNTS OF THE LESSEE

Traditionally most companies disclose their lease commitments by way of footnote to the balance sheet. The question whether leases should be disclosed in the balance sheet itself may than be posed. The disclosure in the balance sheet is usually the capitalized value of all future lease commitments. There are, inter alia, two methods of calculating the capitalized value of a lease. The first is to capitalize the annual net cash outflows of the lease commitments with the lessor's cost of debt capital as illustrated below:

End of Year	*Annual Lease Payments Payable in Advance*	*Executory Expenses Borne by Lessor (including repairs and maintenance)*
	$	$
0	50,000	0
1	50,000	5,000
2	50,000	6,000
3	0	8,000

Lessor's cost of capital = 8% per annum
Puchase price of asset = $131,285
No scrap value
Capitalized Value of Lease

$$= \sum_{t=0}^{n-1} M_t(1 + r)^{-t} - \sum_{t=1}^{n} E_t(1 + r)^{-t} \quad (11.2.1.)$$

Where M_t = annual lease payment in year t payable in advance,
E_t = annual costs of repairs, maintenance, and other executory expenses borne by lessor,
r = lessor's cost of debt,
n = number of years of lease agreement.

Applying equation (11.2.1.) gives the following solution:

End of Year	*Years to Go*	*Capitalized Value of Lease shown in the Balance Sheet*
0	3	$123,039
1	2	$ 78,882
2	1	$ 36,593
3	0	0

The main difficulty with the first method is lack of knowledge of the lessor's cost of debt and the executory expenses. The second method involves discounting the annual lease payments with the internal rate of return to arrive at the purchase price of the equipment.

$$\text{Purchase Price} - S(1 + i)^{-n} = \sum_{t=0}^{n-1} M_t(1 + i)^{-t} \quad (11.2.2.)$$

where S is the scrap value.

With the illustration given i is found to be 15%. The solution is shown below:

End of Year	*Years to Go*	*Capitalized Value of Lease shown in the Balance Sheet*
0	3	131,285
1	2	93,478
2	1	50,000
3	0	0

Whether leases should be disclosed in the balance sheet of the lessee depends firstly on the definitions of assets and liabilities, and secondly, the disclosed and perceived effects of different methods of disclosure.

If an asset is defined as property legally owned by the company and a liability as a debt due from the company, then obviously a lease is not an asset and should not be disclosed in the balance sheet. It can be so disclosed, however, if an asset is considered to be a store of services which are released for use in revenue-earning activities over the years of its economic life and if a liability is defined as a contractual commitment to pay for such services.

More important considerations are the disclosed and perceived effects of disclosure. The reported total liabilities and total assets are both increased by the capitalized value of the lease, thereby increasing the debt/equity ratio and decreasing the profit/total assets ratio. Their impact on decision-making must be considered both by the company and by outside parties. This is so in spite of the fact that the financial burden or obligation of the company remains the same whether lease commitments are disclosed by way of footnote or as a capitalized value in the balance sheet.

11.2.1. Disklouse Ltd

The following statements are prepared from the records of Disklouse Limited:

Disklouse Ltd.
Profit and Loss Statement
for the year ended 31st December, 19X8

	($'000)
Sales	200
Less Cost of sales and operating expenses	120
Net profit for the year	$ 80

Balance Sheet as at 31st December, 19X8

	($'000)
Land at cost	200
Current assets	100
	$300
Share capital	100
Retained earnings	70
Long-term liabilities	50
Current liabilities	80
	$300

Disklouse Limited has decided to invest in a new machine in its expansion programme. The two alternative methods of finance available are:

(1) Buy the machine at a cash price of $50,000 with a loan at 10% interest per annum. The loan is repayable in 5 equal annual instalments starting at the end of the first year.
(2) Lease the machine on a 5-year financial lease for $13,000 per year payable in advance.

The machine is estimated to have an economic life of 5 years with no salvage value at the end of its life. If the machine is purchased, annual costs of repairs and maintenance are expected to be $1,000; such costs are borne by the lessor if the machine is leased.

Disklouse Limited's significant accounting policies which it does not intend to change include:

(1) Depreciation is calculated on the straight line method to write off the cost or valuation of fixed assets other than land over their estimated useful lives.
(2) Financial commitments, such as future lease payments, are shown by way of footnote to the balance sheet, and are not included among the liabilities in the balance sheet.

The installation of the machine is expected to increase annual sales revenue as well as cost of sales and operating expenses by 20%. This increase in cost and operating expenses does not include depreciation, repairs and maintenance and the interest on the loan raised if the machine is purchased, nor does it include the annual lease payment if the machine is leased.

Required:

(*a*) Prepare projected profit and loss statements for the year ended and balance sheets as at 31 December, 19x9 (one year after the proposed expansion) under the two alternative

Diskhouse Limited
Projected Profit and Loss Statement
for the year ended 31st December 19X9

	(*a*) *Buy*	(*a*) & (*b*) *Lease*
	$	$
Sales	240,000	240,000
Less Cost of sales	144,000	144,000
Lease payment		13,000
Depreciation	10,000	
Interest	5,000	
Repairs & Maintenance	1,000	
	160,000	157,000
Net Profit	$80,000	$83,000

Balance Sheet as at 31st December 1979

	(*a*) *Buy*	(*a*) *Lease*	(*b*) *Lease*
	$	$	$
Share capital	100,000	100,000	100,000
Retained earnings	150,000	153,000	153,000
Long-term debt	80,000	50,000	50,000
Current liabilities	90,000	80,000	80,000
Liability on lease (using equation 11.2.2.)	—	—	45,584
	$420,000	$383,000	$428,584
Fixed assets	240,000	200,000	200,000
Current assets	180,000	183,000	183,000
Capitalised lease	—	—	45 584
	$420,000	$383,000	$428,584
(c) Net profit/total assets	$\frac{80}{420} \simeq 0.19$	$\frac{83}{383} \simeq 0.22$	$\frac{83}{428} \simeq 0.19$
Debt/equity	$\frac{80}{250} \simeq 0.32$	$\frac{50}{253} \simeq 0.1976$	$\frac{50 + 32,584}{253} \simeq 0.33$

methods of financing to comply with the company's accounting policies. Ignore taxation.

(*b*) Prepare a projected profit and loss statement for the year ended and a balance sheet as at 31st December 19x9 using the internal rate of return method of capitalizing the annual lease payments. To simplify matters you may debit the annual lease payment to the profit and loss statement.

(*c*) Calculate relevant accounting ratios from the statements prepared in your answer to (*a*) and (*b*) to indicate difference in rates of return and leverage.

11.3. LEASE FINANCING

There are many approaches to the problem of lease financing; some of the approaches consider this as a choice between leasing and borrowing and others, as a choice between leasing and buying.

In the first approach, the capital expenditure decision is supposed to have already been made, that is, it is desirable to invest in the fixed asset. The problem then becomes a financing one: to buy the asset from borrowed funds or to lease it. Thus the actual comparison is between borrowing and leasing. Even here there is disagreement in the use of the discounting rate. Some advocate discounting the lease payments at the minimum borrowing rate and the tax savings on the payments at the cost of capital. Others use a single discounting rate for both. The former argue that since finance is limited in supply and the firm's capacity and cost of borrowing will be affected by a change in its capital structure, the discounting rate for tax savings should be the cost of capital. The latter contend that it is the net after-tax cash flows which are relevant for decision-making and since the lease payments as well as their tax savings are the result of the same decision they should be discounted at the same rate. Let us illustrate this with the following simple example:

Z Limited has decided to invest in a machine which has an economic life of 3 years with no scrap value. It can buy the machine for $91,200 or lease it for $35,000 per year payable in advance. The income tax rate is 40% and the straight-line depreciation basis is allowed with no initial allowance. The company's minimum borrowing rate is 10% and its cost of capital is 15%.

11.3.1. An Adaptation of the R. F. Vancil's Method (Similar to the Bower-Herringer-Williamson's Method)

Step 1
The present value of the total lease payments (using the firm's borrowing rate) = $\sum_{t=0}^{n-1} M_t(1 + c)^{-t}$,
where n = years of lease payments, M_t = lease payment in the tth year and c = the minimum cost of borrowing. This is equal to

$$35{,}000 + \frac{35{,}000}{(1.10)} + \frac{35{,}000}{(1.10)^2} = \$95{,}742$$

The financial disadvantage of leasing is \$95,742 − \$91,200 = \$4,542.

Step 2
The financial charge implicit in the lease w, is obtained thus:

$$\text{Purchase Price} = \sum_{t=0}^{n-1} M_t(1 + w)^{-t}$$

$$91{,}200 = 35{,}000 + (35{,}000)(1 + w)^{-1} + (35{,}000)(1 + w)^{-2}$$
$$\therefore \quad w = 16\%$$

The following table is prepared to show the interest and financing charges implicit in the lease:

Year	*Principal at beginning of Year*	*Lease Payment*	*Interest at 10%*	*Financial charge at 6%*	*Principal Repayment*
0	\$91,200	\$35,000	—	—	\$35,000
1	56,200	35,000	\$5,620	\$3,372	26,000
2	30,200	35,000	3,020	1,811	30,169

In step 2, the annual repayment of the loan raised to buy the asset is assumed to be the same as the annual lease payment in respect of both the amount and the timing of repayment. This is to render the alternatives of leasing and borrowing comparable in the sense that the financial burden is the same.

In the Bower-Herringer-Williamson's version, however, the amount of the annual loan repayment is arrived at by solving the following equation:

$$\text{Purchase price} = \sum_{t=0}^{n-1} x(1 + c)^{-t} \qquad (11.3.1.1.)$$

where x is the annual loan repayment.

Step 3
The present value of the tax savings from lease payments =

$$\sum_{t=1}^{n} TM_t(1 + k)^{-t},$$

where T = tax rate, and k = the cost of capital. This amounts to $.4[(35{,}000)(1.15)^{-1} + (35{,}000)(1.15)^{-2} + (35{,}000)(1.15)^{-3}] =$ \$31,962

Step 4
The present value of the tax savings provided by depreciation =

$$\sum_{t=1}^{n} TD_t(1 + k)^{-t}$$

where D_t = the deductible allowance for depreciation in the tth year. This is equal to

$$.4[(30{,}400)(1.15)^{-1} + (30{,}400)(1.15)^{-2} + (30{,}400)(1.15)^{-}3] = \$27{,}764$$

Step 5
The present value of the tax savings provided by interest =

$$\sum_{t=1}^{n-1} TI_t(1 + k)^{-t},$$

I_t = the deductible allowance for interest in the tth year. This is $.4[(5{,}620)(1.15)^{-1} + (3{,}020)(1.15)^{-2}] =$ \$2,868

Step 6
The present value of the tax savings provided by borrowing is therefore \$(27,764 + 2,868) = \$30,632

Step 7
The operating advantage of leasing is \$31,962 − \$30,632 = \$1,330

Step 8

Financial disadvantage of leasing	=	\$4,542
Operating advantage of leasing	=	1,330
Net disadvantage of leasing	=	\$3,212

Hence from the viewpoint of quantifiable economic factors, it is better to buy the machine.

The Vancil's method compares leasing with borrowing and while the lease payments are discounted with the minimum before-tax borrowing rate, both the tax advantages of leasing and those of borrowing are discounted with the after-tax cost of capital. Thus two rates of discount are used. The main criticism of the Vancil's (BHW) method is that the evaluation of the tax advantages (the operating advantages) by using the cost of capital tantamounts to the application of an investment criterion rather than a financing one.

The Vancil's method assumes 100% debt financing with the purchase alternative. This implies an overstatement of tax advantages from the deductible interest expense if the purchase is more properly financed with less than 100% debt.

11.3.2. Internal Rate of Return Method

In this method the after-tax cost of leasing is assumed to be the internal rate of return i which is determined by solving the following equation:

$$\begin{aligned} A + (1 - T)\sum_{t=1}^{n} R_t(1 + i)^{-t} - T\sum_{t=1}^{n} D_t(1 + i)^{-t} \\ - TI - [S - T_g(S - B)](1 + i)^{-n} \\ = \sum_{t=0}^{n-1} M_t(1 + i)^{-t} - T\sum_{t=1}^{n} M_{t-1}(1 + i)^{-t} \end{aligned} \qquad (11.3.2.1.)$$

where A is the purchase price of the asset,

R_t is the annual repairs and maintenance and other expenses in year t incurred if the asset is purchased,

D_t is the annual depreciation in year t,

T is the tax rate

I is the initial allowance for income tax,

S is the scrap value of the asset,

B is the written-down book value of the asset when scrapped

T_g is the tax rate on balancing charge or allowance, and

M_t is the annual lease payment in year t payable in advance.

The decision rule is:
Buy the asset if $i > r$

where r is the minimum after-tax cost of borrowing.

The decision rule indicates clearly that the comparison is between the cost of leasing and the cost of borrowing. The left side of equation (11.3.2.1.) gives the net present value of the net cash outflows associated with buying the asset and the right side gives the net present value of the net cash outflows associated with leasing the asset. Using the data in Section (11.3) gives:

$$
\begin{aligned}
&91{,}200-(0.4)[30{,}400(1+i)^{-1}+30{,}400(1+i)^{-2}+30{,}400(1+i)^{-3}] \\
&=[35{,}000+35{,}000(1+i)^{-1}+(35{,}000)(1+i)^{-2}] \\
&\quad-(0.4)[35{,}000(1+i)^{-1}+35{,}000(1+i)^{-2}+35{,}000(1+i)^{-3}]
\end{aligned}
$$

Trial and error calculations give i as approximately 0.10. Since this is greater than the minimum after-tax cost of borrowing of 0.06, the decision is to buy the machine.

The main advantage of the internal rate of return method is that there is no necessity of deciding on the rate of interest to be used for discounting and thus the problem is considered to be a financing one alone when the cost of leasing i is compared with the minimum borrowing rate, r.

Using the internal rate of return method fails to consider the risk element in the cash streams of the alternative proposals and suffers the same problems as the internal rate of return method in capital budgeting.

11.3.3. Present Value Method

The present value method is also a method which compares leasing with borrowing. The best way of explaining this method is through an illustration.

Lis Ltd. has decided to invest in a machine which has an economic life of eight years and a scrap value of $10,000. It could buy the machine for $100,000 or lease it for $20,000 per year, payable in advance. The income tax rate is 40%. The annual repairs cost is estimated at $5,000. This will be borne by the lessor if the machine is leased.

The company's before-tax minimum borrowing rate is 10% and its investment opportunity rate is 15%.

Step 1
The present value of the net cash outflows if the asset is leased is:

$$PVO(L) = \sum_{t=0}^{n-1} M_t(1 + r)^{-t} - T \sum_{t=0}^{n-1} M_t(1 + r)^{-(t+1)} \quad (11.3.3.1.)$$

where M_t is the annual lease payment in year t payable in advance, r is the after-tax minimum borrowing rate, and T is the tax rate.

$$\begin{aligned} PVO(L) &= [20{,}000(1.06)^{-0} + 20{,}000(1.06)^{-1} + (20{,}000)(1.06)^{-2} \\ &\quad + \cdots + (20{,}000)(1.06)^{-7}] \\ &\quad -(0.4)[20{,}000(1.06)^{-1} + \cdots + 20{,}000(1.06)^{-8}] \\ &= \$81{,}968 \end{aligned}$$

Step 2
The annual constant amount of loan repayment, x, is obtained thus:

$$\text{Purchase price} = \sum_{t=0}^{n-1} x(1 + c)^{-t} \quad (11.3.3.2.)$$

where c is the before-tax minimum borrowing rate

$$100{,}000 = x + x \sum_{t=1}^{7} (1.10)^{-t}$$

$$100{,}000 = x + 4.868x$$

Therefore $\quad x = \$17{,}042$

Year	Principal	Loan Repayment	Interest at 10%	Principal Repayment
	$	$	$	$
0	100,000	17,042	0	17,042
1	82,958	17,042	8,296	8,746
2	74,212	17,042	7,421	9,621
3	64,591	17,042	6,459	10,583
4	54,008	17,042	5,401	11,641
5	42,367	17,042	4,237	12,805
6	29,562	17,042	2,956	14,086
7	15,476	17,042	1,548	15,494

Step 3

The present value of the net cash outflows if the machine is purchased is:

$$PVO(P) = \sum_{t=0}^{n-1} x_t(1 + r)^{-t} + (1 - T) \sum_{t=1}^{n} R_t(1 + r)^{-t} - T \sum_{t=1}^{n-1} N_t(1 + r)^{-t} - T \sum_{t=1}^{n} D_t(1 + r)^{-t} - TI - [S - T_g(S - B)](1 + r)^{-n} \qquad (11.3.3.3.)$$

where x_t is the annual constant loan repayment including interest in year t

R_t is the annual repairs, maintenance and other costs incurred in year t if the machine is purchased,

D_t is the depreciation allowance deductible in year t,

I is the deductible initial allowance,

T is the tax rate,
T_g is the tax rate on balancing charge or allowance,
N_t is the interest deductible in year t,
S is the scrap or salvage value, and
B is the book or written down value when scrapped.

$$\begin{aligned} PVO(P) &= [17{,}042 + 17{,}042(1.06)^{-1} + \cdots + 17{,}042(1.06)^{-7}] \\ &\quad + (.6)[5{,}000(1.06)^{-1} + \cdots + 5{,}000(1.06)^{-8}] \\ &\quad - .4[8{,}296(1.06)^{-1} + 7{,}421(1.06)^{-2} + 6{,}459(1.06)^{-3} \\ &\quad + 5{,}401(1.06)^{-4} + 4{,}237(1.06)^{-5} + 2{,}956(1.06)^{-6} \\ &\quad + 1{,}548(1.06)^{-7}] \\ &\quad - (.4)[33{,}333(1.06)^{-1} + 33{,}333(1.06)^{-2} \\ &\qquad + 33{,}333(1.06)^{-3}] \\ &\quad - 0 \\ &\quad - [10{,}000 - .4(10{,}000 - 0)](1.06)^{-8} \\ &= \$(112{,}170 + 18{,}630 - 30{,}216 - 35{,}640 - 3{,}762) \\ &= \$61{,}182 \end{aligned}$$

Step 4
Buy if $PVO(L) > PVO(P)$

Since $PVO(L)(= \$81{,}968)$ is greater than $PVO(P)$ $(= \$61{,}182)$, the decision is to purchase the machine.

The present value method assumes 100% debt financing and tends to favour the purchase alternative if less than 100% debt financing is more appropriate in the given situation. Using one single rate of discount for both the lease and purchase cash streams is also criticised for ignoring their different risks in their different probability distributions.

11.3.4. Johnson and Lewellen's Method

Under this method the proposition is that the comparison should be between leasing and purchasing. It is considered that the investment decision is not a separate decision that must be evaluated first since an unattractive investment proposal may be made attractive by advantageous lease terms. The approach compares the present value of the net cash inflows from a project based on a purchase proposal with that based on a lease proposal.

The present value of the net cash inflows from the proposed project based on a purchase proposal is:

$$NPV(P) = \sum_{t=1}^{n} [(y_t - C_t - R_t) - T(y_t - C_t - R_t - D_t)](1 + k)^{-t}$$
$$+ [S - T_g(S - B)](1 + k)^{-n} - A \qquad (11.3.4.1.)$$

And the present value of the net cash inflows from the proposed project based on a lease proposal is:

$$NPV(L) = (1 - T) \sum_{t=1}^{n} (y_t - C_t)(1 + k)^{-t}$$
$$- (1 - T) \sum_{t=1}^{n} M_t(1 + r)^{-t} \qquad (11.3.4.2.)$$

where for both (11.3.4.1.) and (11.3.4.2.)
y_t is the cash revenue from the asset in year t,
C_t is the pre-tax cash cost required to operate the asset in year t,
R_t is the repairs and other costs incurred in year t if the asset is purchased,
D_t is the deductible depreciation in year t,
T is the tax rate,
T_g is the tax rate on any balancing charge or allowance,
k is the cost of capital,
r is the after-tax minimum borrowing rate,
S is the salvage or scrap value,
B is the book value or written down value when the asset is scrapped,
A is the cash purchase price of the asset, and
M_t is the annual lease payment in year t payable in advance.

$$\Delta NPV = NPV(P) - NPV(L)$$
$$= T \sum_{t=1}^{n} D_t(1 + k)^{-t} + (T - 1) \sum_{t=1}^{n} R_t(1 + k)^{-t}$$
$$+ (1 - T) \sum_{t=1}^{n} M_t(1 + r)^{-t}$$
$$+ [S - T_g(S - B)](1 + k)^{-n} - A \qquad (11.3.4.3.)$$

Using the data of Lis Ltd. in Section 11.3.3 and applying equation (11.3.4.3.) gives:

$$\begin{aligned}\Delta NPV &= (.4)[33{,}333(1.15)^{-1} + 33{,}333(1.15)^{-2} \\ &\quad + 33{,}333(1.15)^{-3}] \\ &\quad + (-.6)[5{,}000(1.15)^{-1} + 5{,}000(1.15)^{-2} + \cdots \\ &\quad + 5{,}000(1.15)^{-8}] \\ &\quad + (.6)[20{,}000(1.06)^{-1} + 20{,}000(1.06)^{-2} + \cdots \\ &\quad + 20{,}000(1.06)^{-8}] \\ &\quad + [10{,}000 - .4(10{,}000 - 0)](1.15)^{-8} \\ &\quad - 100{,}000 \\ &= \$[30{,}440 - 13{,}461 + 74{,}520 + 1{,}962 - 100{,}000] \\ &= -\ \$6{,}539\end{aligned}$$

Since ΔNPV is negative, the present value of the net cash inflows of the proposed project based on the lease proposal is greater than that based on the purchase proposal and the decision is to lease the machine.

If the distinction is made that lease payments are made at the beginning of the year while tax advantages are earned at the end of the year, equation (11.3.4.3.) becomes:

$$\begin{aligned}\Delta NPV &= NPV(P) - NPV(L) \\ &= T\sum_{t=1}^{n} D_t(1+k)^{-t} + (T-1)\sum_{t=1}^{n} R_t(1+k)^{-t} \\ &\quad + \sum_{t=0}^{n-1} M_t(1+r)^{-t} - T\sum_{t=0}^{n-1} M_t(1+r)^{-(t+1)} \\ &\quad + [S - T_g(S-B)](1+k)^{-n} - A \qquad (11.3.4.4.)\end{aligned}$$

Applying equation (11.3.4.4.) to the data in Lis Ltd gives:

$$\begin{aligned}\Delta NPV &= \$[30{,}440 - 13{,}461 + 81{,}960 + 1{,}962 - 100{,}000] \\ &= \$901\end{aligned}$$

Since ΔNPV is positive, it is economically better to buy the machine.

In the Johnson and Lewellen's Method, the financing of the proposed asset is not explicitly analysed. As a matter of fact, the problem of leasing vis-a-vis buying is simply treated as an investment problem and the method is essentially the net present value method of investment evaluation using the cost of capital as the discount rate except for the lease payments which are discounted with the after-tax minimum borrowing rate. Hence, the alternatives, lease or purchase, are treated as two alternative proposed investment projects, and the one with the higher expected net present value is the one preferred.

Some of the criticisms of this method suggest that ignoring the tax benefits from deductible expenses like interest and discounting the cash streams from both the lease and the purchase proposals with the same cost of capital may lead to decisions that do not maximize the firm value; it is suggested by some critics that the lease and purchase cash streams have different probability distributions and different risk-adjusted discount rates should therefore be used.

11.3.5. L.D. Schall's Model

L.D. Schall criticizes all the other models previously explained for misspecifying the relevant cash flows associated with the lease and buy proposals and for applying improper discount rates. He suggests that the two decisions concerning the proposed asset are first, whether it should be acquired and second, how it should be financed if it is acquired. He maintains that an asset should be acquired only if its acquisition increases the firm value, and that the method of financing should be the one which increases the firm value by the largest amount.

The relevant cash flows must be identified and since the different cash flows are different in their probability distributions and risk, they must be discounted at different appropriate rates. His formulae (modified) are:

The present value of the net cash inflows of the lease proposal (by which the firm value is expected to increase) is:

$$NPV(L) = (1 - T) \sum_{t=1}^{n} X_t(1 + k_X)^{-t} - \sum_{t=0}^{n} M_t(1 + k_M)^{-t} + T \sum_{t=0}^{n-1} M_t(1 + k_M)^{-(t+1)} \quad (11.3.5.1.)$$

The present value of the net cash inflows of the purchase proposal (by which the firm value is expected to increase) is:

$$NPV(P) = (1 - T) \sum_{t=1}^{n} (X_t - Q_t)(1 + k_p)^{-t} + T \sum_{t=1}^{n} D_t(1 + k_p)^{-t} + T \sum_{t=1}^{n} E_t(1 + k_E)^{-t} + [S - T_g(S - B)](1 + k_p)^{-n} - A \qquad (11.3.5.2.)$$

where for both (11.3.5.1.) and (11.3.5.2.),

X_t is the expected cash revenues less cash costs and expenses associated with the asset in period t (before deducting lease payments),

M_t is the expected lease payment in period t payable in advance,

Q_t is the expected cash costs in period t that are incurred if the asset is purchased but not if it is leased, such as repairs and maintenance,

D_t is the expected deductible depreciation if the asset is purchased,

E_t is the expected interest expense in period t on any new debt incurred to finance the purchase,

S is the expected salvage value of the asset when scrapped,

B is the expected book value or written down value when asset is scrapped.

T_g is the tax rate on any balancing charge or allowance on disposing of the asset,

A is the cash purchase price of the asset, and

k_X, k_M, k_p and k_E are the proper discount rates for the different cash streams.

The decision rules are:
Acquire the asset if either

$$NPV(L) > 0, \text{ or}$$
$$NPV(P) > 0 \qquad (11.3.5.3.)$$
$$\text{And Lease if } NPV(L) > NPV(P) \qquad (11.3.5.4.)$$

An illustration:

$$X_t = \$1{,}100 \text{ for } t = 1, 2, 3$$
$$M_t = \$800 \text{ for } t = 0, 1, 2$$
$$A = \$2{,}100$$

Debt finance of \$450 at 10% and equity finance of \$1,650 if the asset is purchased,

$$
\begin{aligned}
Q_t &= \$50,\ t = 1,\ 2,\ 3\\
T &= T_g = 0.4\\
D_t &= \$700 \text{ for } t = 1,\ 2,\ 3\\
S &= \$100\\
k_X &= 0.15,\ k_M = 0.12,\ k_p = 0.10,\ k_E = 0.06
\end{aligned}
$$

Applying equation (11.3.5.1.) gives:

$$
\begin{aligned}
NPV(L) &= (.6)[(1{,}100)(1.15)^{-1} + (1{,}100)(1.15)^{-2}\\
&\quad + (1{,}100)(1.15)^{-3}]\\
&\quad -[800 + (800)(1.12)^{-1} + (800)(1.12)^{-2}]\\
&\quad + (.4)[(800)(1.12)^{-1} + (800)(1.12)^{-2} +\\
&\qquad (800)(1.12)^{-3}]\\
&= 1{,}507 - 2{,}152 + 769\\
&= \$124
\end{aligned}
$$

Applying equation (11.3.5.2.) gives:

$$
\begin{aligned}
NPV(P) &= (.6)[(1{,}050)(1.10)^{-1} + (1{,}050)(1.10)^{-2}\\
&\quad + (1{,}050)(1.10)^{-3}]\\
&\quad + (.4)[(700)(1.10)^{-1} + (700)(1.10)^{-2} + (700)(1.10)^{-3}]\\
&\quad + (.4)[(45)(1.06)^{-1} + (45)(1.06)^{-2} + (45)(1.06)^{-3}]\\
&\quad + [100 - .4(100 - 0)](1.10)^{-3}\\
&\quad - 2{,}100\\
&= 1{,}567 + 696 + 48 + 45 - 2{,}100\\
&= \$256
\end{aligned}
$$

Since $NPV(P) > NPV(L)$, it is better to purchase.

Schall's model is very much more difficult to apply than the other methods. The cash flows associated with the proposed asset must be forecasted and the different proper discount rates must be known. The assumptions of the model are very restrictive: that capital markets are competitive and that there are no transactions and bankruptcy costs.

11.4. SELECTED BIBLIOGRAPHY

1. R.S. Bower, F.C. Herringer, and J.P. Williamson: Lease Evaluation, Accounting Review, April 1966.
2. R.W. Johnson and W.G. Lewellen: Analysis of the Lease-or-Buy Decision, Journal of Finance, September 1972.
3. Ronald Ma: Comparative Analysis of Lease Evaluation Models (A Review Article), *Accounting and Business Research*, Spring 1981.
4. K.A. Middleton: The Evaluation of Lease Proposals, The Australian Accountant, April 1972.
5. G.B. Mitchell: After-Tax Cost of Leasing, Accounting Review, April 1970.
6. L.D. Schall: The Lease-or-Buy And Asset Acquisition Decisions, Journal of Finance, September 1974.
7. R.F. Vancil: Lease or Borrow-New Method of Analysis, Harvard Business Review, September 1961.
8. J.F. Weston and E.F. Brigham: Managerial Finance.

CHAPTER 12

Securities Investment Analysis

12.1. BUY OR SELL

One of the most elementary problems of securities investment analysis is to decide whether to buy or sell a particular share. The theoretical consideration is not very abstruse; it is easy to see the logic of the following decision rule: Buy if the present value of a share exceeds its quoted market price and sell if the latter exceeds the former. The difficulty lies in estimating the present value of the share, which necessitates not only forecasting future cash flows but also evaluating the risks of such cash flows in arriving at the minimum acceptable rate of return, the risk-adjusted discount rate. Some of the common models of securities investment analysis will be explained in this chapter.

12.2. NET PRESENT VALUE

The kinds of information available usually comprise the quoted prices of the securities, the annual dividends and the annual earnings. One may therefore have to apply the income approach to share valuation: the Net Present Value and the Internal Rate of Return techniques.

Under the Net Present Value technique, the future dividends including the liquidating dividend are discounted to their present value and this is compared with the quoted price of the share to decide to buy or to sell.

$$P = \sum_{t=1}^{n} D_t(1 + i)^{-t} \tag{1}$$

where P = present value of the share, D_t = annual dividend per share at the end of the tth year and i = minimum acceptable rate of return.

If the annual dividends are constant and will be distributed annually forever, we have:

$$P = \lim_{n \to \infty} \sum_{t=1}^{n} D_t(1 + i)^{-t} = \frac{D}{i} \tag{2}$$

If the annual dividends are expected to grow at the rate e per annum, we have:

$$P = \sum_{t=1}^{n} D_1(1 + e)^{t-1}(1 + i)^{-t} + D_m(1 + i)^{-n} \tag{3}$$

where $D_1 = D_0(1 + e)$, that is D_1 is the dividend at the end of the first year, D_0 is the dividend at the beginning of the first year, and D_m is the liquidating dividend.

If the dividends grow at the rate e per year and will be distributed forever, we have:

$$P = \sum_{t=1}^{\infty} D_1(1 + e)^{t-1}(1 + i)^{-t} = \frac{D_1}{i - e} \tag{4}$$

If the dividends grow at the rate e per year from year o to year n, and thence at the rate g per year to year m, after which the annual dividend remains a constant amount that will be distributed forever, we have:

$$\begin{aligned} P = &\sum_{t=1}^{n} D_1(1 + e)^{t-1}(1 + i)^{-t} \\ &+ \sum_{t=n+1}^{m} D_{n+1}(1 + g)^{t-(n+1)}(1 + i)^{-t} \\ &+ \frac{D_{m+1}}{i}(1 + i)^{-m} \end{aligned} \tag{5}$$

12.3. INTERNAL RATE OF RETURN

Under the Internal Rate of Return technique, the future dividends are discounted by trial and error so that the present value of their sum s, is equal to the presently quoted market price, q, in order to ascertain the discounting rate, k.

$$q = s = \sum_{t=1}^{n} D_t(1 + k)^{-t} \tag{6}$$

where D_t = the annual dividend at the end of the tth year.

Similarly as in equations (2) to (4) we obtain:

$$q = s = \sum_{t=1}^{\infty} D_t(1 + k)^{-t} = \frac{D}{k} \tag{7}$$

where D is the annual dividend

$$q = s = \sum_{t=1}^{n} D_1(1 + e)^{t-1}(1 + k)^{-t} \tag{8}$$

Where D is expected to grow at e annually,

$$q = s = \sum_{t=1}^{\infty} D_1(1 + e)^{t-1}(1 + k)^{-t} = \frac{D_1}{k - e} \tag{9}$$

The decision rule under this technique is: Buy if $m = k$, and Sell if $m > k$ where m is the minimum acceptable rate of return.

In applying the above decision rules one must always bear in mind that the quoted market price is a marginal price and any substantial sale or purchase will certainly change it.

12.3.1. An Illustration

The market price of the shares of ZYX Ltd. on 31st December 1979 is $50.00. The company has been distributing all its earnings in cash. The average annual growth rate in earnings is expected to last only another 10 years from 31st December 1979 and then annual earnings are expected to remain constant. The following past earnings are obtained from the records of the company:

1976	\$1.32
1977	1.56
1978	1.74
1979	2.00

REQUIRED:

Estimate the rate of discount that will ensure that the sum of the present values of all future dividends is equal to the market price of \$50.00.

The annual growth rate is:

$$e = \sqrt[3]{2/1.32} - 1 \simeq 0.15$$

$$q = \sum_{t=1}^{10} D_0(1 + e)^t(1 + k)^{-t} + D_{10}(k)^{-1}(1 + k)^{-10}$$

$$50 = \sum_{t=1}^{10} 2(1.15)^t(1 + k)^{-t} + 2(1.15)^{10}(k)^{-1}(1 + k)^{-10}$$

$k \simeq 0.11$ (obtained by trial and error)

12.4. LINEAR REGRESSION

It is widely held that the earnings of a share and its market price are important information in securities investment analysis and price earnings ratios, that is market price divided by earnings, are quoted in publications on securities. There are many models (using linear regression) for predicting price earnings ratio. Linear regression models are explained in the next chapter. Once the parameters are estimated, the linear equation is used for forecasting the price earnings ratio of a share. The following is a typical example:

$$\begin{aligned}\text{PER of XYZ Ltd} &= a + bx_1 + cx_2 - dx_3 \\ &= 9.5 + 2.1x_1 + 4.2x_2 - 1.1x_3\end{aligned}$$

where x_1 could be forecasted earnings growth rate
x_2 could be forecasted proportion of dividend payout out of profit
x_3 could be standard deviation in past growth rates

Other independent variables may also be introduced. The parameters, a, b, c and d are estimated usually from past data. The limitations of such models lie in their assumptions; these are explained in Appendix B.

12.5. PORTFOLIO SELECTION

The second facet of our securities investment analysis is the selection of an efficient investment portfolio. The problem here is to choose a portfolio $X = [x_1\ x_2\ \dots\ x_n]^T$ where x_j is the proportion of the total funds invested in the jth security, $j = 1, 2, \dots, n$. The return on the portfolio is EX where E is a given row vector of mean returns on the n securities. The risk on the portfolio is indicated by the quadratic form: X^TNX, where N is a given $n \times n$ matrix of variances and covariances of returns. N is assumed positive definite. The choice of an investment portfolio can then be expressed as a quadratic programming problem.

Minimize $X^TN\,X$
Subject to $EX \geqq R$, where R is the minimum acceptable rate of return

$$\sum_{j=1}^{n} x_j = 1 \qquad (10)$$

$$X \geqq 0$$

This is a quadratic programming problem because the objective function contains no terms of degree higher than 2 and the constraints are all linear. The portfolio given by the programme will be efficient in the sense that no other portfolio can give a higher return without increasing risk nor the same return with less risk. It can be demonstrated that the folowing programme is also efficient:

Maximize $E\,X$
Subject to $X^TN\,X \leqq D$, where D is the maximum acceptable risk

$$\sum_{j=1}^{n} x_j = 1$$

$$X \geqq 0 \qquad (11)$$

The following data may be used as an illustration, assuming that returns are measured in terms of both capital gains and dividends, and dividends declared and paid have been taken into account in arriving at the values of the shares, and that $R = 0.08$:

Table 12.4.1.

Year	Values of Shares		
	x_1 $	x_2 $	x_3 $
0	10.0	20.0	30.0
1	11.0	21.0	28.0
2	11.5	26.0	32.0
3	10.0	30.0	36.0
4	14.0	29.0	40.0

The annual rates of return are displayed in Table 12.4.2.

Table 12.4.2

Year	Rates of Return		
	r_1	r_2	r_3
1	0.100	0.050	−.067
2	0.045	0.238	0.143
3	−.130	0.154	0.125
4	0.400	−.033	0.111

The geometric means of the rates of return are:

$$\bar{r}_1 = \sqrt[4]{14/10} - 1 = 0.087$$
$$\bar{r}_2 = \sqrt[4]{29/20} - 1 = 0.097$$
$$\bar{r}_3 = \sqrt[4]{40/30} - 1 = 0.074$$

We obtain:

$$N = \begin{bmatrix} .037 & -.015 & -.001 \\ -.015 & .011 & .004 \\ -.001 & .004 & .007 \end{bmatrix}$$

$$E = [\ .087 \quad .097 \quad .074\ ]$$

Minimize $$F(X) = .037x_1^2 + .011x_2^2 + .007x_3^2 - .03x_1x_2 - .002x_1x_3 + .008x_2x_3$$

Subject to $$0.087x_1 + .097x_2 + .074x_3 \geq .08$$
$$x_1 + x_2 + x_3 = 1$$
$$x_1, x_2, x_3 \geqq 0$$

The optimal solutions are:

$$x_1^* = 0.33, \quad x_2^* = 0.66, \quad x_3^* = 0.01$$
$$F^* = 0.0023338$$

12.6. VALUATION OF GOODWILL

12.6.1. Explanation of Goodwill

Goodwill is something intangible which has value. A purchaser of a business sometimes pays for it a sum which is greater than its net worth as professionally assessed. The excess must be paid for something which in the opinion of the purchaser has some value. This value is the goodwill of the business. What factors contribute or have contributed to the value of goodwill? A businessman will not buy a business for a sum in excess of the market price of its net assets unless he expects the business to be comparatively profitable. In other words, he pays for the goodwill because he expects to make good profits from the business. Goodwill and profits are closely inter-related. The factors that contribute to the value of goodwill must, therefore, be the same factors that contribute to the expectations of profits which can be caused, inter alia, by one or more of the following:

(1) Thc location of the business. For instance, a newsagent at a busy railway station should normally bring more sales than one at a small local market place. Goodwill attaches to the place of business.
(2) The reputation of the people operating the business for their efficient and courteous service and/or other attributes. Goodwill attaches to people.
(3) The brand of the product. Customers are attracted to the business because they are brand-conscious. Goodwill attaches to products.

(4) The probability of the future market. Goodwill attaches to the forces at work in the market.

Since goodwill value may be the result of various factors, it is very desirable to identify the pertinent ones when the goodwill of a particular business is evaluated.

12.6.2. Circumstances Requiring Valuation

There are broadly two types of situations where the goodwill of a business must be valued:

(1) On the death, retirement or admission of a partner in a firm of partnership. In this case, the partnership agreement must be examined closely to see if the methods of valuation are provided therein. In the absence of such provisions, either the partners must come to a mutually acceptable method or an arbitrator is usually appointed to assess the value of goodwill.
(2) When one person intends to buy over the business of another, both parties would like to know the goodwill value in order to arrive at the purchase consideration.

12.6.3. Goodwill Valuation in Theory

Theoretically the goodwill of a firm is the excess of the present value of the firm over the present value of its net assets. Symbolically:

$$G = V - (A - L) \qquad (12.6.3.)$$

where G is the value of the goodwill of the firm,
V is the present value of the firm as defined in equation (2.1) of Chapter 2,
A is the present value of all the assets of the firm, and
L is the present value of the firm's liablities.

The selling prices of assets have been justified to be good surrogates of their present values in Section 2.5. of Chapter 2. Hence, A may be the sum of the selling prices of all the firm's assets. The concept of goodwill is thus one which explains why the firm as a going concern is worth more than its net assets at current selling prices.

12.6.4. Goodwill Valuation in Practice

There are five principal methods of goodwill valuation often adopted in practice:

(1) By a certain number of years' purchase of past profits.
(2) By a certain number of years' purchase of super profits.
(3) By a certain number of years' purchase of "gross takings."
(4) By capitalizing expected future profits.
(5) By discounting the expected future profits to their present value.

1. Years' Purchase of Past Profits
Under this method, the past profits of a number of years are averaged to arrive at the average annual profit. The goodwill is calculated as so many years' purchase of such average annual profit. The past profits may be gross or net and the profit trend is expected to continue in the future.

Example
A, *B* and *C* share profits and losses in the proportions 3:2:1 respectively. The partnership agreement provides that goodwill is to be three years' purchase of the average annual net profit of the past five years. The past five years' profits are as follows:

19x1	$5,000
19x2	6,000
19x3	5,500
19x4	6,500
19x5	6,500
Total Profits for past 5 years	$29,500

What is *A*'s share of the firm's goodwill?

$$\text{Average Annual Profit} = \frac{29{,}500}{5} = \$5{,}900$$

3 years' purchase of average annual profit = 3 × 5,900 = $17,700.
∴ Total goodwill = $17,700.
A's share of goodwill = 3/6 × 17,700 = $8,850.

It should be noted that in practice it is often assumed that the partners' profit sharing ratios are the same as their goodwill sharing ratios.

2. Years' Purchase of Super Profits

Under this method it is first necessary to arrive at a figure of average super annual profit. This is usually the average annual profit remaining after deducting therefrom

(1) the expenses that must be paid which hitherto had not been deducted and
(2) the amount representing a reasonable return on the net assets of the business.

It is the future profits that must be estimated. To do this the past profits are often used as a basis to which all necessary adjustments are made in the light of the circumstances that are likely to prevail in the future. The amount of goodwill is arrived at on the assumption that it represents profits which are in excess of the normal return expected from similar businesses. The main problem is to determine the number of years' purchase of the average super annual profit; this in practice is decided by the parties concerned as a result of bargaining.

Example

A Ltd. is to buy over B Ltd. The value of goodwill is to be four years' purchase of the average annual super profit to be based on the past five years' profits of B Ltd. The two directors of B Ltd. whose services have not so far been remunerated are to serve on the board of A Ltd. at a sum of $5,000 each per annum. The average net assets of B Ltd. amount to $100,000 and the normal rate of return for such businesses is considered to be 12%. The past five years' profits before tax are: $30,000, $35,000, $40,000, $35,000 and $45,000. What is the goodwill value of B Ltd.?

Total past five years' profits	= $185,000
Average annual profit $\frac{185,000}{5}$	= $ 37,000
Less Directors' Fees	10,000
	$ 27,000
Less Income Tax at 40%	10,800
Average annual profit after tax	$ 16,200
Less Interest on capital invested (12% of $100,000)	12,000
	$ 4,200
∴ Goodwill = 4 × 4,200	= $ 16,800

3. Years' Purchase of "Gross Takings"
This method is considered by most people to be suitable for calculating the goodwill of professional practices. A professional practice often has two types of gross revenue, the recurring and the non-recurring. Only the gross fees of the recurring type are taken into account in arriving at goodwill. So many years' purchase of such gross takings is the basis used. For instance, the goodwill of a medical practice may be one year's purchase of the average gross fees of the past three years. Other types of businesses where this method has been applied include bakery, newsagents, butchers, grocers and estate agents.

4. Capitalization of Expected Future Profits
This is considered by many people to be the most logical method of valuing goodwill. The average net profit is used as a starting point. From it is deducted

(1) the expenses of the buying business if this has not been done and will be incurred, and
(2) the income tax payable on the profit in the case of a limited company.

If there are items of expenditure that will not recur and/or that will be incurred, these must necessarily be taken into account. The figure thus obtained is then capitalized at a rate which represents the normal return on capital invested in similar businesses. The goodwill value is the difference between this capitalized net profit and the value of the net assets (total assets less total liabilities) used in the business.

Example
X Ltd. is desirous of buying over Y Ltd. which has made an average annual net profit of $100,000 before tax. It is considered that the profit trend will continue in the future. But X Ltd. need not pay the directors' fees of $20,000 nor the annual rent of $10,000 which have always been paid by Y Ltd. The net assets of Y Ltd. amount to $740,000 and 10% on capital invested is the reasonable rate of return for similar businesses. What is the goodwill value of Y Ltd.?

Average Annual Net Profit		$100,000
Add Non-recurring expenses:		
Directors' Fees	$20,000	
Rent	10,000	30,000
Estimated future annual profit before tax		$130,000
Less Income tax at 40%		52,000
Estimated future annual profit after tax		$ 78,000
Capitalize this at 10% we get $\frac{78{,}000 \times 100}{10}$		= $780,000
Capitalized future profit		$780,000
Less net tangible assets		740,000
Y's goodwill value		$ 40,000

5. Discounting Expected Future Profits

It is first necessary to determine the expected average annual super profit which is arrived at as in method 2 (Years' Purchase of Super Profits). The average annual super profit is discounted at an appropriate rate of interest over a period of years. This is so because a sum of money (goodwill) must be paid now in order to receive an annual super profit at the end of each year for an estimated number of years. A dollar received today is worth more than a dollar received at some future date because interest must be paid for the use of money. The appropriate interest rate to be used is the rate at which the sum to be paid now for goodwill can be invested elsewhere.

Example

Average annual super profit	$10,000
Number of years super profit will be earned	2
Appropriate rate of interest per annum	10%

The present value of an annuity of $1 can be obtained from tables or from the following formula (from equation 9 of Appendix A):

$$P_0 = \frac{1 - (1 + i)^{-n}}{i}$$

where P_0 = present value of an annuity of $1
n = the number of years
i = the annual rate of interest.

$$\text{Hence, } P_0 = \frac{1 - (1 + .10)^{-2}}{.10}$$

$$= \$1.73553$$

∴ Goodwill (which is the present value of an annuity of \$10,000 for 2 years)

$$= 10{,}000 \times 1.73553$$

$$= \$17{,}355$$

12.7. VALUATION OF SHARES

When valuation of shares is a topic under discussion, it is essential at the outset to divide all shares of companies into two classes:

(1) quoted shares, and
(2) unquoted shares.

Quoted shares are shares which are listed on the Stock Exchange, bought and sold on stock exchange market, and having their prices quoted. Only shares of public companies can be quoted; shares of private companies are not freely transferable and hence, are not quoted. For shares quoted on the Stock Exchange, valuation is facilitated because their prices are known. But in valuing a business whose ownership is represented by its share capital, the quotation of the Stock Exchange may not give a true value of the shares. First, the prices quoted are marginal prices; any substantial purchase or sale of a particular company's shares will change their price; in other words all the shares of a company are unlikely to be sold at the quoted price at any point of time. Secondly, under or over-valuation of a company's assets may influence the price quoted for its shares. Thirdly, the dividend policy of management affects the share price of the company. And finally, other factors, including the following, also influence share prices quoted on the Stock Exchange:

(1) Political and economic trends of the country where the company is operating.
(2) Government policies which affect interest rates and taxes on income.
(3) The prospects of the industry to which the company belongs.

(4) The reputation of the company's top management for efficiency and skill or otherwise.
(5) The probability of the company's future capital structure, such as, capital gearing, issue of bonus shares, and rights issue.

Hence, for shares of private companies and even those of public companies, accountants are sometimes asked to value them. Specifically valuation of shares, especially unquoted shares, is necessary in the following situations:

(1) In cases of take-over bids.
(2) Where a member of a private company wishes to dispose of his shares.
(3) Where a company amalgamates with or absorbs another company, their shares may have to be valued.
(4) Shares held by partners in a partnership may have to be valued when the partnership property is to be distributed in the event of its dissolution.
(5) For the purpose of assessing death duties, the shares held by a deceased person must be valued.

12.7.1. Methods of Share Valuation Often Adopted in Practice

There are three methods of share valuation which can be discussed, namely,

(1) Net Assets Method,
(2) Dividend Yield Method, and
(3) Earnings Yield Method.

It is important to note that none of these methods can give an absolute figure; hence, the results obtained from one or more of the methods may be modified by judgment or negotiation to suit the particular needs of the purpose on hand. The value of a business should theoretically be dependent on its earning power, its prospective dividend payments and its net assets. Some assets, such as plant and machinery which is very specific in use, may have very little realizable value. And in the case of a prosperous company, its goodwill may be worth a substantial amount though goodwill account may not be in the books. Hence, the assets of a company are sometimes revalued for the purpose of valuing its shares. Fictitious assets, such as discount on debentures, are of course excluded.

1. Net Assets Method

Under this method, the net assets of the company (total assets less total liabilities) is divided by the number of issued shares to arrive at the value per share.

Example

Balance Sheet as at 31st December 19x6

Issued Capital		**Land and Buildings**	$40,000
10,000 7% Preference shares	$ 10,000	**Plant and Machinery**	50,000
40,000 ordinary shares	40,000	**Preliminary Expenses**	15,000
Paid-up Capital	$ 50,000		
Revenue Reserves	40,000	**Current Assets**	35,000
Mortgage on Land and Buildings	20,000		
Current Liabilities	30,000		
	$140,000		$140,000

Other Information:

(1) The land and buildings are considered to be worth $80,000.
(2) Goodwill is valued at $30,000.
(3) Other assets are worth their book values.

The net assets of the company are arrived at as follows:

Land and buildings			$ 80,000
Plant and Machinery			50,000
Current Assets			35,000
Goodwill			30,000
		Total Assets	$195,000
Less Mortgage on land and buildings	$20,000		
Current Liabilities	30,000		
		Total Liabilities	50,000
Total Net Assets			$145,000
Less Value of Preference Shares			10,000
Net assets attributable to ordinary shareholders			$135,000

$$\therefore \text{Net Asset Value per ordinary shares} = \frac{135,000}{40,000}$$

$$= \$3.375$$

NOTE: Since the preference share capital is many times covered by the net assets, it is considered to be worth its book value.

2. Dividend Yield Method

The dividend yield method has stringent assumptions and may not be suitable for valuation of shares for these reasons: first, dividend rate may fluctuate from year to year for various reasons, such as ploughing back profits; and second, capital gains may be more important than dividends for some people with very high tax rates. However, it may be used as a guide or in conjunction with other methods.

Example

(1) Using the same example as before.
(2) The net profit after tax but before appropriation has been averaged at $8,000 per annum.
(3) Average ordinary dividends have been at 11%.
(4) The dividend yield on ordinary shares of similar businesses is 8% and on preference shares is 6%.

(a) Value of Ordinary Share on Dividend Yield Method

$$= \frac{11\%}{8\%} \times \$1 = \$1.375$$

or alternatively,

Ordinary dividend = $4,400.
Normal return for similar business = 8%

$$\text{The dividend capitalized} = \frac{4{,}400 \times 100}{8}$$

$$= \$55{,}000$$

$$\therefore \text{ Value per ordinary share} = \frac{55{,}000}{40{,}000} = \$1.375$$

(b) Value of Preference Share on Dividend Yield Method

$$= \frac{7\%}{6\%} \times \$1 = \$1.167$$

3. Earnings Yield Method

Under this method the earnings of the company rather than dividends declared form the basis on which the ordinary share value is calculated. In the example given before, the value of one ordinary share is arrived at as shown below:

Net Profit after tax	=	$8,000
Less preference dividend (7%)	=	700
Net profit available to ordinary shareholders	=	$7,300

Normal return is given as 8%

$\therefore$ The net profit capitalized at 8% $= \dfrac{7{,}300}{8} \times 100 = \$91{,}250.$

Hence, the value per ordinary share $= \dfrac{91{,}250}{40{,}000} = \$2.281$

12.7.2. Effect of Bonus Issues

Bonus shares are issued either to existing shareholders in the proportions of their present holdings or to debenture holders in discharge of the debentures. No funds are derived from bonus issues. Hence, the price of the company's shares is affected by any bonus issue. Let us suppose that a company has 100,000 ordinary shares of $1 each fully paid and that the market value of the shares is $2 each. If the company issues bonus shares to existing shareholders on the basis of one bonus share for every share now held out of the reserves of the company, the price per share should fall to $1. The reasoning can be illustrated below:

Before Bonus Issue: 100,000 shares at $2 = $200,000
After Bonus Issue: 200,000 shares at $1 = $200,000

This must be correct because the mere issue of bonus shares does not increase the company's net worth or assets nor its earning prospects. When bonus shares are issued out of revenue reserves, debenture holders, if any, stand to benefit, because the revenue reserves being capitalized are no longer distributable as cash dividend and thus enhance the debenture holders' security. From the viewpoint of return of capital in the event of liquidation of the company, preference shareholders benefit in the same way as debenture holders by a bonus issue out of revenue reserves if the preference shareholders enjoy priority right in respect of capital return. But should future earnings decline they may suffer since the revenue reserves are no longer available for paying preference dividend.

12.7.3. Effect of Rights Issues

A rights issue is often offered to existing shareholders because this is a cheaper way of raising capital than a public issue. The procedure involved is simple. Provisional allotment letters are sent to existing shareholders giving them the right to take up a specified number of shares in proportion to their existing holdings. These "rights" may be sold by the shareholders, and since the price per share offered by the company is usually less than the market price, a rights issue, if resorted to, is very seldom unsuccessful. The success of a rights issue of any particular company of course depends on the prospects of the company. To ensure success the difference between the price of the rights issue and the market price of the existing shares must be sufficiently large to act as an inducement.

Let us assume that a company decides to have a rights issue, which is on the basis of one share for every two now held. The positions before and after the rights issue can be shown as follows:

	Total Value
Before Rights Issue:	
500,000 shares of \$1 each fully paid at a market price of \$2 per share	= \$1,000,000
Rights Issue:	
250,000 shares of \$1 each fully paid (rights issue) at a price of \$1.50 per share	= \$ 375,000
After Rights Issue:	
750,000 shares at a total market value of	= \$1,375,000

$$\therefore \text{ The new market price per share} = \frac{1{,}375{,}000}{750{,}000} = \$1.833$$

In discussing the effect on the market price of shares of a bonus or a rights issue, it is important to remember that share prices may not in practice be determined in such a precise manner as the arithmetics may indicate. The prospective earning capacity of the company as well as the other factors which have been discussed may have contributory effects.

12.8. SELECTED BIBLIOGRAPHY

1. A.V. Adamson and M.G. Gorey: The Valuation of Company Shares and Businesses.
2. T.A.H. Baynes: Share Valuations
3. J.C. Bonbright: Valuation of Property
4. J.C.G. Boot: Quadratic Programming
5. Michael Firth: The Valuation of Shares and the Efficient Markets Theory
6. M. Keenan: Models of Equity Valuation (The Great Serum Bubble), *Journal of Finance*, May 1970
7. H. Markowitz: Portfolio Selection, Cowles Foundation Monograph No. 16, 1959.
8. W.F. Sharpe: A Simplified Model for Portfolio Selection Analysis, Management Science, January 1963.
9. R.L. Sidey: The Valuation of Shares
10. V.S. Whitbeck and M. Kisor Jr.: A New Tool in Investment Decision Making, *Financial Analysts Journal*, May–June 1963.

CHAPTER 13

Financial Forecasting

13.1. PLANNING AND FORECASTING

The use of mathematical models to enhance the quality of decision-making entails availability of relevant information. Many of these kinds of information relate to predictions of the future. Hence, forecasting becomes increasingly an important management tool. Forecasting total market demand and market share, product price and product development, production and input requirements, plant capacity and expansion, cash flows and capital as well as manpower requirements—all these are examples.

A forecast is an estimate of future events without the conscious efforts of management to change or influence the course of such events. A detailed plan of action, on the other hand, is an adjusted forecast after intended management actions to change or modify such future events and after all the known constraints under which the firm is operating have been taken into account. Forecasting is therefore an essential element in the planning process.

A significant aspect of most quantitative forecasting techniques is the use of past data. It is on historical data that the parameters of most forecasting models are estimated. This may suggest that where the future events are unlikely to be influenced to the same extent by the same forces operating in the past or where new forces are likely to emerge, qualitative judgment may have to be exercised in one way or another in the forecasting process.

13.2. FORECASTING METHODS

Methods or techniques of forecasting have increased over the years. While some methods may be used in combination, it is obviously too costly to use many methods for the same purpose. A choice of models may be necessary. Besides the question of cost, there are other factors to be considered. The planning horizon affects this choice. Generally, the accuracy of a forecast decreases as the forecast extends further into the future, and some methods may be more suitable for short-term forecasting while others may give better long-term results. Different forecasting techniques require different amount of detailed data; the keeping of statistical records may be costly. Availability of data sometimes precludes the use of some models. The degree of accuracy desired as well as difficulty of application may also have significant bearing on the selection.

Both qualitative and quantitative methods are used in forecasting. Surveys are sometimes made where decision-makers are asked to state their anticipated actions which are then weighted and evaluated by experts in arriving at a forecast. The well-known Delphic Method elicits the opinions of a panel of experts. These are reviewed and revised until consensus or maximum degree of agreement among them is obtained. Some forecasts are based on the method of leading indicators. For instance, certain production statistics may indicate an increase or a decline in business activities. Usually the final forecast is the result of the inter-play between objective data and value judgment.

Most of the techniques explained in this chapter are linear models and give either point or interval estimates. Hence, they are generally more suitable for short-term forecasting though there is no reason why they cannot be used for long-term forecasting provided their limitations and assumptions are borne in mind when interpreting their results. Before using past data for estimating parameters of a forecasting model, it is always advisable to analyse the raw data, for instance by drawing scatter graphs to ascertain whether linear relationships are in fact appropriate. Sometimes exponential trends may be more accurate, for instance, $y = ab^x$. In this case, taking logarithm of both sides of the equation converts it into a linear one: $(\log y) = (\log a) + (\log b)x$. And linear analysis may then be applied. Without first linearizing the equation, linear analysis will yield misleading forecasts.

13.3. TREND ANALYSIS

The purpose of trend analysis is to ascertain the direction in which a series is moving. And if the direction as well as the intensity of its growth is constant, this can be represented by a straight line. If the past characteristics of the series are assumed to be present in the future, the straight line obtained from a study of the given series can be projected into the future. This is called extrapolation. The conclusions drawn from extrapolation are, therefore, only estimates and are based on the assumption that the past trend will continue into the future. Extreme or exceptional observations which are not expected to recur are usually left out, otherwise they may distort the trend line. The number of observations chosen for estimating the trend line depends on the pattern of the trend line and the experience and judgment of the analyst. For instance, if the trend line is to be used for forecasting the next two years' figures, the last ten years' observations may not be suitable if there is a clear new pattern emerging eight years ago. In this case, the last seven years' observations may be more appropriate.

Data given:

Year	*Production (in '000 units)*
1	9
2	11
3	15
4	13
5	14
6	13
7	15
8	16
9	18

The original data are plotted on a graph as shown in Figure 13.3.1. (on page 247 *infra*), and by inspection, a trend line is drawn. This method is, therefore, subject to personal bias and can be used only by an experienced person.

The Semi-Average Method

Under this method the series is divided into two parts. A simple average is calculated for each part. A straight line passing through the two averages is assumed to represent the growth factor of the series. This method may give reasonably accurate results only if there are no extreme values as it is affected by extremes.

Figure 13.3.1. (see text on page 246 *supra*.)

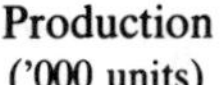

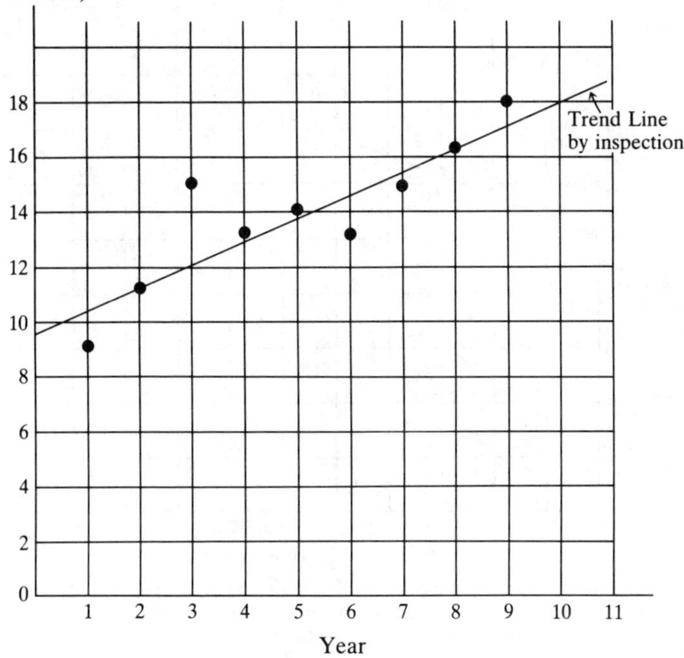

Year	*Production*	*Semi-average*
1	9	
2	11	
3	15	12.4
4	13	
5	14	
6	13	
7	15	
8	16	16.3
9	18	

The Least-Squares Method

The least-squares method requires computation and the mechanics of it can be shown as in Table 13.3.1.

Figure 13.3.2.

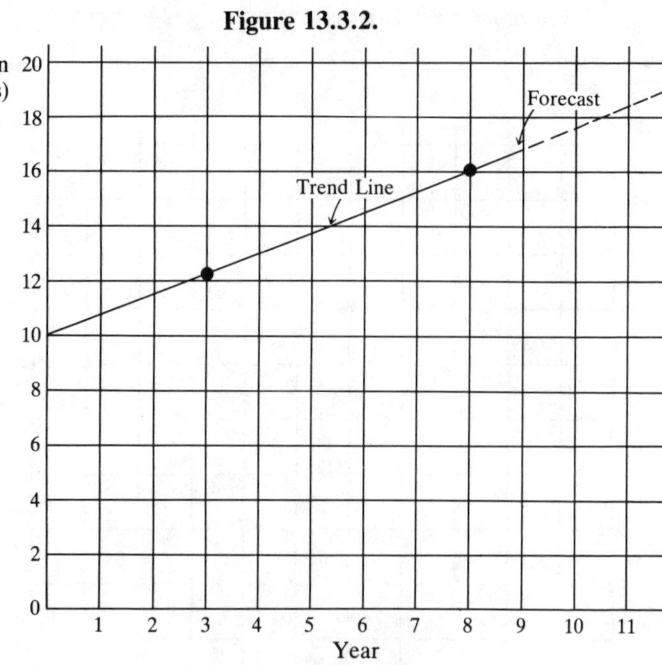

By Semi-Average Method

For year 10, production is estimated to be 17,800 and for year 11 it is estimated to be 18,500

Table 13.3.1.

Year	*Production* *Y*	*X*	*XY*	X^2
1	9	−4	−36	16
2	11	−3	−33	9
3	15	−2	−30	4
4	13	−1	−13	1
5	14	0	0	0
6	13	+1	+13	1
7	15	+2	+30	4
8	16	+3	+48	9
9	18	+4	+72	16
	$\sum Y = 124$	$\sum X = 0$	$\sum XY = 51$	$\sum X^2 = 60$

The purpose of the above computation is to arrive at the linear equation: $Y = a + bx$, the variables of which are found as follows:

$$a = \frac{\sum Y}{N} = \frac{124}{9} = 13.777 \qquad (13.3.1.)$$

$$b = \frac{\sum XY}{\sum X^2} = \frac{51}{60} = 0.85 \qquad (13.3.2.)$$

The equation is, therefore: $Y = 13.777 + .85X$. Say two values of X can be calculated, preferably two which are far apart. The two trend values thus obtained are plotted on a graph, and when the two points are joined, the trend line is obtained. The trend line can be produced to forecast the future.

For year 2, $Y = 13.777 + (.85)(-3) = 11.227$

For year 9, $Y = 13.777 + (.85)(4) = 17.777$

The graph can now be drawn as shown in Figure 13.3.3.

Figure 13.3.3.

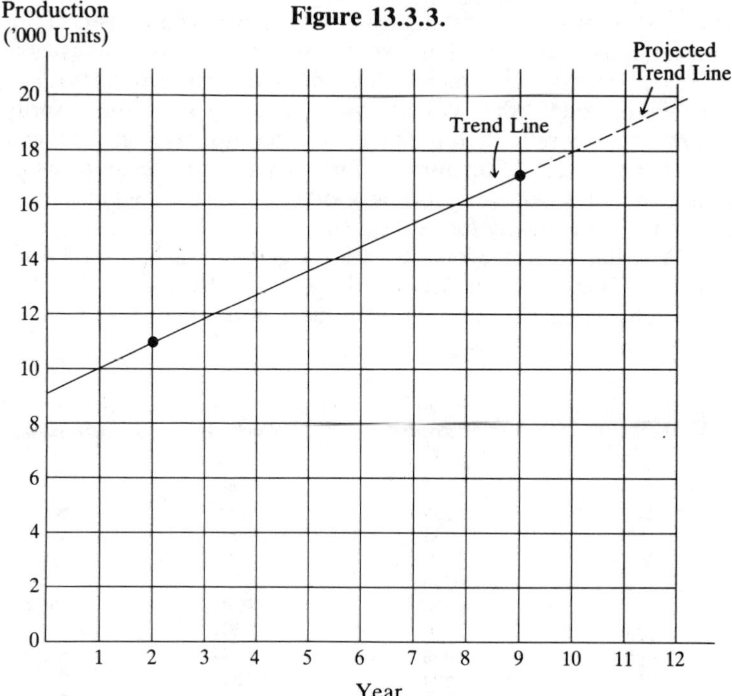

By Method of Least-Squares

The least-square method provides more accurate results than the other methods. From the graph by inspection, production for year 10 is estimated to be 17,700 units.

13.4. CORRELATION ANALYSIS

It is found from empirical evidence that many events move together. For instance, the annual demand for baby milk powder may go together with the number of babies born yearly; the sales of a certain type of rubber shoes may vary with the number of employed workers; and so on. This relationship or varying together of a series of paired items is called co-variation. If we know the number of babies born in any year we can, therefore, estimate the demand for baby milk powder in that year. Solving this kind of problem by statistical techniques is known as correlation analysis. The fact that two events vary together does not, however, necessarily indicate that one is the cause of the other. Correlation establishes co-variation but it does not necessarily follow that there is a functional relationship between the two events. Because two or more events vary together enables us to predict one if we know the other or others. Correlation analysis is, therefore, often used for forecasting.

Whether or not events do vary together can be established either by means of a scatter diagram or by calculating the coefficient of correlation. We shall use the following data as an illustration:

Number of Employed Workers *X*	*Demand for "M" Brand* *Y*	*Number of Employed Workers* *X*	*Demand for "M" Brand* *Y*
410	250	795	560
440	255	850	600
460	265	890	650
500	300	940	710
540	310	975	750
578	320	1,000	790
620	390	1,050	830
665	450	1,100	860
710	500	1,150	906
760	520	1,195	941

Scatter Diagram By plotting the paired items on a graph, we get a scatter diagram as shown in Figure 13.4.1.

Figure 13.4.1.

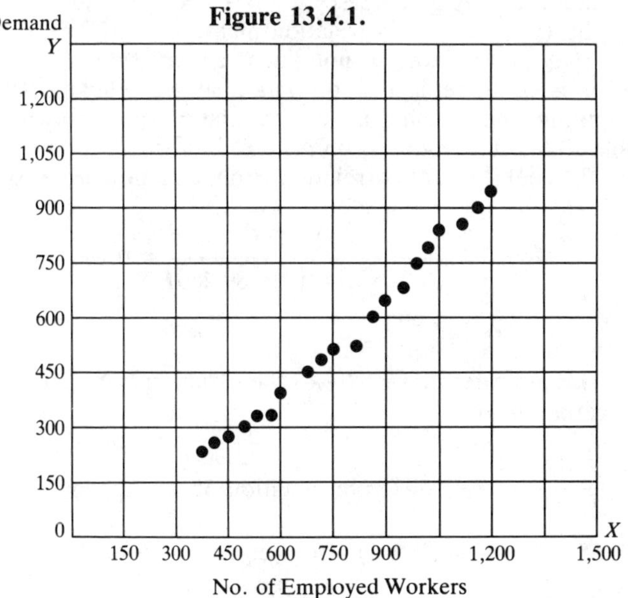

From the above scatter diagram it can be seen that the dots form themselves into the pattern of an almost straight line when they are joined together. This means that correlation is marked, or that the number of employed workers and the demand for "M" Brand do vary together. If we know what the number of employed workers will be in the future, we can predict the future demand for "M" Brand.

13.5. LINEAR REGRESSION

13.5.1. Simple

The scatter diagram gives us only a rough idea. If we want a more accurate measurement of the degree of correlation, we must compute what is known as the coefficient of correlation. This can either be positive or negative. If correlation is perfect and positive, the coefficient will be +1. That means that the paired items will be in straight line and they move in the same direction. If correlation is perfect and negative, the coefficient will be −1.0, meaning that the paired items vary in opposite directions. The coefficient of correlation in any given case is $-1 \leq r \leq 1$. It should be noted that the coefficient of correlation measures only linear covariation. It does not indicate non-linear co-variation.

If if is 0, there is no correlation at all. The mechanics of computing the coefficient of correlation are shown in the Table 13.5.1. (reproduced on page 253 *infra.*).

The coefficient of correlation (from equation 58 of Appendix B) is:

$$r_{xy} = \frac{1{,}118{,}373}{\sqrt{(1{,}058{,}940)\,(1{,}189{,}466)}} \cong 0.996$$

$$r_{xy}^2 = 0.992$$

This indicates that 99.2% of the variation in Y is explained by the variation in X.

$$\hat{b} = \frac{1{,}118{,}373}{1{,}189{,}466} \triangleq 0.94 \text{ (from equation 55 of Appendix B)}$$

$$\hat{a} = 557.85 - 0.94\,(781.4) \text{ (from equation 56 of Appendix B)}$$
$$= -176.667$$

Hence, $\hat{Y} = \hat{a} + \hat{b}X$

$\hat{Y} = -176.667 + \quad 0.94X$

From equations 68 and 69 of Appendix B

95% confidence interval: (± 32) (± 0.04)

Standard error : $(S_0 = 15.218)$ $(s_1 = 0.019)$

From equation 76 of Appendix B : $(t_0 = 11.621)$ $(t_1 = 50.574)$

From Table 4 of Appendix C $t_{.025} = 2.10$ (with 18 degrees of freedom)

If the number of employed workers has been forecasted (say from official statistics) to be 1,250, then the demand for "*M*" Brand in the next period is estimated as:

$$\hat{Y} = -176.667 + 0.94(1{,}250) \cong 998$$

Table 13.5.1.

Y Actual	X Actual	$Y - \overline{Y} = y$	$X - \overline{X} = x$	xy	y^2	x^2	$\hat{Y}$ Fitted	$Y - \hat{Y}$ Residual	$(Y - \hat{Y})^2$
250	410	−307.85	−371.4	114,335	94,772	137,938	208.647	41.353	1,710.07
255	440	−302.85	−341.4	103,393	91,718	116,554	236.854	18.146	329.28
265	460	−292.85	−321.4	94,122	85,761	103,298	255.659	9.341	87.25
300	500	−257.85	−281.4	72;559	66,487	79,186	293.268	6.731	45.31
310	540	−247.85	−241.4	59,831	61,430	58,274	330.878	−20.878	435.89
320	578	−237.85	−203.4	48,379	56,573	41,372	366.606	−46.606	2,172.12
390	620	−167.85	−161.4	27,091	28,174	26,050	406.096	−16.096	259.08
450	665	−107.85	−116.4	12,554	11,632	13,549	448.407	1.593	2.54
500	710	−57.85	− 71.4	4,130	3,347	5,098	490.717	9.283	86.17
520	760	−37.85	−21.4	810	1,433	458	537.729	−17.729	314.28
560	795	2.15	13.6	29	5	185	570.637	−10.637	113.15
600	850	42.15	68.6	2,891	1,777	4,706	622.350	−22.35	499.52
650	890	92.15	108.6	10,007	8,492	11,794	659.959	−9.959	99.18
710	940	152.15	158.6	24,131	23,150	25,154	706.971	3.029	9.17
750	975	192.15	193.6	37,200	36,922	37,481	739.879	10.121	102.43
790	1,000	232.15	218.6	50,748	53,894	47,786	763.385	26.615	708.36
830	1,050	272.15	268.6	73,099	74,066	72,146	810.397	19.605	384.36
860	1,100	302.15	318.6	96,265	91,295	101,506	857.409	2.591	6.71
906	1,150	348.15	368.6	128,328	121,208	135,866	904.42	1.58	2.50
941	1,195	383.15	413.6	158,471	146,804	171,065	946.731	−5.731	32.84
11,157	15,628	0	0	1,118,373	1,058,940	1,189,466		0	7,400.00
$\overline{Y}$ =557.85	$\overline{X}$ =781.4								

A comparison of each t value (from equation 76 of Appendix B) with the critical $t_{.025}$ value from Student's t Critical two-tail test (from Table 4 of Appendix C) indicates that both a and b are significantly different from zero.

The standard deviation [See equation (61) of Appendix B] is:

$$s = \left[\frac{1}{n-2}\sum (Y_i - \hat{Y}_i)^2\right]^{1/2} = \left[\frac{1}{18}(7{,}400)\right]^{1/2}$$

$$= 20.276 \qquad (13.5.1.1.)$$

The 95% confidence interval estimate for b [See equation (68) of Appendix B] is:

$$b = \hat{b} \pm t_{.025}\frac{s}{\sqrt{\sum x^2}}$$

$$= 0.94 \pm (2.10)\frac{20.276}{\sqrt{1{,}189{,}466}}$$

$$= 0.94 \pm 0.04 \qquad (13.5.1.2.)$$

The 95% confidence interval estimate for a [See equation (69) of Appendix B] is:

$$a = \hat{a} \pm t_{.025}s\sqrt{\frac{1}{n} + \frac{\bar{X}^2}{\sum x_i^2}}$$

$$= -176.667 \pm 32 \qquad (13.5.1.3.)$$

The 95% confidence interval estimate for Y for the next period [See equation (71) of Appendix B] is:

$$Y = \hat{Y} \pm t_{.025}s\left[\left(\frac{1}{n} + \frac{x_0^2}{\sum x^2} + 1\right)\right]^{1/2}$$

$$= 998 \pm (2.10)(20.276)\left[\left(\frac{1}{20} + \frac{468.6}{1{,}189{,}466} + 1\right)\right]^{1/2}$$

$$= 998 \pm 44 \qquad (13.5.1.4.)$$

Thus we are 95% confident that the demand for "M" Brand will be between 954 and 1,042.

13.5.2. Multiple

In multiple correlation, we try to establish how closely y, the dependable variable, is associated with two or more explanatory variables. What we are trying to do is to arrive at the multiple regression equation with estimated parameters a, b, c, etc.:

$$y = a + bx + cz + \cdots + r \qquad (13.5.2.1.)$$

where r is assumed random with zero mean. This equation can then be used for forecasting. The estimated parameters a, b, $c, \ldots,$ can be obtained through solving the following set of equations (from equation 80 of Appendix B):

$$\hat{A} = (X^T X)^{-1} X^T Y \qquad (13.5.2.2.)$$

Where $A = (a\ b\ c\ \ldots)^T$, $Y = (y_1\ y_2\ \ldots\ y_m)^T$, and

$$X = \begin{bmatrix} 1 & x_1 & z_1 & \cdots \\ 1 & x_2 & z_2 & \cdots \\ \vdots & \vdots & \vdots & \vdots \\ 1 & x_m & z_m & \cdots \end{bmatrix}$$

Let us illustrate this with the following data:

Year	*y*	*x*	*z*
1	110	95	50
2	120	95	60
3	130	100	54
4	140	105	56
5	150	110	58
6	160	115	65
7	180	120	62
8	175	125	64
9	190	130	66
10	200	135	68
11	220	140	70
12	230	145	80
13	?	150	90

Substituting the given data into equation (13.5.2.2.) results in the estimated parameters:

$$\hat{A} = \begin{bmatrix} -100.425 \\ 2.004 \\ 0.498 \end{bmatrix}$$

Hence, the estimated multiple regression equation is:

$$\hat{y} = -100.425 + \quad 2.004X + \quad 0.498z$$

From equation 95 of Appendix B 95% confidence interval	:	(± 26.9)	(± 0.466)	(± 1.006)
Standard error	:	$(s_0 = 11.911)$	$(s_1 = 0.206)$	$(s_2 = 0.446)$
From equation 100 of Appendix B	:	$(t_0 = -8.431)$	$(t_1 = 9.728)$	$(t_2 = 1.117)$
From Table 4 of Appendix C		$t_{.025} = 2.26$ (with 9 degrees of freedom)		
From equation 90 of Appendix B		$F = 326$		

Since 326 > 4.26 (obtained from F table with 2 and 9 degrees of freedom) the entire regression equation with respect to all the slope coefficients is significant. 4.26 is the critical 5% point of F from F table (Table 5 of Appendix C).

The forecast for year 13 is:

$$\hat{y}_{13} = -100.425 + 2.004(150) + 0.498(90)$$
$$\cong 245$$

From equation 84 of Appendix B,

$$R^2 = \frac{16{,}297.885}{16{,}522.918} \cong 0.9864 \qquad (13.5.2.3.)$$

$$R = \sqrt{0.9864} \cong 0.99317 \qquad (13.5.2.4.)$$

Table 13.5.2.

Year	$\hat{y}$	$(\hat{y} - \bar{\hat{y}})^2$	$(y - \bar{y})^2$	$(y - \hat{y})^2$
1	114.818	2,731.630	3,258.469	23.213
2	119.794	2,236.250	2,216.809	.042
3	126.827	1,620.546	1,375.149	10.068
4	137.842	855.036	733.489	4.657
5	148.856	332.224	291.829	1.309
6	162.358	22.326	50.169	5.560
7	170.885	14.455	166.849	83.083
8	181.899	219.514	62.679	47.596
9	192.914	667.241	525.189	8.491
10	203.928	1,357.554	1,083.529	15.429
11	214.942	2,290.484	2,800.209	25.583
12	229.937	3,950.625	3,958.549	.004
Total	2,005.000	16,297.885	16,522.918	225.035

$\bar{\hat{Y}} = 167.083$

R, like the simple correlation coefficient, r, is within the range $0 \leq R^2 \leq 1$, and R^2 gives the percentage of the variation of y that is explained by the variations in both x and z. In the numerical example above, 98.1% of the variation in y can be explained by both the variations in x and z. For forecasting purposes, it is desirable to have R very close to 1.

From equation (88) of Appendix B, the variance S^2 is:

$$S^2 = \frac{1}{n - m} (y - \hat{y})^T (y - \hat{y})$$

$$= \frac{1}{9} (225.035) \simeq 25$$

$$S = \sqrt{25} = 5 \qquad (13.5.2.5.)$$

From equation (94) of Appendix B, the 95% prediction interval for year 13 is:

$$y_{13} = \hat{y}_{13} \pm St_{.025} \, [X_{13}(X^TX)^{-1}X_{13}^T + 1]^{1/2} \qquad (13.5.2.6.)$$

where $X_{13} = [1\ \ 150\ \ 90]$; and

$$(X^T X)^{-1} = \begin{bmatrix} 5.67359 & .00888 & -.10577 \\ .00888 & .00170 & -.00334 \\ -.10577 & -.00334 & .00796 \end{bmatrix}$$

$$\begin{aligned} y_{13} &= 245 \pm (5)(2.26)(1.6867) \\ &= 245 \pm 19 \end{aligned}$$

Thus we are 95% confident that for year 13 y will be between 264 and 226.

13.6. MOVING AVERAGE

The moving average is a smoothing process used for forecasting. Suppose we are given the following data:

Date	*Data*
1	40
2	45
3	42
4	48
5	50

One way of forecasting the event for the 6th is to average the past five observations:

$$(40 + 45 + 42 + 48 + 50) \div 5 = 45$$

Should the actual event turn out to be 50, our forecast error is 5. Our forecast for the 7th will be:

$$(45 + 42 + 48 + 50 + 50) \div 5 = 47$$

In the above method of forecasting, equal weight is given to the five observations. If recent data are more valid than old data we may use three observations instead of five. Our forecast for the 6th is now:

$$(42 + 48 + 50) \div 3 \cong 47$$

And our forecast for the 7th will be:

$$(48 + 50 + 50) \div 3 \cong 49$$

In the original forecast, the most recent observation was given a weight of 1/5, whereas in the revised forecast, it was given a weight of 1/3. The optimal number of observations to use is determined by the rate of change in the process. However, once this optimal number is decided, equal weighting is given to each observation. If we think recent data should be given more weight than old data, exponential smoothing may be applied.

13.7. EXPONENTIAL SMOOTHING

In exponential smoothing, more weight is given to recent data and less to old data. The formula is:

$$\begin{aligned} f_n &= f_{n-1} + \alpha(a_{n-1} - f_{n-1}) \\ &= \alpha a_{n-1} + (1 - \alpha)f_{n-1} \end{aligned} \qquad (13.7.1.)$$

where a_{n-1} is the actual result, f_{n-1} is the old forecast, f_n is the new forecast, and $0 < \alpha < 1$ is the smoothing constant. By induction, the formula can be expanded into:

$$\begin{aligned} f_n = \alpha[a_{n-1} &+ (1 - \alpha)a_{n-2} + (1 - \alpha)^2 a_{n-3} + \cdots \\ &+ (1 - \alpha)^{n-1} a_0] + (1 - \alpha)^n f_0 \end{aligned} \qquad (13.7.2.)$$

The above formula shows clearly that weights given to the observations decrease with age. The forecast errors should be carried forward as a means of checking the stability of the process as well as the proximity of the forecast to the true mean. If the forecast errors sum to zero, the processs is stable and the forecast is close to the true mean. However, if the sum of the errors increases in the positive direction, the mean of the process has probably increased, and the reverse holds true if the sum of errors increases in the negative direction. This may warrant an increase in the smoothing constant. A good guide may be provided by the difference between the average of the forecast errors and the estimated standard deviation of the process.

13.7.1. An Illustration

Table 13.7.1. provides an illustration of the method of exponential smoothing (from equation 13.7.1.). The first actual observation is used as the first forecast.

Table 13.7.1.

Actual	*Forecast with* $\alpha = .1$	*Error*	*Forecast with* $\alpha = .5$	*Error*	*Forecast with* $\alpha = .8$	*Error*
95	—	—	—	—	—	—
100	95	− 5	95	− 5	95	− 5
110	96	−14	98	−12	99	−11
120	97	−23	104	−16	108	−12
100	99	− 1	112	+12	118	+18
130	99	−31	106	−24	104	−26
120	102	−48	118	−32	125	+ 5
130	104	−26	119	−11	121	− 9
125	107	−18	125	0	128	+ 3
135	109	−26	125	−10	126	− 9
—	112	—	130	—	133	—
Sum of squared errors		5,692		2,390		1,486
Mean squared error		632		266		165

13.8. MARKOV CHAIN PROCESSES

This technique is very often used in market research, especially in forecasting the firm's demand, and is best illustrated with an example. Let us assume that at time t_0, the total demand in the market is shared by three brands of a certain product:

$$X_0 = [.1 \quad .3 \quad .6]^T$$

The vector X_0 shows that the first brand shares 10% of the total demand, the second brand 30%, and the third brand 60%, all at time t_0. We would like to forecast the market share of each brand in time t_1. In order to do this we need a transition matrix, A.

Let us assume

$$A = \begin{bmatrix} .6 & .4 & .1 \\ .2 & .5 & .2 \\ .2 & .1 & .7 \end{bmatrix}$$

It should be noted that each column of A sums to 1, and may be explained thus. In the next period, 60% of the first brand demand remains in the first brand, 20% of its demand switches to the second brand and 20% switches to the third brand. The second column explains what will happen to the second brand; 50% will remain in the second brand, 40% will switch to the first brand and 10% to the third brand. The third column shows that 70% of the demand for the third brand will remain with the third brand, 10% will turn to the first brand, and 20% to the second brand. The shares of the market by the three brands in time t_1 may be denoted by the vector X_1, in time t_2 by X_2 and so on.

$$X_1 = AX_0 = \begin{bmatrix} .6 & .4 & .1 \\ .2 & .5 & .2 \\ .2 & .1 & .7 \end{bmatrix} \begin{bmatrix} .1 \\ .3 \\ .6 \end{bmatrix} = \begin{bmatrix} .24 \\ .29 \\ .47 \end{bmatrix}$$

X_1 shows that in period t_1, the first brand will share 24% of the total market, the second brand 29% of the total market, and the third brand 47%.

$$X_2 = AX_1 = AAX_0 = A^2X_0$$

And $$X_3 = AX_2 = A^3X_0$$

The difficulty in applying this technique lies in arriving at the transition matrix A and in detecting structural changes that may occur in the matrix over time.

13.8.1. Another Illustration

There are three brands of a certain standard product in the market: "Big", "Great" and "Large". They are manufactured and sold at the same ruling market price by three different autonomous companies. "Great" is manufactured and sold by Grand Limited.

For the year ended 31st December 19x0, the brands enjoyed the following market shares:

"Big"	...	80,000 units
"Great"	...	20,000 units
"Large"	...	100,000 units
Total Demanded	...	200,000 units

The board of directors of Grand Ltd would like to have a forecast of the demand for "Great" for the year ended 31st December 19x1. The total demand for 19x1 has been estimated by the official statistics bureau as 150,000 units.

Grand Ltd has approached you to help them in their forecast. You have arrived at the following transition probability matrix after a careful market survey:

$$A = \begin{array}{r} \\ \text{Big} \\ \text{Great} \\ \text{Large} \end{array} \begin{array}{c} \begin{array}{ccc} \text{Big} & \text{Great} & \text{Large} \end{array} \\ \begin{bmatrix} .80 & .22 & .05 \\ .10 & .70 & .10 \\ .10 & .08 & .85 \end{bmatrix} \end{array}$$

REQUIRED:

(a) Estimate the demand for "Great" for the year ended 31st December 19x1.

(b) The actual market shares for the year ended 31st December 19x1 turned out to be as follows:

"Big"	...	44,000 units
"Great"	...	19,000 units
"Large"	...	57,000 units
Total Demanded	...	120,000 units

The managing director of Grand Ltd attributed the fall of sales volume from 20,000 units in 19x0 to 19,000 units in 19x1 to the poor performance of the sales department.

Do you agree with the managing director? Give reasons.

(a) The demand composition at time t_0 is:

80/200, 20/200 and 100/200

Hence, $x_0 = [.4 \quad .1 \quad .5]^T$

$$\therefore \quad X_1 = \begin{bmatrix} .80 & .22 & .05 \\ .10 & .70 & .10 \\ .10 & .08 & .85 \end{bmatrix} \begin{bmatrix} .4 \\ .1 \\ .5 \end{bmatrix} = \begin{bmatrix} .367 \\ .160 \\ .473 \end{bmatrix}$$

The forecast for "Great" for the year ended 31st December 19x1 is 16% of the total market demand or [(0.16)(150,000) = 24,000] units.

(b) (.16)(120,000) = 192,000 units.

It turned out that "Great" enjoyed 19/120 or 15.8% of the total market demand in 19x1, not far from its forecast of 16%. Actually, Grand Ltd performed very well in comparison with its competitors; it increased its market share from 10% to 15.8% over the year.

13.9. INPUT-OUTPUT ANALYSIS

In many a manufacturing firm using process costing, its activities and operations are comparable to those of an economy. Its many processes of manufacturing can be compared to the many industries of a nation. The output of an industry becomes the inputs of itself and the other industries as well as satisfying the final demand of consumers; in thc same way, the output of a process becomes the inputs of itself and the other processes as well as satisfying the demand for finished goods. These similarities enable us to use the technique of input-output analysis (which is usually applied to establish the inter-relationships of the industries of an economy) to solve the process costing problems of an individual firm.

We assume a firm uses many processes in its manufacturing activities. Process 1 produces x_1; Process 2, x_2, and so on. Each process produces a homogeneous product. If a process produces two or more products, these can be assumed to be one homogeneous product provided they are produced in fixed combinations. The total output of each process is used as input requirement for itself and the other processes as well as finished goods for sale. If we represent x_i as the total output of process i, d_i as the proportion of the total output of process i, that is finished goods for sale; and x_{ij} as the amount of process i that goes into process j as input, the inter-relationships among these processes and variables can be expressed as a system of equations:

$$\begin{aligned} x_{11} + x_{12} + x_{13} + \cdots + x_{1n} + d_1 &= x_1 \\ x_{21} + x_{22} + x_{23} + \cdots + x_{2n} + d_2 &= x_2 \\ \vdots \\ x_{n1} + x_{n2} + x_{n3} + \cdots + x_{nn} + d_n &= x_n \end{aligned} \qquad (13.9.1.)$$

Let $\frac{x_{ij}}{x_j} = [a_{ij}]$ be the matrix of input coefficients. a_{ij} indicates the amount of process i which is required for the unit production of process j. Equation (13.9.1.) can be written as:

$$(I - A)X = D \qquad (13.9.2.)$$

where

$$A = \begin{bmatrix} a_{11} & a_{12} \cdots a_{1n} \\ a_{21} & a_{22} \cdots a_{2n} \\ \vdots & \\ a_{n1} & a_{n2} \cdots a_{nn} \end{bmatrix}; X = \begin{bmatrix} x_1 \\ x_2 \\ \vdots \\ x_n \end{bmatrix}; \text{ and } D = \begin{bmatrix} d_1 \\ d_2 \\ \vdots \\ d_n \end{bmatrix}$$

Treating our model as an open one, that is

$$\sum_{i=1}^{n} a_{ij} < 1, \ (j = 1, 2, \ldots, n)$$

where the summation is over i, we have

$$a_{oj} = 1 - \sum_{i=1}^{n} a_{ij} \qquad (13.9.3.)$$

a_{oj} is the amount of material, labour and overheads (called primary input) necessary to produce one unit of process j. If $\bar{x}_j$ is known, the primary input can be thus obtained as:

$$\sum_{j=1}^{n} a_{oj}\, \bar{x}_j \qquad (13.9.4.)$$

If $\sum_{i=1}^{n} |a_{ij}| < 1$, $(j = 1, 2, \ldots, n)$, $(I - A)$ is non-singular; hence the solution vector is:

$$\bar{X} = (I - A)^{-1}\, D \text{ from (13.9.2.)} \qquad (13.9.5.)$$

This static open input-output model can be manipulated to arrive at various kinds of information for decision-making and control. If $\bar{X} = (I - A)^{-1}D$ (from 13.9.5.) is in terms of physical units, the unit cost of $\bar{X}$ denoted by $\bar{X}_c$ can be derived as follows:

$$\frac{\partial \bar{X}}{\partial D} = (I - A)^{-1} \qquad (13.9.6.)$$

where $(I - A)^{-1} = B = \begin{bmatrix} b_{11} & b_{12} & \ldots & b_{1n} \\ b_{21} & b_{22} & \ldots & b_{2n} \\ \vdots & & & \\ b_{n1} & b_{n2} & \ldots & b_{nn} \end{bmatrix}$

$$\therefore \quad \bar{x}_{c,j} = \sum_{i=1}^{n} x_{g,i}\, b_{ij} \qquad (j = 1, 2, \ldots, n)$$

where $x_{g,i}$ is the primary input cost per unit of process i, (commodity i), that is, the total primary input cost divided by the total output, both of process i,

$$\text{or } \bar{X}_c = B^T \cdot [x_{g,1} \quad x_{g,2} \quad \ldots \quad x_{g,n}]^T \qquad (13.9.7.)$$

From this the input cost exhibit can be constructed, and the cost input coefficient matrix can be obtained.

If $\bar{X} = (I - A)^{-1}D$ (from equation (13.9.5.) is in terms of dollar amounts, the cost input coefficient matrix can be obtained directly:

$$[a_{ij}] = A$$
$$\bar{X} = (I - A)^{-1}D \qquad \text{(from equation (13.9.5.))}$$
$$\frac{\partial \bar{X}}{\partial D} = (I - A)^{-1}$$
$$= G = \begin{bmatrix} g_{11} & g_{12} & \cdots & g_{1n} \\ g_{21} & g_{22} & \cdots & g_{2n} \\ \vdots & & & \\ g_{n1} & g_{n2} & \cdots & g_{nn} \end{bmatrix} \qquad (13.9.8.)$$

This matrix gives the input cost requirements of the various processes to produce the unit dollar cost of product x_j. Hence, the unit dollar cost of $\bar{X}$ denoted by $\bar{X}_d$ is analysed into the various processes as follows for each process:

$$\bar{x}_{d,j} = \sum_{i=1}^{n} a_{oi} g_{ij} \qquad (13.9.9.)$$

where a_{oi} represents the cost of primary input requirement for the production of one unit of process i.

$\sum_{j=1}^{n} a_{oj}\bar{x}_j$ represents the primary input cost (material, labour and overheads)—from equation (13.9.4.) If we denote the total variable primary input cost as V_j, then $\frac{V_j}{a_{oj}}$ gives us the total variable cost of process j.

Hence the variable unit cost of process j is:

$$\frac{V_j}{a_{oj}} \div t_j \qquad (13.9.10.)$$

where t_j, is the total output of process j in physical units.

The following is an example. Exhibit 1 gives us the information relating to a firm producing three products x_1, x_2 and x_3 in three processes 1, 2, and 3 respectively. The total output of 1,000,000 units of process 1 (x_1) is accounted for as follows: 500,000 units become the input requirement of process 1 itself, 150,000 units become the input requirement of process 2,

10,000 units become the input of process 3, and the remaining 340,000 units form the finished goods for sale. The total output of 300,000 units and 40,000 units of processes 2 and 3 respectively can be similarly explained. The primary input cost of process 1 is \$2,000,000 made up of material \$1,200,000, labour \$600,000 and overheads \$200,000. The primary input cost of processes 2 and 3 are \$900,000 and \$100,000 respectively as indicated in Exhibit 1.

Exhibit 1

To / *From*	*Process 1*	*Process 2*	*Process 3*	*Finished Goods For Sale*	*Total Output*
	Units	Units	Units	Units	Units
x_1	500,000	150,000	10,000	340,000	1,000,000
x_2	150,000	10,000	30,000	110,000	300,000
x_3	10,000	5,000	10,000	15,000	40,000
	\$	\$	\$	\$	\$
Material	1,200,000	150,000	10,000	—	—
Labour	600,000	450,000	40,000	—	—
Overheads	200,000	300,000	50,000	—	—
Total	\$2,000,000	\$900,000	\$100,000	—	—

The physical input coefficients $\left[\frac{x_{ij}}{x_j}\right] = \left[a_{ij}\right]$

are given by the following matrix:

$$\begin{bmatrix} 0.500 & 0.500 & 0.250 \\ 0.150 & 0.033 & 0.125 \\ 0.010 & 0.017 & 0.250 \end{bmatrix}$$

Using equation (13.9.6.), we have $\frac{\partial \bar{X}}{\partial D} = (I - A)^{-1} = B$

$$= \begin{bmatrix} 2.430 & 1.293 & 2.102 \\ 0.409 & 1.270 & 1.406 \\ 0.042 & 0.046 & 1.392 \end{bmatrix}$$

The unit costs of $\bar{X}$ are therefore $B^T \cdot [x_{g,1} \quad x_{g,2} \quad x_{g,3}]^T$ from equation (13.9.7.) that is:

$$\bar{X}_c = \begin{bmatrix} \bar{x}_{c,1} \\ \bar{x}_{c,2} \\ \bar{x}_{c,3} \end{bmatrix} = \begin{bmatrix} 2.430 & 0.409 & 0.042 \\ 1.293 & 1.270 & 0.046 \\ 2.102 & 1.406 & 1.392 \end{bmatrix} \begin{bmatrix} 2 \\ 3 \\ 2.5 \end{bmatrix} = \$ \begin{bmatrix} 6.192 \\ 6.511 \\ 11.902 \end{bmatrix}$$

With the unit costs of $\bar{X}$ thus obtained, the cost input table is constructed as shown in Exhibit 2.

Exhibit 2 ($'000)

To / From	*Process 1*	*Process 2*	*Process 3*	*Finished Goods*	*Total Output*
	($'000)	($'000)	($'000)	($'000)	($'000)
x_1	3,096	929	62	2,105	6,192
x_2	977	65	195	716	1,953
x_3	119	59	119	179	476
Primary Input	2,000	900	100	—	3,000
Total	$6,192	$1,953	$476	$3,000	$11,621

The cost input coefficient matrix $\begin{bmatrix} \frac{x_{ij}}{x_j} \end{bmatrix} = \begin{bmatrix} a_{ij} \end{bmatrix}$ is constructed from Exhibit 2.

$$\begin{bmatrix} 0.500 & 0.4757 & 0.1300 \\ 0.159 & 0.0333 & 0.4097 \\ 0.019 & 0.0302 & 0.2500 \end{bmatrix}$$

Hence, using equation (13.9.3.), $a_{oj} = 1 - \sum_{i=1}^{n} a_{ij}$, we have

$$a_{o1} = 0.322; \; a_{o2} = 0.4608; \text{ and } a_{o3} = 0.2103$$

Using equation (13.9.8.), we have

$$(I - A)^{-1} = G = \begin{bmatrix} 2.4307 & 1.2312 & 1.0945 \\ 0.4334 & 1.2716 & 0.7699 \\ 0.0785 & 0.0824 & 1.3922 \end{bmatrix}$$

From equation (13.9.9.), $\bar{x}_{dj} = \sum_{i=1}^{n} a_{oi} \; g_{ij}$, Exhibit 3 is constructed:

Exhibit 3
Analysis of Unit Dollar Cost of x_j

	Process 1	*Process 2*	*Process 3*	*Total*
	$	$	$	$
$\bar{x}_{d1}$	0.783	0.200	0.017	1.000
$\bar{x}_{d2}$	0.397	0.586	0.017	1.000
$\bar{x}_{d3}$	0.352	0.355	0.293	1.000

The information in Exhibit 3 enables us to analyse the cost per physical unit of x_j into the various processes as shown in Exhibit 4.

Exhibit 4

	Process 1	*Process 2*	*Process 3*	*Total cost per unit*
	$	$	$	$
x_1	4.8483	1.2384	0.1053	6.192
x_2	2.5849	3.8154	0.1107	6.511
x_3	4.1895	4.2252	3.4873	11.902

Exhibit 4 can be expanded to show the individual elements of cost: material, labour and overheads. This is done by using the proportions of the three elements of cost given in Exhibit 1. The results are shown in Exhibit 5.

Exhibit 5
Analysis of Cost Per Physical Unit

Product	*Elements of Cost*	*Process 1*	*Process 2*	*Process 3*	*Total*
		$	$	$	$
x_1	Material	2.90898	.20640	.01053	3.12591
	Labour	1.45449	.61920	.04212	2.11581
	Overheads	.48483	.41280	.05265	.95028
		$4.84830	$1.23840	$0.10530	$6.19200
x_2	Material	1.55094	.63590	.01107	2.19791
	Labour	.77547	1.90770	.04428	2.72745
	Overheads	.25849	1.27180	.05535	1.58564
		$2.58490	$3.81540	$0.11070	$6.51100
x_3	Material	2.51370	.70420	.34873	3.56663
	Labour	1.25685	2.11260	1.39492	4.76437
	Overheads	.41895	1.40840	1.74365	3.57100
		$4.18950	$4.22520	$3.48730	$11.90200

It is very often necessary to know the variable cost per unit of production. To see how the variable cost per unit can be obtained from our example, we assume that the primary input cost is divided into their fixed and variable components as shown in Exhibit 6.

Exhibit 6
Primary Input Cost

Cost \ *Product*	x_1	x_2	x_3	*Total*
	$	$	$	$
Fixed cost	500,000	300,000	10,000	810,000
Variable Cost	1,500,000	600,000	90,000	2,190,000

Equation (13.9.4.) $\sum_{j=1}^{n} a_{oj}\bar{x}_j$ tells us how the primary input cost can be obtained once $\bar{x}_j$ is known. If, therefore, a_{oj} and the primary input cost are known, $\bar{x}_j$ can be obtained. We have

$$\bar{x}_j = \frac{p_j}{a_{oj}} \qquad (13.9.11.)$$

where p_j is the primary input cost of commodity j.

This formula can be used to arrive at the total variable cost of each commodity if the assumption is made that all costs are variable costs, that is, x_j consists of only variable cost. Once the total variable cost is obtained, the total fixed cost and the unit variable cost follow immediately. The results, using equations (13.9.10.) and (13.9.11.), are given in Exhibit 7.

Exhibit 7
Analysis of Costs into their Fixed and Variable Components

	x_1		x_2		x_3	
	Total	Unit	Total	Unit	Total	Unit
	($'000)	$	($'000)	$	($'000)	$
Fixed Cost	1,557	1.557	651	2.1702	48	1.2
Variable Cost	4,635	4.635	1,302	4.3403	428	10.7
	$6,192	$6.192	$1,953	$6.5105	$476	$11.9

The variable cost per unit thus derived is the breakeven price for deciding whether the firm should buy the article or manufacture it. Other techniques used for decision-making and control purposes can be applied to the information derived from the analysis of the input-output model.

In a full cost pricing system, the results in Exhibit 4 will enable prices to be fixed for the commodities and in differential or variable cost pricing system, the information in Exhibit 7 will be useful. If the final demand of the output D is known, equations (13.9.3.) and (13.9.4.) can be used to forecast the requirements of the primary inputs: raw materials, labour and factory overheads.

The input-output model can be used in other ways for forecasting, such as the total demand of an industrial output.

In using the model, however, we must ensure that the operating conditions of the firm are approximately true to the assumptions made in the Leontief input-output model. Besides those already mentioned it is also important to remember that the firm is assumed to operate at constant returns to scale and that the input requirements are in fixed combinations; the input coefficients must remain constant.

13.10. SELECTED BIBLIOGRAPHY

1. R.G. Brown: Smoothing, Forecasting and Predicting of Discrete Time-Series.
2. S.K. Chambers: How to Choose the Right Forecasting Technique, Harvard Business Review, July-August, 1971.
3. R.K. Chisholm and G.R. Whitaker: Forecasting Methods.
4. K.H. Han: (1) Process Costing Using Input-Output Model, The Singapore Accountant, Vol. 6, 1971
   (2) Cost and Management Accounting
5. Y, Ijiri: Input-Output Analysis in Cost Accounting, Management Accounting, N.Y., April 1968.
6. S. Makridakis and S.C. Wheelwright: Forecasting–Methods and Applications
7. O. Morgenstern: On the Accuracy of Economic Observations.
8. See the Selected Bibliography listed at the end of Appendix B.

CHAPTER 14

Business Combinations

14.1. KINDS OF COMBINATIONS

There are various forms of business combinations and there are no standard terms for describing them. Nevertheless, the more common terms will be used in this chapter. When two or more companies manufacturing and/or selling competing products or services combine, a horizontal merger takes place. This is the case of the merger of supermarkets, of oil refineries, and of rubber plantations. The term vertical merger is used to describe the combination of two companies where the output of one is the input of the other, for instance, a sugar plantation and a sugar refinery, a shoes manufacturer and a distributor of its shoes. A conglomerate refers to the combination of companies engaged in unrelated business activities, for instance, a glass manufacturer and a ship builder. Business combinations take place because of the many benefits which are expected to be derived.

14.2. BENEFITS OF MERGERS

The economic benefits of horizontal and vertical mergers are mainly the economies of scale. Buying in large quantities may get better discounts and better and more secure sources of supply may result from a merger. Larger markets may become possible. Cost savings become possible. Cost savings become possible with the avoidance of duplication in research and development, heavy plant and equipment, and management personnel. Distribution and selling costs may be reduced. If the merger is with a distributor, intermediaries are avoided and the company can now have its own distribution system. In the case of a horizontal merger, competition is reduced and price war avoided. A bigger company can engage better and specialist personnel. The financial standing and credit-worthiness of a bigger company should enhance.

14.3. SYNERGY

While many of the economies of operations should accrue to vertical and horizontal mergers, most of such economies and benefits are not available to a conglomerate. Yet, conglomerates do take place. Besides providing psychic satisfaction to captains of industry, there must be other more tangible reasons. Synergism or synergy is the term coined by experts in corporate mergers to refer to the benefits of business combinations in the sense that the whole is greater than the sum of the parts. Whether such synergism materialized in past mergers must be demonstrated by empirical surveys. Nevertheless, earnings per share can be shown in a theoretical illustration to increase in some situations.
Let us use the following as illustration:

Table 14.3.1.

	Company *U*	Company *V*
Net profit after tax	Π_u = \$100,000	Π_v = \$40,000
Number of ordinary shares	S_u = 50,000	S_v = 40,000
Earnings per share	E_u = \$2	E_v = \$1
Market price per share	P_u = \$50	P_v = \$15
Price-Earnings ratio	R_u = 25	R_v = 15
Net assets value per share	\$40	\$15

Suppose Company *U* acquires Company *V* by issuing its shares to the shareholders of Company *V* at the exchange ratio of 3/10, that is, 3/10 of one share in Company *U* is exchanged for one share in Company *V*. The expected earnings per share of the merged company is:

Table 14.3.2.

	Merged Company
Net profit after tax	Π_{uv} = \$140,000
Number of ordinary shares [(50,000) + 3/10 (40,000)]	S_{uv} = 62,000
Earnings per share	E_{uv} = \$ 2.258

The above illustration demonstrates that the shareholders of Company *U* benefit by the increase in earnings per share of their holdings from $2 to $2.258. If the merged company can maintain the acquiring company's price-earnings ratio of 25, the market price of its share will increase from $50 to $56.45, enabling the shareholders of both companies to reap capital gains.

If Company *V* acquires Company *U* at the exchange ratio of 10/3, the earnings per share of the merged company is:

Net profit after tax	$140,000
Number of ordinary shares	
(40,000) + 10/3 (50,000)	206,667
Earnings per share	$ 0.677

It can be seen that it is not immediately beneficial for Company *V* to acquire Company *U* at the exchange ratio of 10/3. As a matter of fact, whenever the paid price-earnings ratio (price per share offered divided by the earnings per share of the acquired company) exceeds the price-earnings ratio of the acquiring company, earnings per share of the merged company becomes less than that of the acquiring company, and vice versa.

The above analysis is made on the assumption that total earnings of the merged company are equal to the combined earnings of the two separate companies and that other things such as the price-earnings ratio of the acquiring company remain equal. The expected earnings as well as the price-earnings ratio of the merged company, which may not materialize in the way illustrated above, are key factors to be considered in a combination proposal. Sometimes a combination takes place even if there is dilution in the earnings per share of the acquiring company provided the expected earnings per share will increase in time to compensate for such initial disadvantages.

14.4. BASES USED FOR EXCHANGE RATIO

14.4.1. Book Values

Book values are seldom useful for decision-making, but may be used in addition to other bases, especially when accounting ratios are important considerations in the combination proposal. A company may acquire another company in order to bolster up its accounting ratios if these are significant ratios in the eyes of the financial world. For example, if the combination can be construed as a pooling of interest, the earnings per share ratio as well as the book value debt-equity ratio may be improved.

14.4.2. Earnings

Earnings per share may sometimes serve as an exchange ratio if it is believed that the price of a share is a function of its earnings. Using this basis ignores the quality of the earnings in the sense that risks are associated with earnings. For instance, the share of a highly-geared company, that is, a company with a high debt-equity ratio, is expected to have higher earnings than the share of a company with a lower leverage, other things being equal. For merger of companies belonging to the same equivalent risk class, earnings per share may sometimes be used as a basis for arriving at the exchange ratio. In our illustration previously given, (Table 14.3.1.) the exchange ratio using this basis is $\frac{1}{2}$ of one share in Company *U* for every share held in Company *V* if the former acquires the latter, the earnings per share being $2 for Company *U* and $1 for Company *V*.

Earnings per share are important because an acquiring company does not wish to dilute its earnings per share ratio.

14.4.3. Market Price Per Share

Market price per share is a figure determined by the forces of supply and demand in the Stock Exchange Market, and if the market is a perfect one and the shares of the acquiring and acquired company are broadly and deeply traded, then the market price per share should be a good indicator of the value of the company represented by that share. Sometimes, however, for various reasons such as low dividends declared by a company and under-utilization of its resources resulting in poor earnings, the market price of the company's share may not indicate its real value. Nevertheless, it can be strongly contended that the market price at least represents the floor value of the company. So in many mergers shareholders of the acquired company are expected to demand a price which is higher than this minimum, the margin of this difference being dependent on their bargaining power.

If market price per share is used as a basis for arriving at the exchange ratio for the previous illustration (Table 14.3.1.), the exchange ratio is 3/10 of one share in Company *U* for one share in Company *V* if the former acquires the latter.

14.4.4. Dividends

If the acquired company has adopted a stabilized dividend policy its shareholders may expect regular dividends, and if this is the case, dividends may form a basis for determining the exchange ratio. Its shareholders may accept a price only if they can be assured of a regular dividend or its equivalent that is no less favourable than before the merger.

Dividends seldom form a basis for negotiation mainly because the merged company may not follow the dividend policies of the previous separate companies.

14.4.5. Net Asset Value

Instead of accepting the market price per share, many companies engage professional valuers to value the assets of the companies to arrive at their selling prices. All liabilities are then deducted to arrive at the net assets value. When this is divided by the number of shares, the result is net assets value per share. In our illustration (Table 14.3.1.) using this basis gives an exchange ratio of 3/8 (15:40).

Net assets value per share is a fair basis if the market price does not represent the real value of the company. This basis is also used in cases where the acquiring company intends to dispose of some of the assets and discharge some of the liabilities. But the net aggregate of the selling prices of individual assets less liabilities ignores intangible values that may be attached to the establishments and their personnel.

14.5. A MODEL BY K.D. LARSON AND N.J. GONEDES

Larson and Gonedes describe a model which arrives at the maximum exchange ratio acceptable to the acquiring company. Using the symbols of the illustration in Table 14.3.1., the following equations may be obtained:

The market price per share of the acquiring company, Company U, is:

$$P_u = \frac{R_u \Pi_u}{S_u} \qquad (14.5.1.)$$

The market price per share of the acquired company, Company V, is:

$$P_v = \frac{R_v \Pi_v}{S_v} \qquad (14.5.2.)$$

If R_{uv} is designated as the expected price-earnings ratio of the merged company, the expected market price per share of the merged company is:

$$P_{uv} = \frac{R_{uv}(\Pi_u + \Pi_v)}{S_u + XS_v} \qquad (14.5.3.)$$

where X is the exchange ratio.

Equating equation (14.5.1.) with equation (14.5.3.) and solving for X gives the maximum exchange ratio acceptable to Company U as:

$$X_u = \frac{R_{uv}(\Pi_u + \Pi_v) - R_u\Pi_u}{(R_u\Pi_u)\left(\frac{S_v}{S_u}\right)} \qquad (14.5.4.)$$

$$= 0.07R_{uv} - 1.25 \qquad (14.5.5.)$$

For Company V equation (14.5.3.) becomes:

$$\frac{R_{uv}(\Pi_u + \Pi_v)}{S_v + \frac{S_u}{X}} \qquad (14.5.6.)$$

Equating equation (14.5.2.) with equation (14.5.6.) and solving for X gives the minimum exchange ratio acceptable to Company V as:

$$X_v = \frac{R_v \Pi_v \, S_u/S_v}{R_{uv}(\Pi_u + \Pi_v) - R_v \Pi_v} \tag{14.5.7.}$$

$$= \frac{7.5}{1.4R_{uv} - 6} \tag{14.5.8.}$$

The graphic representation of equations (14.5.5.) and (14.5.8.) are shown in figure (14.5.1.). The intersection of the two curves at ($X = 0.3$, $R_{uv} = 22.143$) gives the weighted average price-earnings ratio of the two companies:

$$R^*_{uv} = \frac{P_u S_u + P_v S_v}{\Pi_u + \Pi_v} \tag{14.5.9.}$$

$$= \frac{3{,}100{,}000}{140{,}000} = 22.143$$

And $X^* = 0.3$ (14.5.10.)

Figure 14.5.1.
(*Not drawn to scale*)

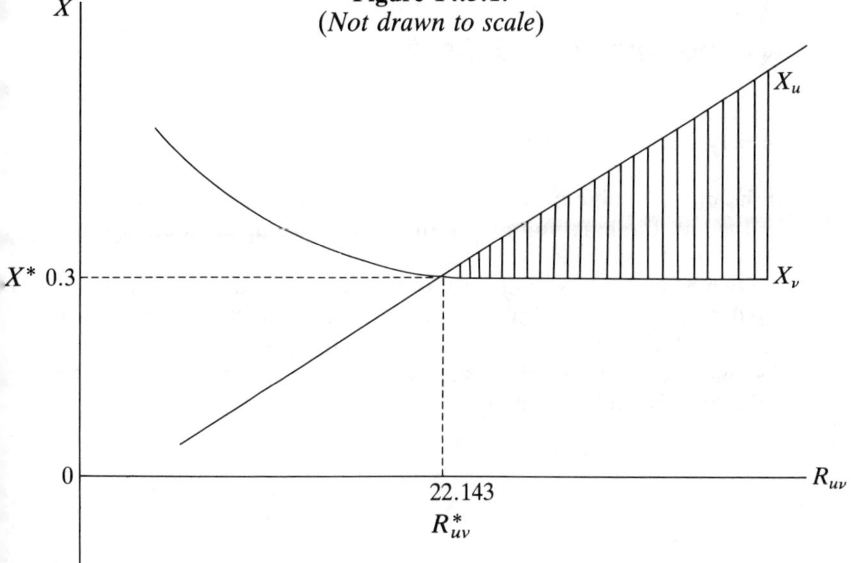

If the formula of price-earnings ratio is used for arriving at the market price per share, the earnings and market price per share of the merged company at the point of intersection are:

$$E^*_{uv} = \frac{140{,}000}{62{,}000} = \$2.258 \qquad (14.5.11.)$$

$$P^*_{uv} = (22.143)(2.258) = \$50 \qquad (14.5.12.)$$

Any exchange ratio above and to the left of the X_u curve will not be acceptable to Company U and any exchange ratio below the X_v curve will not be acceptable to company V. Any exchange ratio to the left of R^*_{uv}, that is to the left of the point of intersection, will not be acceptable to one of the two companies. Therefore, only exchange ratios in the shaded area are acceptable to both companies and represent the area for negotiation. Company U will try to strike a bargain for an exchange ratio as close to the X_v curve as possible, and Company V, as close to the X_u curve as possible.

The model is useful for arriving at an exchange ratio when the expected R_{uv} of the merged company cannot be predicted with certainty. It also indicates the minimum R_{uv} below which a merger will not usually take place since it is to the disadvantage of one party.

14.6. DISCOUNTED CASH FLOW

14.6.1. Market Price Plus Synergy

If the market value of the acquired company's shares represents its real value, the maximum price that the acquiring company should be willing to pay is its total market value plus the present value of the synergy which is expected to accrue to the merged company. Assuming an annual synergistic net cash inflow of $\$X_t$ to be generated for n years after the proposed merger and using a rate of discount adjusted for the risks of the expected synergy gives the following formula for arriving at the maximum price:

$$M_s = S_v P_v + \sum_{t=1}^{n} X_t (1 + k)^{-t} \qquad (14.6.1.1.)$$

where M_s is the maximum price the acquiring company is willing to pay,
S_v is the total number of shares of the acquired company,
P_v is the market price per share of the acquired company, and
k is the risk-adjusted rate of discount.

Assuming k is 15%, X_t is a constant flow of \$15,000, $n \to \infty$, and using Table 14.3.1. for data relating to the acquired company, Company V, gives M as:

$$M_s = (40{,}000)(15) + \frac{15{,}000}{0.15}$$

$$= \$700{,}000 \qquad (14.6.1.2)$$

14.6.2. Incremental Cash Flows

Another way of arriving at the valuation of the acquired company is to compare the present value of the net cash inflows of the acquiring company without the merger and that of the merged company with the merger, both from the date of the proposed merger. The difference less the market value of the acquired company's liabilities is the maximum price. In symbols:

$$M_d = \sum_{t=1}^{n} I_t(1 + r)^{-t} + I_{n+1}(r - e)^{-1}(1 + r)^{-n} - L \quad (14.6.2.)$$

where M_d is the maximum price the acquiring company is willing to pay for the acquired company,
I_t is the annual differential after-tax cash flows in year t, that is, the annual after-tax net cash flows of the merged company less the annual after-tax net cash flow of the acquiring company assuming that the merger does not take place.
r is the appropriate rate of discount,
e is the constant annual growth rate of I_n after the nth year, and
L is the market price of the acquired company's liabilities on the date of acquisition.

In the above model, the individual I_t for the first n years must be forecasted after which the annual growth rate is assumed to stabilize at e per annum, and the planning horizon is infinite.

14.7. METHODS OF FINANCING

Methods of financing that can be used by the acquiring company include: issue of ordinary shares, issue of preference shares, issue of debentures and payment in cash.

If the acquiring company has surplus cash which has no other better investment opportunity, payment in cash will enhance greatly the earnings per share of the merged company since its total number of shares remain the same while the combined total earnings increase. However, the desire of the acquired company's shareholders to participate in the ownership of the merged company as well as lack of surplus cash of the acquiring company often constitutes two main obstacles to the adoption of this method of finance.

The issue of ordinary shares is very common, but from the viewpoint of the acquiring company this method may dilute control, and earnings per share will not be as high as in the case of cash payment. In order to preserve as high as possible the earnings per share ratio, debentures and preference shares are sometimes issued in settlement. Such debentures and preference shares may be attractive to the acquired company's shareholders who wish to receive constant annual income but may not be sufficient inducement to those who desire ownership participation. To the latter convertible preference shares, or a combination of ordinary shares and convertibles, may be appealing. While the primary earnings per share ratio is not affected by the issue of convertibles, the diluted earnings per share is, and this must be taken into account before the final decision is made.

14.8. GROWTH BY MERGER VIS-A-VIS BY INTERNAL EXPANSION

Besides the benefits of business combinations briefly mentioned in Section 14.2, growth by merger, especially through purchasing the shares of a company making it a subsidiary, has many advantages over growth by internal expansion. Its goodwill, reputation, expertise, personnel, organizational structure, marketing and distributing system and so on may be retained intact if so desired by the acquiring company. It is sometimes easier to improve on what is already established than to start from scratch. Tax advantages may be possible.

A subsidiary is a separate legal entity so that should it fail because of the risky nature of its business, the loss is limited to the amount of the shares paid for by the acquiring company; expansion into a risky venture may ruin the company otherwise. Acquiring a subsidiary through issue of shares and/or debentures becomes the best choice if lack of liquid resources prevents a company from growing by means of internal expansion.

By a process known as pyramiding the acquiring company can control many companies with a total amount of paid-up capital many times its own. This is illustrated in Figure (14.8)

Figure 14.8

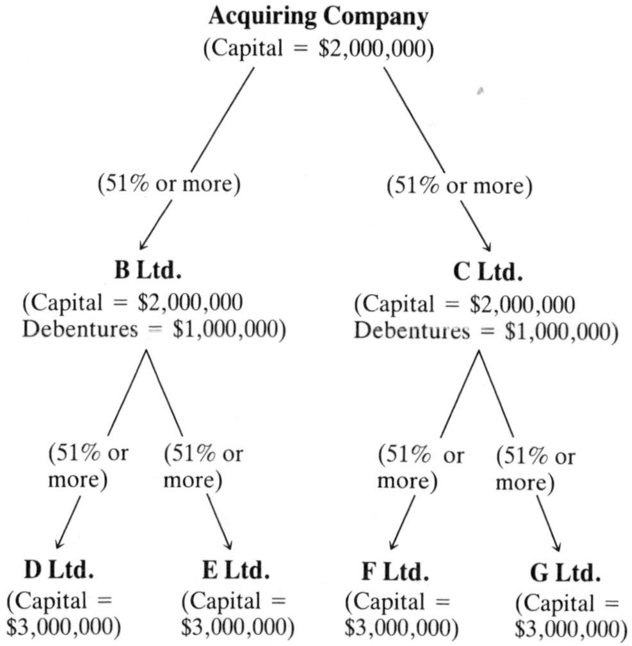

Acquiring Company
(Capital = $2,000,000)

(51% or more) → **B Ltd.** (Capital = $2,000,000 Debentures = $1,000,000)

(51% or more) → **C Ltd.** (Capital = $2,000,000 Debentures = $1,000,000)

B Ltd.:
(51% or more) → **D Ltd.** (Capital = $3,000,000)
(51% or more) → **E Ltd.** (Capital = $3,000,000)

C Ltd.:
(51% or more) → **F Ltd.** (Capital = $3,000,000)
(51% or more) → **G Ltd.** (Capital = $3,000,000)

14.9. SELECTED BIBLIOGRAPHY

1. W.W. Alberts and J.E. Segall, eds.: The Corporate Merger.
2. K.D. Larson and N.J. Gonedes: "Business Combinations: An Exchange—Ratio Determination Model," Accounting Review, October 1969.
3. G.D. McCarthy: Acquisitions and Mergers.
4. R.W. Moon: Business Mergers and Take-Over Bids.
5. D.C. Mueller: "A Theory of Conglomerate Mergers", Quarterly Journal of Economics, November 1969
6. G.C. Philippatos: Essentials of Financial Management.
7. J.F. Weston and E.F. Brigham: Managerial Finance.

CHAPTER 15

Financial Analysis

15.1. USES OF FINANCIAL STATEMENTS

Management need information for performing their functions of control and planning. Accounting information is one of the most important sources of quantitative data used in this regard. If managerial decisions are based on accounting data, their correctness and rationale must be greatly influenced by the adequacy and accuracy of these data. But accounting information is the end-product of accounting processes. Hence, management and those who use accounting data must have an understanding of these processes.

Accounting has been defined as the recording, classifying and summarizing of business transactions in a systematic manner and the making of reports on them. Management requires quantitative data which can be measured in two ways: in physical units (like tons and metres) and in monetary units. The accounting process records all business transactions in a common unit of measurement, that is, in monetary units. This does not mean that non-quantifiable data, such as social and political changes, are not important in the decision-making process since many a good entrepreneur would adopt measures to cope with such changes long before they can be reduced to measurable terms. But accounting can perform its function only if the business activities to be recorded are capable of being expressed in terms of money.

Besides management there are other people who find accounting information useful: investors, creditors, employees, governmental agencies and the general public. Investors need to decide whether to buy or sell shares; creditors, to reject or grant loans and credit; employees to claim or not to claim for wage increases; governmental agencies need to decide how much tax to collect and what statistics to compile; and the general public wish to see that the company charges a fair price for its product. Accounting information is available in various forms, but mainly from the Revenue Statement and the Balance Sheet.

15.2. PRACTICAL TOOLS OF ANALYSIS

We will now describe some of the tools of analysis which can be employed as aids to interpreting these statements. The main tools include:

(1) Funds Flow Statement.
(2) Cash Flow Statement.
(3) Accounting Ratios.

15.3. FUNDS FLOW STATEMENT (TOTAL RESOURCES)

The term "funds" is explained as having the meaning of means of payment or resources with which business transactions can be financed. A balance sheet indicates the sources and applications of an enterprise's funds, but it is a static device showing a position at a specific point of time. A funds flow statement, on the other hand, attempts to analyse the changes of the position between two dates, which may be a month or a year apart. In other words, a funds flow statement shows the funds which are generated in a period and how such funds are applied in the period.

The funds flow statement has been widely used by both internal and external analysts of financial statements. When the funds statement is reviewed over a number of accounting periods, the financial policies of management may be revealed, and the strength or weakness of such policies. The funds statement also provides guidance to management in planning future operations. It helps to explain or answer questions such as:

(1) Why is there a shortage of funds despite good profits?
(2) Should the dividend policy of the company be reviewed?
(3) Has plant expansion been financed from external borrowing or ploughed-back profits or capital contributions?
(4) What finance was resorted to in redeeming the redeemable preference shares:

The funds statement reveals the effects of efficient or poor financial planning, and thus serves a useful purpose together with other budgets in helping management to measure operating efficiency and formulate financial policies for the future. In this respect a forecasted funds flow statement should be prepared. This is done through the preparation of a forecasted balance sheet and a profit and loss statement.

Business transactions which result in accounting entries being recorded on them can be divided into two main groups:

(A) other-affecting transactions
(B) non-other-affecting transactions

Transactions of (A) type affect other entities external to the accounting entity with which we are concerned. Every transaction of (A) type creates a source and an application of funds. This can be illustrated diagrammatically:

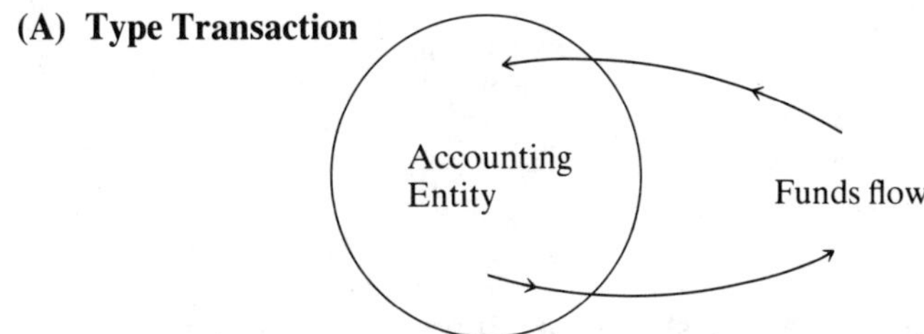

The following transactions show how funds are derived and applied:

Type (A) Transactions	*Source of Funds*	*Application of Funds*
1. Purchase of merchandise on credit	+Creditor	+Stock
2. Sale of merchandise on credit	−Stock	+Debtor
3. Payment of a debt	−Cash at bank	−Creditor
4. Receipt of a debt	−Debtor	+Cash at bank
5. Issue of shares payable in full on application	+Paid-up Capital	+Cash at bank
6. Redemption of shares	−Cash at bank	−Paid-up Capital
7. Payment of expenses	−Cash at bank	+Expenses (which reduces net profit)
8. Sale of a fixed asset for cash	−Fixed asset	+Cash at bank
9. Purchase of a fixed asset for cash	−Cash at bank	+Fixed asset
10. Finance the purchase of a building by mortgaging it	+Mortgage on land & building	+Land and building
11. Redeem the mortgage, i.e. repayment of the loan	−Cash at bank	−Mortgage on land and building

Transactions of (B) type do not affect other entities: hence they do not involve funds flow. Type (B) transactions include revaluation of assets, writing off goodwill or preliminary expenses and issue of bonus shares. They may be represented diagrammatically below:

(B) Type Transaction

When a funds statement is prepared, only type (A) transactions are considered; type (B) transactions do not involve funds and are not shown. From what has been discussed by us, we can discern four sources of funds and four applications of funds in the (A) type transactions of a company:

Sources: (1) Capital contributions
(2) Funds earnings from trading operations
(3) Increases in liabilities
(4) Decreases in assets

Uses: (1) Capital withdrawals
(2) Funds loss from trading operations
(3) Decreases in liabilities
(4) Increases in assets

There are different ways of presenting a funds flow statement. The following are illustrative examples:

Illustration 1
The following accounting information is extracted from the annual reports of Recurd Ltd., for the years ended 31st December:

REVENUE STATEMENT

	19x6	19x7
Sales	$18,000,000	$16,500,000
Less Cost of Sales	13,500,000	12,540,000
Gross Profit	$ 4,500,000	$ 3,960,000
Operating Expenses:-		
Selling	$ 2,160,000	$ 1,320,000
Administration	1,140,000	1,215,000
	$ 3,300,000	$ 2,535,000
Net operating revenue	$ 1,200,000	$ 1,425,000
Interest received	75,000	30,000
	$ 1,275,000	$ 1,455,000
Less Loss on Sale of Investment	—	255,000
Net profit for year	$ 1,275,000	$ 1,200,000
Less Dividends paid	675,000	450,000
	$ 600,000	$ 750,000
Balance of unappropriated profits brought forward from previous year	2,985,000	3,585,000
Balance of unappropriated profits carried forward	$ 3,585,000	$ 4,335,000

Balance Sheets as at 31st December

		19x6		19x7
Paid-up Capital		$4,500,000		$ 4,500,000
Profit and Loss Appropriation		3,585,000		4,335,000
Creditors		900,000		1,050,000
Bills Payable		450,000		525,000
Total Equities		$9,435,000		$10,410,000
Plant at cost 1st January	$6,000,000		$6,150,000	
Additions	150,000		1,575,000	
	6,150,000		7,725,000	
Less Provision for Depreciation	1,725,000		2,340,000	
		$4,425,000		$ 5,385,000
Investments		960,000		300,000
Stock		750,000		1,500,000
Bills Receivable		375,000		1,005,000
Debtors		1,500,000		2,055,000
Cash at Bank		1,425,000		165,000
Total Assets		$9,435,000		$10,410,000

Additional Information:

(1) It was proposed to sell the remaining Investments in early 19x8.

(2) There were no sales of plant in 19x6 and 19x7.

REQUIRED:

A statement of sources and application of funds for the year ended 31st December 19x7.

RECURD LIMITED
Statement of Sources and Applications of Funds
for the year ended 31st December 19x7

		($'000)
Sources		
1. Trading Operations		
Net operating revenue	$1,425	
Add non-cash item—		
Depreciation on plant	615	$2,040
2. Interest received		30
3. Proceeds from sale of investments		405
4. Decrease in cash at bank		1,260
5. Increase in current liabilities—		
Creditors	$ 150	
Bills Payable	75	225
Total Source of Funds		$3,960
Applications		
1. Payment of dividends		$ 450
2. Purchase of plant		1,575
3. Increases in current assets—		
Stock	$ 750	
Bills receivable	630	
Debtors	555	1,935
Total Application of Funds		$3,960

Illustration 2

The following information is extracted from the annual report of Fantasy Limited:

(1) Balance sheet as at 31 December

	19x5	*19x6*	*19x7*
Paid-up Capital			
$1 fully paid redeemable preference shares	$ 50,000	$ 50,000	$ 25,000
$1 fully paid ordinary shares	100,000	110,000	110,000
Capital Redemption Reserve	—	—	25,000
Profit & Loss Appropriation	4,151	8,000	12,578
Debentures	40,000	33,000	25,500
Creditors	31,462	29,400	27,158
Taxation Payable	6,000	3,600	2,000
Dividend Payable	2,000	2,000	2,000
	$233,613	$236,000	$229,236
Goodwill	$ 40,000	$ 34,000	$ 25,000
Land and buildings	92,620	102,620	102,620
Plant and machinery	17,000	17,000	16,000
Stock	29,378	39,800	44,453
Debtors	46,195	40,200	35,623
Bank	8,420	2,380	5,540
	$233,613	$236,000	$229,236

(2) During the period 1st January 19x6 to 31st December, 19x7, dividends paid = $14,500, Taxation paid = $8,200.

(3) In 19x7, some of the redeemable preference shares were redeemed.

(4) Plant and machinery was depreciated by $7,500 and there was no sale of plant and machinery during this period.

(5) $10,000 of the Debentures will be redeemed in early 19x8.

(6) In 19x6, there was an issue of 10,000 fully-paid bonus shares of $1 each out of a capital reserve created by the revaluation of land and buildings.

REQUIRED:

A statement of sources and application of funds for the period 1st January, 19x6 to 31st December, 19x7.

FANTASY LIMITED
Funds Statement for the period 1st January, 19x6 to 31st December 19x7

Sources

1. Trading operations		
Net profit for the period before tax	$67,127	
Add non-cash item:		
Depreciation of plant and machinery	7,500	$74,627
2. Decrease in: (i) Debtors	$10,572	
(ii) Bank	2,880	13,452
Total Source of Funds		$88,079

Applications

1. Purchase of plant	$ 6,500
2. Redemption of redeemable preference shares	25,000
3. Redemption of debentures	14,500
4. Payment of dividends	14,500
5. Payment of taxation	8,200
6. Increase in stock	15,075
7. Decrease in creditors	4,304
Total Application of Funds	$88,079

WORKINGS
Profit and Loss Appropriation

Capital Redemption Reserve	25,000	Balance b/f	$ 4,151
Goodwill written off	15,000	Net profit for the period	67,127
Taxation payable	4,200		
Dividend payable	14,500		
Balance c/f	12,578		
	$71,278		$71,278

Taxation Payable

Cash	$ 8,200	Balance b/f	$ 6,000
Balance b/f	2,000	Profit & Loss Appropriation	4,200
	$10,200		$10,200

Plant and machinery a/c.

Plant at book value on 1st January 19x6	$17,000
Less Depreciation written off	$7,500
	$9,500
Add Purchase of plant during the period	6,500
Plant at book value on 31st December 19x7	$16,000

Illustration 3

The following comparative statements for the years ended 31st December are summarized from the accounting reports of Oedipus Limited:

		19x1		19x2		19x3
Creditors		$ 35,000		$ 40,000		$50,000
Bank		20,000		30,000		30,000
Provision for taxation		6,000		8,000		10,000
Provision for dividend		3,000		4,000		5,000
		$ 64,000		$ 82,000		$ 95,000
Capital (shares of $1 each fully paid)		45,000		45,000		90,000
Capital reserves		—		91,000		46,000
Revenue reserves		90,000		100,000		110,000
Profit & Loss Appropriation		3,000		4,000		10,000
		$202,000		$322,000		$351,000
Cash		$ 1,000		$ 500		$ 500
Debtors		50,000		$ 60,000		50,000
Stock		60,000		80,500		115,500
		$111,000		$141,000		$166,000
Land and buildings		71,000		162,000		162,000
Plant and Machinery at cost	$25,000		25,000		30,000	
Less Provision for Depreciation	5,000		6,000		7,000	
		20,000		19,000		23,000
		$202,000		$322,000		$351,000

Other information relating to the company during this period (that is from 1st January, 19x2 to 31st December, 19x3):

(*a*) Taxation paid to the Comptroller of Income Tax amounted to $52,000.

(*b*) Dividend paid to shareholders amounted to $45,000.

(*c*) A sum of $20,000 was transferred to Revenue Reserves from the Profit and Loss Appropriation Account.

(*d*) The capital reserve of $91,000 in 19x2 arose out of a revaluation of land and buildings. Of this sum, $45,000 was utilized in a bonus issue of ordinary shares in 19x3.

(*e*) A new plant was installed during the period. An old machine, costing $6,000 and depreciated to $4,500, was sold for $4,000 cash.

(*f*) The banker of Oedipus Limited requested that the unsecured bank overdraft should be reduced from $30,00 to $10,000 by the middle of 19x4.

REQUIRED:
A source and application of funds statement for the period 1st January, 19x2 to 31st December, 19x3.

OEDIPUS LIMITED
Funds Flow Statement for the period 1st January 19x2 to 31st December 19x3

Funds were derived from			
1. Trading operations			
Net profit before income tax		$130,000	
Add Non-funds items:			
Depreciation of plant and machinery	$3,500		
Loss on sale of plant	500	4,000	$134,000
2. Proceeds from sale of plant			4,000
3. Increases in Current liabilities:			
Creditors		$ 15,000	
Bank overdraft		10,000	25,000
4. Decreases in Current Assets:			
Cash		$ 500	500
Total Source of Funds			$163,500
Funds were applied to			
1. Purchase of a new plant			$ 11,000
2. Payment of income tax			52,000
3. Payment of dividends			45,000
4. Increase in Current assets			
Stock		$ 55,500	55,500
Total Application of Funds			$163,500

WORKINGS
Profit and Loss Appropriation

Balance, 1.1.19x2		$ 3,000
Add Net Profit for the period before tax		130,000
Available for distribution		$133,000
Distributed as follows:		
Provision for income tax	$ 56,000	
Provision for dividend	47,000	
Revenue Reserves	20,000	123,000
Balance, 31.12.19x3		$ 10,000

Provision for taxation

Balance brought forward	$ 6,000
Add Profit and loss appropriation	56,000
	$62,000
Deduct Amount paid to Inland Revenue Department	52,000
Balance carried forward	$10,000

Provision for dividend

Balance brought forward	$ 3,000
Add Profit and loss appropriation	47,000
	$50,000
Deduct Amount paid to shareholders	45,000
Balance carried forward	$ 5,000

Plant and Machinery at Cost

Balance brought forward	$25,000
Add Purchase	11,000
	$36,000
Deduct Sale of plant	6,000
Balance carried forward	$30,000

Provision for depreciation–Plant and machinery

Balance brought forward	$ 5,000
Add Depreciation provided during the period	3,500
	$ 8,500
Deduct Depreciation on the plant sold	1,500
	$7,000

Sale of Plant

Provision of depreciation on plant sold	$ 1,500
Proceeds from sale of plant	4,000
Loss on sale	500
Cost of plant sold	$ 6,000

15.4. WORKING CAPITAL

The above concept of funds flow is sometimes referred to as total resources flow, that is, the flow of financial resources into and out of the business entity. Another concept of funds flow called the working capital concept, is sometimes used to show the movements of financial resources that result in a net change in working capital for a period of time, working capital being current assets less current liabilities. Under this definition of funds any movement of resources that affects the working capital of a company necessarily results in a funds flow. Hence, depreciation which is a non-funds item under the total resources concept, is a flow of funds under the working capital concept, being a release of services from fixed assets which is a non-current item into inventory which is a current asset. Even if direct costing is used, a depreciation is a flow of working capital, being a release of services from fixed assets which is a non-current item. Since it does not flow into another non-current class, it must necessarily flow into a current class, all items in the total resources being exhaustively divided into two mutually exclusive sets: current and non-current. Depreciation is debited to the profit and loss account which belongs to the current set. Similarly the provision for dividend and the provision for tax in a period are flows of resources from the profit and loss appropriation account (a non-current item) into current liabilities (a component of working capital) and they therefore constitute funds flow. These examples may be represented by the diagram below where the big circle is total resources, *WC* = Working Capital, *FA* = Fixed Assets and *PL* = Profit and Loss Appropriation Account.

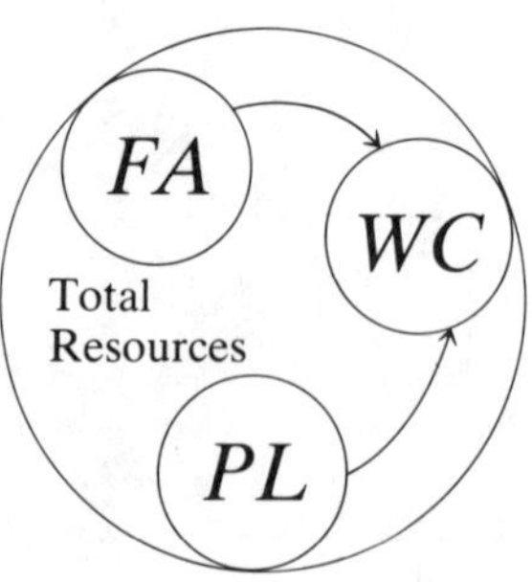

The two concepts of funds flow are illustrated with the example of the Trigola Corporation.

The Trigola Corporation is a medium-sized company which has been operating successfully in Singapore for the past twenty years. To maintain its leadership position in the industry, the board of directors proposes an expansion programme involving an addition of a new plant and other facilities as well as the disposal of old buildings and equipment. The following are the actual and forecasted financial and operating statements which are prepared from the records kept by the company and after making a detailed analysis of the proposed expansion programme, (the way it will be financed, and the consequences on the company's assets, liabilities and capital structure):

TRIGOLA CORPORATION
Balance Sheet as at 31st December

Assets	*19x1 Actual* ($'000)	*19x2 Forecasted* ($'000)
Currents Assets		
Cash	$ 1,167	$1,075
Sundry debtors, less provision for bad debts	1,264	1,318
Government Stock, at cost	1,634	532
Stock	1,999	2,123
Prepaid expenses	374	391
Total	$ 6,438	$ 5,439
Investments		
Government Stocks at cost	$ 1,408	$ 245
Fixed Assets		
Land	$ 389	$ 387
Plant at cost	$14,405	$16,267
Less Provision for depreciation	8,512	9,121
Net	$ 5,893	$ 7,146
Transportation equipment, at cost	$ 2,714	$ 2,919
Less Provision for depreciation	1,140	1,194
Net	$ 1,574	$ 1,725
Total fixed assets	$ 7,856	$ 9,258
Total Assets	$15,702	$14,942
Equities		
Current Liabilities		
Sundry creditors	$ 1,698	$ 1,876
Provision for income tax	2,548	1,375
Provision for dividends	129	129
Long-term debt due within one year	14	16
Total	$ 4,389	$ 3,396
Long-term Debt	$ 274	$ 305
Shareholders' Funds		
7% Preference shares ($1 per share fully paid)	1,801	1,801
Ordinary shares ($1 per share fully paid)	4,351	4,351
Profit and loss a/c (retained earnings)	4,887	5,089
Total	$11,039	$11,241
Total Equities	$15,702	$14,942

Forecasted Profit and Loss Statement for the year ended 31st December 19x2

		($'000)
Sales		$15,686
Less Cost of sales		11,445
Gross Profit		$ 4,241
Less Operating expenses	$ 2,610	
Interest	10	
Miscellaneous taxes	341	2,961
Net operating profit before income tax		$ 1,280
Add Profit from sale of fixed assets		23
Net Profit before income tax		$ 1,303
Less Income tax payable		585
Net Profit after income tax		$ 718
Add Undistributed profit, 1.1.x2		4,887
		$ 5,605
Less Dividends payable		516
Balanced of Undistributed profit, 31.12.x2		$5,089

During 19x2, it is intended to dispose of the following assets:

	Cost	*Accumulated Depreciation*	*Net Value*	*Expected Realizable Value*
Land	$ 2,000	Nil	$ 2,000	$ 2,000
Plant	$231,000	$205,000	$26,000	$44,000
Transportation equipment	$ 44,000	$ 39,000	$ 5,000	$10,000

TRIGOLA CORPORATION
Statement of Funds Flow for the Year ended 31st December 19x2.

Sources	(\$'000)	(\$'000)
1. Trading Operations:		
Net operating profit before tax	\$ 1,280	
Add depreciation	907	
		\$ 2,187
2. Proceeds from the sale of:		
Land	\$ 2	
Plant	\$ 44	
Equipment	\$ 10	
		56
3. Proceeds from the sale of investment		2,265
4. Increase in long-term debt		33
5. Increase in trade creditors		178
6. Decrease in cash		92
		\$ 4,811
Applications		
1. Purchase of plant		\$ 2,093
2. Purchase of equipment		249
3. Payment of tax		1,758
4. Payment of dividends		516
5. Increase in trade debtors		54
6. Increase in stock		124
7. Increase in prepaid expenses		17
		\$ 4,811

Statement of Working Capital Flow for the Year ended 31st December 19x2

	($'000)	($'000)
Working Capital balance, 1.1.19x2		$ 2,049
Add Inflows:		
1. Trading operations	$ 2,187	
2. Proceeds from sale of land	2	
3. Proceeds from sale of plant	44	
4. Proceeds from sale of equipment	10	
5. Increase in long-term debt	31	
6. Proceeds from sale of investment	1,163	
		3,437
		$ 5,486
Less Outflows:		
1. Purchase of plant	$ 2,093	
2. Purchase of equipment	249	
3. Provision for dividend	516	
4. Provision for tax	585	
		3,443
Working Capital balance, 31.12.19x2		$ 2,043

15.5. CASH FLOW STATEMENT

Cash is required for meeting specific business requirements such as the payment of operating costs and expenses at specific times, and the importance of efficient cash management has already been stressed. A funds flow statement may be too general to be of use in such circumstances. A cash flow statement is more useful for short-term planning, such as six months to a year. Beyond that it may be difficult to forecast with fair accuracy the inflows and outflows of cash. Hence, for long-term planning a funds statement should be sufficient in most cases.

In a funds statement, resources derived and used in a period are shown. In a cash flow statement all items of costs or expenses and revenue are treated on a cash basis. This is done by relating all the revenue and expense items to the balance sheet items to disclose the cash inflows and outflows. A cash flow statement is useful because it indicates the efficiency or otherwise of cash management and a forecasted cash flow statement is, of course, part of cash budgeting. A cash flow statement explains that business profits may not necessarily result in a positive net cash flow if other demands on cash resources have been heavy.

Similarly a net loss may not necessarily result in a negative net cash flow if depreciation and other non-cash charges exceed the net loss. A cash flow statement suffers the disadvantage of not showing the timing of the flows.

The following example (which is the same example used in Illustration 1 for the funds flow statement), should explain how a cash flow statement can be prepared:

Revenue Statement for the year ended 31st December 19x7

	Accrual Basis	*Cash Basis*
	($'000)	($'000)
Sales	$16,500	$15,315
Less Cost of Sales	12,540	13,065
Gross Profit	$ 3,960	$ 2,250
Less Operating expenses:		
Selling	$ 1,320	$ 1,320
Administration	1,215	600
Total operating expenses	$ 2,535	$ 1,920
Net Operating revenue	$ 1,425	$ 330

Debtors

Balance b/f	$ 1,500	Cash from sales	$15,315
Bills receivable b/f	375	Bills receivable c/d	1,005
Sales	16,500	Balance c/d	2,055
	$18,375		$18,375

Creditors

Cash on cost of sales	$13,065	Balance b/f	$ 900
Bills payable c/d	525	Bills payable b/f	450
Balance c/d	1,050	Purchases	13,290
	$14,640		$14,640

Purchases

Cost of sales	$12,540
Add increase in stock	750
	$13,290

Administration Expenses

Administration expenses	$1,215
Less non-cash item—depreciation	615
Administration expenses (cash basis)	$ 600

RECURD LIMITED
Cash Flow Statement for the year ended 31st December 19x7

		($'000)
Balance on hand as at 1st January 19x7		$1,425
Add Cash Inflows:		
(1) Net operating revenue (cash basis)	$ 330	
(2) Interest received	30	
(3) Sale of investment	405	765
		$2,190
Deduct Cash Outflows:		
(1) Payment of dividends	$ 450	
(2) Purchase of plant	1,575	2,025
Balance on hand as at 31st December 19x7		$ 165

15.6. ACCOUNTING RATIOS

Accounting ratios are some of the tools used by analysts in interpreting financial statements. They are obtained by relating one item to another item or by relating a group of similiar items to another group in the financial statements. If ratios are calculated on the financial statements of only one accounting period, they reveal structural relationships which are usually of little practical significance unless they can be compared with secondary data. But the trends of the structural relationships obtained from the financial statements of a few accounting periods normally have some importance. Analysis of financial statements can be effected by comparing with:

(1) past results,
(2) results of similar businesses in the same industry, and
(3) budgets and standards.

Comparison of actual results with budgeted and standard performance should be more valuable to management than with past results. But in some cases budgets and standards are not available. Comparison with secondary data is also useful. For instance, a soft drink manufacturer may be able to compare its raw material cost per unit of production with that of other soft drink manufacturers. There are many other areas of comparison with secondary data. However, the practical limitations of comparison with secondary data must be appreciated. Very seldom do two firms, however similar, use identical methods of recording, classifying and preparing accounts or have similar characteristics in managerial policies of production and trading methods.

In analysing trend relationships the accountant must be aware of all the limitations of accounting ratios. At best accounting ratios show possible reasons for changes and indicates areas where further investigations must be made. Unless the analyst realizes this, he may draw faulty conclusions from his analysis. First, because of the inherent limitations of financial statements prepared on the historical cost basis, the analyst must make sure that there has been consistent application of sound accounting principles and practice in the recording, classifying and summarizing of accounting data and in the making of estimates.

Secondly, he must realize that every enterprise has its own peculiar characteristics in respect of its organization, staff, methods of carrying out its business activities, its accounting and internal control systems and the nature of its operations. From a study of these characteristics he should be able to form a good visual picture of the enterprise as an accounting and economic unit. For instance, a business engaged in seasonal trade has the trend of its sales volume in a special pattern; its sales volume is closely related to the seasons. The amount of fares collected by a bus company is closely related to a number of factors, such as, the population of the districts through which the buses run, the availability of other transport facilities, the number of schools in the districts and any other relevant establishments along its routes. A decrease in the fares collected for a period, compared with those of the other periods, may be due to an increase in the number of taxis running along the same route, a decrease in the population of the district due to a re-settlement scheme, the closing down of a famous seaside resort, or it may be due to corruption on the part of the fare collectors. Thirdly, he must be aware of economic conditions prevailing at different times. For instance, the cost of production per unit may be increased not because of the inefficiency of production or errors or fraud, but, may be, because of an increase in the prices of raw materials and labour. And lastly, the analyst must be alert to all other relevant factors. For instance, there may be an abnormal variation in the labour cost per unit of production. This abnormal increase could be due to the inclusion of dummy wages, incorrect classification of costs, or it may be due to the fact that as a result of a wages agreement with the union, arrears of wages for the past two years were charged to the current year's labour cost. This kind of information can be obtained by an alert mind always ready to get information from whatever source, however insignificant it may seem. This incidentally illustrates the importance of appraising the practical business situations and shows the danger of relying solely on the analysis of figures presented on the financial statements.

The accounting ratios used by analysts could be classified under four main groups:

(1) Indications of earning capacity,
(2) Indications of operating efficiency,
(3) Indications of financial stability, and
(4) Indications of leverage.

Most of the ratios in the following paragraphs are calculated from the data given in Exhibit 15.

Exhibit 15
GROWING LIMITED
Profit and Loss Statement
for the year ended 31st December

	19x4	*19x4*	*19x5*	*19x5*
	($'000)	%	($'000)	%
Sales	57,500	100.00	63,250	100.00
Less Cost of sales and operating expenses	51,750	90.00	57,560	91.00
Net profit before tax	5,750	10.00	5,690	9.00
Less Income tax	2,300	4.00	2,276	3.60
Net profit after tax	3,450	6.00	3,414	5.40
Balance of unappropriated profit, 1st January	1,493		632	
Total available for appropriation	4,943		4,046	
Less Appropriations				
Capital reserve	1,840		—	
Dividend (net)	2,471		2,471	
	4,311		2,471	
Balance of unappropriated profit, 31st December	632		1,575	

GROWING LIMITED
Balance Sheet as at 31st December

	19x4	*19x4*	*19x5*	*19x5*
	($'000)		($'000)	
Issued and Paid-up Capital	20,000		25,000	
RESERVES				
Capital	8,900		5,000	
Revenue	632		1,575	
	29,532	74.7	31,575	63.1
10% DEBENTURES			5,000	10.0
CURRENT LIABILITIES				
Trade creditors	6,820		9,075	
Provision for income tax	2,350		2,250	
Provision for dividend	819		1,125	
Bank overdraft	—		1,018	
	9,989	25.3	13,468	26.9
TOTAL EQUITIES	**$39,521**	**100.0**	**$50,043**	**100.0**
FIXED ASSETS	16,000	40.5	25,000	50.0
CURRENT ASSETS				
Stock	9,000		9,800	
Trade debtors	13,870		15,243	
Cash	651		—	
	23,521	59.5	25,043	50.0
TOTAL ASSETS	$39,521	100.0	$50,043	100.0
Current Ratio	2.35		1.86	
Liquid Ratio	1.45		1.22	

NOTES ON THE ACCOUNTS AND ADDITIONAL INFORMATION

	19x4	*19x5*
	($'000)	($'000)
(1) **CAPITAL**		
Authorised:		
50,000,000 shares of $1 each	50,000	50,000
Issued and fully paid:		
Shares of $1 each	20,000	25,000

(2) **Reserves**

CAPITAL: Gains and losses on disposals of fixed assets are transferred to Capital Reserve. In January 19x5, a bonus issue of one fully paid share out of every four shares held was made from Capital Reserve.

(3) **10% Debentures**

The debentures maturing in 19x9 and issued in January, 19x5 are unsecured.

(4) **Fixed Assets**

	19x4	19x5
	($'000)	($'000)
Balance at cost, 1st January	25,000	26,000
Additions at cost	1,200	12,000
	26,200	38,000
Disposals at cost	200	1,500
Balance at cost, 31st December	$26,000	$36,500

(5) **Depreciation**

	19x4	19x5
	($'000)	($'000)
Provision for depreciation, 1st January	9,100	10,000
Annual depreciation charge	1,300	2,200
	10,400	12,200
Accumulated depreciation on fixed assets disposed of during the year	400	700
Provision for depreciation, 31st December	$10,000	$11,500

(6) The expansion project completed in early 19x5 has increased plant capacity by approximately 50%.

(7) From 19x1 to 19x4, Growing Limited experienced an annual growth rate of approximately 10% in sales volume and net profits.

Exhibit 15(a)
GROWING LIMITED
Statement of Sources and Applications of Funds for the year ended 31st December, 19x5

		($'000)
Sources		
(1) Trading Operations:		
Net Operating Profit Before Tax	$5,690	
Add Depreciation	2,200	
		7,890
(2) Proceeds from Disposal of Fixed Assets		1,900
(3) Issue of 10% Debentures		5,000
(4) Increase in Trade Creditors		2,255
(5) Increase in Bank Overdraft		1,018
(6) Decrease in Cash Balance		651
		$18,714
Applications		
(1) Purchase of Fixed Assets		12,000
(2) Payment of Income Tax		2,376
(3) Payment of Dividend		2,165
(4) Increase in Stock		800
(5) Increase in Trade Debtors		1,373
		$18,714

GROWING LIMITED
Statement of Cash Flows
for the year ended 31st December, 19x5

		($'000)
Cash at Bank balance 1.1.x5		651
Add Inflows:		
(1) Trading Operations before Tax	$ 7,972	
(2) Proceeds from disposal of Fixed Assets	1,900	
(3) Issue of 10% Debentures	5,000	
		14,872
		15,523
Deduct Outflows:		
(1) Purchase of Fixed Assets	$12,000	
(2) Payment of Income Tax	2,376	
(3) Payment of Dividend	2,165	
		16,541
Bank Overdraft balance, 31.12.x5		$ 1,018

15.6.1. Indications of Earning Capacity

The earning power of an enterprise is indicated by its return on investment. The return on investment can be measured in various ways.

(*a*) *Return on Asset Investment*

	19x4	*19x5*
(i) $\dfrac{\text{Net Profit after Tax}}{\text{Total Assets}}$	$\dfrac{3{,}450}{39{,}521}$	$\dfrac{3{,}414}{50{,}043}$
	$=0.087$	$=0.068$
(ii) $\dfrac{\text{Sales}}{\text{Total Assets}}$		
$\times\dfrac{\text{Net Profit after Tax}}{\text{Sales}}$	$\dfrac{57{,}500}{39{,}521}\times\dfrac{3{,}450}{57{,}500}$	$=\dfrac{63{,}250}{50{,}043}\times\dfrac{3{,}414}{63{,}250}$
	$=1.455\times 0.06$	$=1.264\times 0.054$
	$=0.087$	$=0.068$

The return on asset investment can be increased by improving either one or both of the total assets turnover and the rate of net profit on sales. The ratio can also be increased by allowing the fixed assets to be increasingly depreciated especially if historical book values are used, but this may be offsetted by the higher costs of operations with old machines which may be indicated by the lower rate of net profit on dollar sales. Price changes of output as well as input factors also affect the ratios.

(*b*) *Return on Shareholders' Funds*

	19x4	*19x5*
$\frac{\text{Net Profit after Tax}}{\text{Shareholders' Funds}}$	$\frac{3,450}{29,532} = 0.117$	$\frac{3,414}{31,575} = 0.108$

This ratio is useful to ordinary shareholders who wish to know the return on the funds they have invested or re-invested in the business. If there are fixed dividends on preference shares that enjoy priority in dividend payment over ordinary shares, these must first be deducted from the net profit after tax. Sometimes, earnings per share is used to indicate the return on each share. This is the total net profit after tax available to ordinary shareholders divided by the number of issued ordinary shares. Similarly, dividends per share may be calculated:

(*c*) Current Dividend Yield

$$= \frac{\text{Dividend}}{\text{Current Market Price Per Share}}$$

(*d*) Current Earnings Yield

$$= \frac{\text{Earnings Per Share}}{\text{Current Market Price Per Share}}$$

The current earnings yield is very often known as the price earnings ratio which is its inverse:

$$PER = \frac{\text{Current Market Price Per Share}}{\text{Earnings Per Share}}$$

If the investor is interested in capital gains, earnings per share would be more indicative, whereas the dividend per share shows the dividend he is likely to receive. The prospective investor will find the (*c*) and (*d*) ratios more useful since he has to pay the current market price of the shares he buys. The use of earnings per share is subject to the remarks made in Section 10.1.6. of Chapter 10.

15.6.2. Indications of Operating Efficiency

We discuss these ratios under three headings:

(*a*) Manufacturing operations,
(*b*) Commercial operations, and
(*c*) Utilization of assets.

(*a*) In measuring the efficiency of manufacturing operations, variance analysis under a system of standard costing is the best method. However, there are two other ways of doing this. The first way is by expressing each element of cost as a percentage of cost of production. Here, a decrease in a percentage simply means that the element of cost concerned forms a smaller proportion of the total cost of production. And any increase in the percentage regarding any element of cost, such as labour, naturally pushes down the percentages in the other elements of cost. Hence, percentages must be used with great caution. The second way of expressing each element of cost as a certain dollar amount per unit of production is, therefore, more informative, especially in firms producing a single product. Where a firm produces more than one product, comparison by unit cost is also more informative provided there are logical bases in the apportionment of joint costs to the different products. If there are no logical bases of joint cost allocation, comparison of direct or variable unit cost may be more meaningful.

(*b*) In measuring the efficiency of commercial operations, cost of sales, gross profit, and each type of operating expense, are all expressed as percentages of sales. They are subject to the same limitations as explained in the previous paragraph (*a*). The gross profit rate indicates the profit margin, and the profit margin for each type of product is usually different from that for another type. Hence, the gross profit rate can be meaningless if a wide range of products with varying profit margins are sold unless the accounts can be rationally departmentalized so that the gross profit rate for each item can be obtained. Generally speaking an increase in the gross profit ratio is a healthy sign, but it could be caused by one or more of the following:

(i) under-valuing the opening stock,
(ii) over-valuing the closing stock,
(iii) suppression of purchase invoices,
(iv) inclusion of fictitious sales,
(v) increasing selling prices without proportionally increasing cost of sales,
(vi) decreasing cost of production without proportionally decreasing selling prices.
(vii) introducing more profitable lines of products or eliminating and curtailing unprofitable ones.

The opposites of all these can cause a decrease in the gross profit ratio.

The usefulness of expressing each type of operating expense as a percentage of sales is enhanced if the expenses can be divided into two categories: (i) those which remain constant irrespective of the levels of sales volume, called fixed expenses, and (ii) those which vary proportionally with sales volume, called variable expenses. If this can be done, then the percentage in each group of fixed expenses ought to decrease as sales volume increases, while the percentage in each group of variable expenses ought to remain constant with any change in sales volume. Should the groups of expenses do not vary as predicted, further investigations might be called for. For instance, one would expect selling and distribution expenses to increase with an increase in sales volume. One might also expect a little increase in administration expenses with an increase in sales volume, but it should not increase proportionately with a sales volume increase, since most of administration expenses is fixed in the normal circumstances. This holds true if there is no increase in operating capacity. Should operating capacity be increased, such as the renting of additional premises, the total fixed administration expenses would increase.

(*c*) The objective of measuring the utilization of assets by calculating their turnovers is to ascertain the extent of their being used in relation to the level of business operations. Some of the ratios are given below:

		19X4	*19X5*
(i)	$\frac{\text{Sales}}{\text{Total Assets}}$	$\frac{57{,}500}{39{,}521} = 1.455$	$\frac{63{,}250}{50{,}043} = 1.264$
(ii)	$\frac{\text{Sales}}{\text{Fixed Assets}}$	$\frac{57{,}500}{16.000} = 3.594$	$\frac{63{,}250}{25{,}000} = 2.53$
(iii)	$\frac{\text{Sales}}{\text{Current Assets}}$	$\frac{57{,}500}{23{,}521} = 2.445$	$\frac{63{,}250}{25{,}043} = 2.526$
(iv)	$\frac{\text{Sales}}{\text{Stock}}$	$\frac{57{,}500}{9{,}000} = 6.389$	$\frac{63{,}250}{9{,}800} = 6.454$
(v)	$\frac{\text{Sales}}{\text{Trade Debtors}}$	$\frac{57{,}500}{13{,}870} = 4.146$	$\frac{63{,}250}{15{,}243} = 4.149$

In calculating the turnover of total assets and of fixed assets in (i) and (ii), sometimes the cost of production or cost of goods manufactured is used instead of sales. This measure of utilization of assets may not be appropriate if production is measured in monetary units since an increase in dollar production may result from increases in dollar costs of production due to price increases of input factors or inefficiency in production or both.

In arriving at the stock turnover ratio in (iv) cost of sales is sometimes used instead of sales and average stock instead of closing stock. If the closing stock figure is not representative, average stock may be more appropriate.

The debtors turnover ratio in (v) is very often used to calculate the average number of days trade debtors take to pay their debts. In this case only credit sales should be used. The ratio is:

$$\frac{365 \times (\text{Trade Debtors} + \text{Bills Receivable})}{\text{Credit Sales}}$$

$$= 365 \times \frac{1}{4.146} \text{ or 88 days for 19X4}$$

$$\text{and } 365 \times \frac{1}{4.149} \text{ or 88 days for 19X5}$$

Cash can be released by reducing debtors turnover. And the trade-off between greater cash discount allowed to induce prompt payment by debtors and the opportunity cost of the money tied up in trade debtors may be calculated.

15.6.3. Indications of Financial Stability

In the ratios calculated to indicate the financial health of the company, we divide them into two groups:

(*a*) short-term, and
(*b*) long-term.

(*a*) By short-term, we mean a year or less. First, we have the current ratio or working capital ratio: $\frac{\text{current assets}}{\text{current liabilities}}$. A ratio of 2.35 means that for every \$100 of liabilities that must be discharged within one year's time the company has \$235 of assets that can be converted into cash within a year to meet these debt obligations. In practice, it is important to ascertain what the current assets actually are and whether they can in fact be converted into so much cash within a year without loss. If the current assets consist mainly of obsolete goods, for example, the current ratio may be misleading. It is also important to ensure that no window-dressing has been resorted to. For instance, if the figures should have been:

current assets = \$300,000
current liabilities = 200,000
current ratio = 150%,

but management, to window-dress the short-term financial position, paid off \$100,000 of liabilities two days before the balance sheet date, the figures become:

current assets = \$200,000
current liabilities = 100,000
current ratio = 200%

The second ratio is the liquid ratio: $\frac{\text{liquid assets}}{\text{liquid liabilities}}$, sometimes called the acid test. The liquid assets are usually taken to mean the current assets less stock; and the liquid liabilities, the current liabilities less bank overdraft. Stock is excluded because stock is considered to take much longer time to convert into cash. Here, the rule must be used with the nature of the business borne in mind. A fishmonger's stock of fish may be sold the next day, may be more than half of it for cash. Bank overdraft is also excluded because it is considered that though it is usually legally repayable on demand, banks seldom exercise their legal rights in this manner. The liquid ratio indicates the company's ability to meet its immediate commitments.

The third ratio is the creditors turnover:

$$\frac{\text{credit purchases}}{\text{creditors + bill payable}}.$$

If this ratio decreases it indicates that the firm takes a longer time to pay off its debts, and this could mean that it has not taken advantage of cash discount because it is short of cash. Financial expenses would increase.

(*b*) By long-term we mean longer than one year. The surest sign of the long-term financial stability of a company is its earning power. If it is short of funds but it can earn exceptional profits, a lot of people are willing to contribute funds. However strong the present financial health of the company may be, if it can be carried on only at a loss, its funds will soon be depleted and its financial strength sapped. The two ratios that are often calculated for measuring long-term financial stability are:

(i) $\frac{\text{shareholders' funds}}{\text{total assets}}$

and (ii) $\frac{\text{shareholders' funds}}{\text{fixed assets}}$

A shareholders' funds to total assets ratio of 63% means that only 63% of the total assets are financed from funds belonging to the shareholders, and 37% are financed from borrowed resources.

A shareholders' funds to fixed assets ratio of 126% means that for every $100 of fixed assets, none of them are financed from indebtedness. A general rule of thumb, which should not be applied indiscriminately, is that all fixed assets should be financed from capital contributions and retained earnings.

15.6.4. Indications of Leverage

There are three ways of measuring leverage.

The ratio, $\dfrac{\text{long-terms liabilities + preference capital}}{\text{shareholders' funds} - \text{preference capital}}$, shows the relation between long-term indebtedness and shareholders' funds. A decrease in the ratio indicates that the company has become less dependent on long-term debt-financing. An increase in the ratio indicates the reverse state of affairs.

The ratio, $\dfrac{\text{preference dividend + fixed interest charges}}{\text{net distributable profit}}$, indicates the proportion of the net profit (which is available for distribution as dividend) which must be used towards meeting the fixed charges (the result of long-term debt-financing). The ratio is considered to be insufficiently comprehensive for two reasons. First, the net distributable profit is not the equivalent of funds generated from trading operations. And secondly, the ratio does not take into account other contractual obligations of the debt, such as contractual sinking fund requirements. For this reason, the following ratio is more often used:

$$\frac{\text{total contractual burden on long-term debt}}{\text{net funds inflow from trading operations}}$$

Total contractual burden on long-term debt includes: (1) the preference dividend, (2) the interest on the debt, and (3) the annual fixed sum that must be set aside from profits to invest outside the business, either for redeeming the preference shares or for repaying the principal of the long-term debt, or for both purposes. The ratio shows the ability of the company to meet its long-term contractual obligations, and hence, the risks involved in long-term debt-financing as an alternative to capital contributions.

To be more exact, the formula for this ratio should be:

$$\frac{\text{total contractual burden on long-term debt}}{\text{net cash inflow from trading operations}}$$

15.7. MORE ILLUSTRATIONS

Illustration 1

Freezer Limited is a company incorporated in the Republic of Singapore. The following annual statements are extracted from the audited accounts of the company.

Consolidated Profit and Loss Statement
for the year ended 31st December

	19X4	*19X5*
	($'000)	($'000)
Sales	100	120
Less Cost of sales	77	90
Gross Profit	23	30
Less Operating expense	10	12
Net Profit before Tax	13	18
Less Income Tax	8	11
Net Profit after Tax	5	7
Less Minority Interest	2	2
	3	5
Balance of unappropriated profit, 1st January	7	6
Total available for Appropriation	10	11
Less Appropriations		
Capital Reserve	2	2
Dividend (Net)	2	3
	4	5
Balance of Unappropriated Profit, 31st December	6	6

Consolidated Balance Sheet
as at 31st December

	19X4 ($'000)	19X5 ($'000)
Capital and Liabilities		
Issued and Paid-Up Capital (See Note 1)	40	45
Capital Reserve (See Note 2)	6	10
Profit and Loss	6	6
	$52	$61
MINORITY INTEREST	13	13
Current Liabilities		
Trade Creditors	5	8
Taxation	10	12
Dividend	1	2
	16	22
Total Equities	$81	$96
Assets		
Fixed Assets (see Note 3)	59	55
Current Assets		
Stock	8	9
Trade Debtors	10	30
Cash	4	2
	22	41
Total Assets	$81	$96

NOTES ON THE ACCOUNTS

	19X4	19X5
(1) **Capital**		
Authorised 50,000 stock units of $1 each	$50,000	$50,000
Issued and paid-up stock units of $1 each	$40,000	$45,000
(2) **Capital Reserve**		
Balance, 1st January	$ 4,000	$ 6,000
Transfer from Profit and Loss Account	2,000	2,000
Revaluation of land and buildings	—	5,000
Profit on sale of plant and equipment	—	1,000
Profit on sale of shares in a subsidiary	—	1,000
	$ 6,000	$15,000
Issue of Bonus Shares	—	5,000
Balance, 31st December	$ 6,000	$10,000

(3) **Fixed Assets**			*19X4*	*19X5*
Land and buildings at cost			$20,000	
As Revalued				$25,000
			Accumulated Depreciation	
	19X4	*19X5*	*19X4*	*19X5*
Plant and equipment at cost	$79,000	$75,000	$40,000	$45,000

During 19X5, some equipment costing $20,000 and depreciated to $5,000 were sold.
Some shares in a subsidiary company were disposed of for $2,000.

FREEZEE LIMITED
Statement of Sources and Uses of Funds (Working Capital Concept) for the year ended 31st December 19X5

Sources		
(1) Trading Operations before Tax		$38,000
Net Profit Before Tax	$18,000	
Add Depreciation	20,000	
(2) Proceeds from sale of plant		6,000
(3) Proceeds from disposal of shares in a subsidiary		2,000
		$46,000
Uses		
(1) Purchase of plant and equipment		$16,000
(2) Payment to reduce Minority Interest		3,000
(3) Provision for taxation		11,000
(4) Provision for dividend		3,000
		$33,000
Resulting in a Net Increase in Working Capital		$13,000

Cash Flows Statement for the year ended 31st December 19X5

Balance, 1st January		$4,000
Add Inflows		
(1) Trading operations	$20,000	
(2) Proceeds from sale of plant	6,000	
(3) Proceeds from disposal of shares in a subsidiary	2,000	28,000
		$32,000
Deduct Outflows		
(1) Purchase of plant and equipment	$16,000	
(2) Payment to reduce Minority Interest	3,000	
(3) Payment of dividend	2,000	
(4) Payment of taxation	9,000	30,000
Balance, 31st December		$ 2,000

Cash Flows Statement for the year ended 31st December 19X5

Alternative Method of Presentation

Balance, 1st January		$4,000
Add Inflows:		
(1) Trade Debtors	$100,000	
(2) Proceeds from Sale of Plant	6,000	
(3) Proceeds from Disposal of Shares	2,000	108,000
		112,000
Deduct Outflows:		
(1) Trade Creditors	$68,000	
(2) Operating Expenses	12,000	
(3) Purchase of Shares to reduce Minority Interest in Subsidiaries	3,000	
(4) Purchase of Plant and Equipment	16,000	
(5) Payment of Dividends	2,000	
(6) Payment of Income Tax	9,000	
		110,000
Balance, 31st December		$ 2,000

In spite of the big amount of cash received from trade debtors in the period the debtors turnover ratio as calculated below indicates a decline from 10 to 4 times a year. In 19X5 trade debtors on the average took about 90 days to settle their debts as compared with about 36 days in 19X4

	19X4	19X5
(i) $\frac{\text{Net Profit before Tax}}{\text{Sales}}$	$\frac{13}{100} \times \frac{100}{81}$	$\frac{18}{120} \times \frac{120}{96}$
$\times \frac{\text{Sales}}{\text{Total Assets}}$	$= .13 \times 1.23$	$.15 \times 1.25$
	$\cong .16$	$\cong .19$
(ii) Earnings before Tax per share	$\frac{13}{40}$ or $\frac{13}{45}$	$\frac{18}{40}$ or $\frac{18}{45}$
	$\cong \$.325 \quad \cong \$.29$	$\cong \$0.45 \quad \cong \$.40$
(iii) $\frac{\text{Current Assets}}{\text{Current Liabilities}}$	$\frac{22}{16}$	$\frac{41}{22}$
	$\cong 1.37$	$\cong 1.86$
(iv) $\frac{\text{Liquid Assets}}{\text{Current Liabilities}}$	$\frac{14}{16}$	$\frac{32}{22}$
	$\cong .875$	$\cong 1.45$
(v) Stock Turnover	$\frac{\text{Sales}}{\text{Closing Stock}}$	
	$\frac{100}{8}$	$\frac{120}{9}$
	$\cong$ 12.5 times	$\cong$ 13.3 times
(vi) Debtors Turnover	$\frac{100}{10}$	$\frac{120}{30}$
	$\cong$ 10 times	$\cong$ 4 times

Plant & Equipment

Balance b/f	79	Sale	20
Cash	16	Bal. c/d	75
	$95		$95

Provision for Depreciation

Sale of Plant & Machinery	15	Balance b/f	40
Balance c/d	45	Depreciation	20
	$60		$60

Sale of Plant & Machinery

Plant & Machinery	20	Prov. for Depreciation	15
Capital Reserve	1	Cash	6
	21		21

Minority Interest

Capital Reserve	1	Balance b/f	13
Payment (net)	1	Profit & Loss App.	2
Balance c/d	13		
	15		15

Funds from Trading Operations		$38,000
Add Increase in Trade Creditors		3,000
		41,000
Less Increase in Stock	$1,000	
Increase in Trade Debtors	20,000	
		21,000
Cash from Trading Operations		20,000

Illustration 2

The following balance sheets are extracted from the Ledger of Short-term Vision Ltd.:

		31st Dec., 19X2 ($'000)		*31st Dec., 19X3* ($'000)
Shareholders' Funds				
Issued and paid-up capital		10,000		15,000
Profit and loss		5,000		6,000
		15,000		21,000
Current Liabilities				
Trade creditors		20,000		30,000
Bank overdraft		30,000		45,000
Income tax payable		400		600
		50,400		75,600
Total Equities		$65,400		$96,600
Fixed Assets				
Land and buildings		15,000		20,000
Plant and machinery at cost	$20,000		$50,000	
Less Provisions for deprec.	10,000	10,000	11,000	39,000
		25,000		59,000
Current Assets				
Stock		10,400		15,600
Trade debtors		28,000		21,000
Prepaid expenses		2,000		1,000
		40,400		37,600
Total Assets		$65,400		$96,600

The following additional information is obtained after careful investigation:

(i) The amount of income tax paid in 19X3 was $420,000.

(ii) A machine costing $5,000,000 and depreciated to $2,000,000 was sold for $2,200,000.

(iii) The land and buildings were revalued in 19X3. There was no purchase or sale of land and buildings during the year.

Short-term Vision Ltd.
Funds Statement for the year ended 31st December, 19X3

	($'000)	($'000)
Sources		
(1) Trading operations:		
Net operating profit before tax	1,420	
Add depreciation	4,000	
		5,420
(2) Proceeds from sale of machine		2,200
(3) Trade creditors increase		10,000
(4) Bank overdraft increase		15,000
(5) Decrease in trade debtors		7,000
(6) Decrease in prepaid expenses		1,000
		$40,620
Uses		
(1) Purchase of machine		35,000
(2) Income tax paid		420
(3) Increase in stock		5,200
		$40,620

Cash Flows Statement
for the year ended 31st December, 19X3

Bank overdraft, 1.1.19x3		$30,000
Less Cash inflows:		
(1) Trading operations	$18,220	
(2) Proceeds from sale of machine	2,200	
		20,420
		9,580
Add Cash outflows:		
(1) Purchase of machine	$35,000	
(2) Income tax paid	420	
		35,420
Bank overdraft, 31.12.19x3		$45,000

Profit and Loss

Income Tax payable	620	Balance b/f	5,000
Balance c/d	6,000	Profit on sale of fixed asset	200
		Net operating profit before tax	1,420
	$6,620		$6,620

Cash Inflow from Trading Operations

		($'000)
Net operating profit before tax		1,420
Add depreciation	4,000	
trade credit increase	10,000	
trade debts decrease	7,000	
prepaid expense decrease	1,000	
		22,000
		23,420
Deduct Increase in stock		5,200
Cash inflow from trading operations		$18,220

Illustration 3

The following information is obtained from Funds Flows Berhad:

	Balance Sheets as at 31st December		
	19x0	*19x1*	*19x2*
	$	$	$
$1 fully paid preference share capital	400,000	400,000	—
$1 fully paid ordinary share capital	400,000	800,000	800,000
Capital redemption reserve	—	—	400,000
Revenue reserve	35,000	70,000	100,000
Debentures	100,000	60,000	50,000
Trade Creditors	110,000	100,000	90,000
Provision for income tax	60,000	40,000	50,000
Provision for dividend	20,000	30,000	40,000
	$1,125,000	$1,500,000	$1,530,000
Land and Buildings	400,000	800,000	800,000
Plant and Machinery	70,000	70,000	70,000
Preliminary Expenses	300,000	250,000	220,000
Bank	35,000	10,000	40,000
Trade Debtors	210,000	200,000	300,000
Stock	110,000	170,000	100,000
	$1,125,000	$1,500,000	$1,530,000

Additional information:

(i) In 19X1, the land and buildings were revalued. There was no sale or purchase of land and buildings during the period.
(ii) There was no sale of plant and machinery. The depreciation charges were:

	19x1	*19x2*
	$20,000	$20,000

(iii) The payment of dividends and income taxes were:

	19x1	*19x2*
Dividends	$25,000	$30,000
Income Tax	20,000	28,000

(iv) There was an issue of bonus shares.

FUNDS FLOWS BERHAD
Statement of Sources and Applications of Funds for the Period 1st January, 19x1 to 31st December, 19x2

Sources		
1. Trading operations:		
Net profit before tax	$658,000	
Add depreciation	40,000	$698,000
2. Decrease in stock		10,000
Total		$708,000
Applications		
1. Redemption of preference shares		$400,000
2. Redemption of debentures		50,000
3. Purchase of plant and machinery		40,000
4. Payment of income tax		48,000
5. Payment of dividends		55,000
6. Decrease in trade creditors		20,000
7. Increase in trade debtors		90,000
8. Increase in bank balance		5,000
Total		$708,000

PROFIT AND LOSS ACCOUNT

Income tax provision	$ 38,000	Balance b/f	$ 35,000
Provision for Dividends	75,000	Net Profit before Tax	658,000
Capital Redemption Reserve	400,000		
Preliminary Expenses	80,000		
Balance c/d	100,000		
	$693,000		$693,000

15.8. BUSINESS FAILURE AND ACCOUNTING RATIOS

15.8.1. Liquidation or Reconstruction

Technically a firm is insolvent when it cannot meet its financial commitments. From the accounting point of view its assets are insufficient to discharge its liabilities. There can be various reasons why a company has come into a state of bad financial health. It may have suffered trading losses because its products have gone out of vogue and it has not been able to diversify or compete successfully. Its management may have been inefficient and inexperienced; its financial management is ineffective; it has relied too heavily on debt financing; it has expanded too rapidly; and so on. Whatever the cause or causes, the top management of the company must decide whether the company can be reconstructed or it should be liquidated. Liquidation of a company is a legal process governed by the provisions of the Companies Act. Here a public accountant should be consulted as to whether a voluntary liquidation is possible or the company has to undergo a compulsory liquidation under a court's order.

15.8.2. Reconstruction and Steps Taken

By reconstruction is meant the reorganization of a company in a very drastic manner very often involving a reduction of its paid-up capital because it is no more represented by available assets, and the raising of new finance in order to put the company on a sound financial footing again. The purpose of reconstruction is to save the company from going into liquidation.

The first thing to do is to find out whether the adverse factors operating against the company which have been the cause of its financial plight can be removed. There is no point in reconstructing the company if after the reconstruction the same adverse forces will operate again. In such a case the company should in fact go into liquidation. If the fault lies mainly in inefficient management, the management team or some of them may have to be replaced. If its product is no more in demand, it is necessary to investigate into the feasibility of producing new products which have a ready market.

The next step is to discover the extent of the loss of capital. Here it is necessary to draw up a balance sheet on the date when the actual cleaning up of the balance sheet is to take place. The following is an illustrative example:

A & COMPANY LIMITED
Balance Sheet as at 31st December 19x6

Paid-up Capital		Fixed Assets	$390,000
Ordinary Capital		Current Assets	120,000
($1 fully paid shares)	$80,000	Profits & Loss a/c	10,000
6% Preference Capital			
($1 fully paid shares)	40,000		
	$120,000		
Long-term Liabilities	100,000		
Current Liabilities	300,000		
	$520,000		$520,000

Other Information:

(1) The fixed assets are assessed to be worth only $340,000.
(2) Among the current assets, $20,000 of the debts are considered to be bad.

The assets should be professionally assessed and new values arrived at; all liabilities of the company whether in the books or not must be taken into account. The loss of capital is ascertained as follows:–

Fixed assets as revalued		$340,000
Current assets as revalued		100,000
Total Assets		$440,000
Less Long-term liabilities	$100,000	
Current liabilities	300,000	400,000
Net Assets		$ 40,000
Total paid-up capital		120,000
Loss of Capital		$ 80,000

Share of Loss of Capital

Since there are two classes of shares, it becomes essential to decide who shall bear the loss, or if both classes should bear the loss, in what proportions. From the outset, one fact must be borne in mind, and that is, ordinary shareholders will not lose anything if their shares are reduced from $1 to any smaller value so long as they are not entirely eliminated, whereas any reduction in the nominal or paid-up value of preference shares affects the preference shareholders adversely. Suppose, for example, the ordinary shares and the 6% preference shares are all reduced from $1 to $0.50 per share. On a net distributable profit of $10,400 per annum to be earned by the company, the profit-sharing before and after capital reduction is illustrated below:

BEFORE CAPITAL REDUCTION

Preference shareholders get: 6% on $40,000	$ 2,400
Ordinary shareholders get: the balance	8,000
Total Net Distributable Profit	$10,400

AFTER CAPITAL REDUCTION

Preference shareholders get: 6% on $20,000	$ 1,200
Ordinary shareholders get: the balance	9,200
Total Net Distributable Profit	$10,400

In the example given above, the ordinary shareholders, in fact, gain at the expense of the preference shareholders. Hence, it can be stated that under ordinary circumstances the preference shareholders will not normally agree to share the loss of capital proportionately with the ordinary shareholders. If the preference shareholders enjoy priority right in the return of capital, they may prefer a liquidation of the company, where in this case, they will get back all the $40,000 which they can invest elsewhere at, perhaps, a higher rate of interest than 6%. On the other hand, the ordinary shareholders who normally have the voting power, may want the company to continue. If no reconstruction is to be undertaken the preference shareholders will not get their dividend since the company will presumably go on making losses, and ultimately they may lose their capital as well. Hence, in practice some compromise is usually arrived at where the ordinary shareholders may have to bear a major share of the loss of capital while the preference shareholders agree to bear part of the loss. The proportions in which the two classes of shares actually bear the loss of capital are more the result of their bargaining power rather than that of any precise formula. However, in some cases, the Articles of Association of the company may contain provisions governing the sharing of capital loss. If that is the case, they must be complied with.

New Finance

Having reduced the paid-up capital, and having reorganized the company in all the appropriate aspects, the newly-constituted board of directors may now decide on whether new finance is required, the size of such new finance, in what form or forms it will be, for instance, long-term debt or share capital, and how the various types of new finance are to be raised. A merger with another company should not altogether be ruled out.

Capital Reduction

A company may reduce its capital by complying with the necessary statutory provisions (capital reduction is governed by Section 64 of the Companies Act) which may be briefly summarized below:

(1) The reduction of capital must be authorized by the company's Articles of Association.
(2) It must be carried out by a special resolution.
(3) The reduction may be either one or more of the following:
    (i) reducing or cancelling the uncalled capital,
    (ii) writing off paid-up capital which is no more represented by available assets,
    (iii) refunding to shareholders any paid-up capital which is in excess of the wants of the company,
    (iv) cancelling unissued shares, which is the same as reducing the authorized capital.
(4) The Memorandum of Association may have to be altered accordingly.
(5) After the special resolution has been passed, the company may apply by petition to the court for an order confirming the reduction.
(6) The court may make an order to confirm the reduction only after the claims and/or objections of creditors of the company have been settled.
(7) The court may require that the name of the company for a certain period shall include the words: "and reduced," and may cause the company to publish its capital reduction for the information of the public.

(8) The reduction of capital shall take effect only after a copy of the court order and a copy of a minute approved by the court showing the effects of reduction in respect of the company's capital have been registered by the Registrar of Companies.

(9) The Certificate of Registration issued by the Registrar shall be conclusive evidence that all the requirements with respect to share capital reduction have been complied with.

An examination of the statutory provisions governing share capital reduction reveals the various reasons for capital reduction.

15.8.3. Business Failure and Accounting Ratios

A number of empirical surveys have been carried out very often using discriminant analysis to predict business failure using various financial ratios. They seem to indicate that the financial ratios of failed businesses did show rapid deterioration as they approached tight financial straits. Very often the market prices of their shares fell rather quickly towards the end of their corporate existence. It is an open question whether recognising the signs and symptoms of approaching demise management can take steps to arrest their advance and reverse the process to put their companies on a sound financial footing again. It is sad to contemplate that with a knowledge of such prognosis management cannot but stand and wait for the inevitable.

15.9. SELECTED BIBLIOGRAPHY

1. E.I. Altman: Financial Ratios, Discriminant Analysis and Prediction of Corporate Bankruptcy, *Journal of Finance*, September 1968.
2. William H. Beaver: Market Prices, Financial Ratios, and the Prediction of Failure, *Journal of Accounting Research*, Autumn 1968.
3. L.A. Bernstein: Financial Statement Analysis (Theory, Application, and Interpretation).
4. A.A. Fitzgerald and L.A. Schumer: Classification in Accounting.

5. V.L. Gold: Fitzgerald's Analysis and Interpretation of Financial Statements.
6. Han Kang Hong: Cost and Management Accounting.
7. E.A. Helfert: Techniques of Financial Analysis.
8. R.K. Jaedicke and R.T. Sprouse: Accounting Flows–Income, Funds and Cash.
9. J.N. Myer: Financial Statement Analysis.

APPENDIX A

Review of Mathematics of Finance

If we examine closely most of our formulae in Mathematics of Finance, we find that a certain number of variables are often involved. Our task is to express their inter-relationships in a single formula.

If a sum of money at time zero is represented by P_0 and it earns interest at a rate of i, and a constant amount R is either added or subtracted from the amount at the end of each period, we have the following relationship at the end of the first period:

$$P_1 = P_0 + iP_0 + R = P_0(1 + i) + R$$

where P_1 is the amount at the end of the first period.

Similarly the amount at the end of the second period is:

$$P_2 = P_1(1 + i) + R$$

and the amount at the end of the third period is:

$$P_3 = P_2(1 + i) + R$$

By induction we have

$$P_{n+1} - P_n(1 + i) = R \tag{1}$$

where n is the end of the nth period.

Substituting $P_n = Mh^n$ into equation (1), we have

$$Mh^{n+1} - (1 + i)Mh^n = R$$

And we have a difference equation.

The complementary function P_c is:

$$Mh^{n+1} - (1 + i)Mh^n = 0$$

Hence $$h = (1 + i)$$

and

$$P_c = Mh^n = M(1 + i)^n \tag{2}$$

Substituting $P_n = C$ (a constant) into equation (1) we get

$$C - C(1 + i) = R$$

$$C = -\frac{R}{i}$$

And the particular integral is:

$$P_p = -\frac{R}{i} \tag{3}$$

Hence the general solution of our difference equation is:

$$\begin{aligned} P_n &= P_c + P_p \\ &= M(1 + i)^n - \frac{R}{i} \end{aligned} \tag{4}$$

[from equations (2) and (3)]
Definitizing the solution, we have:

$$P_n = P_0 \text{ when } n = 0$$

$$P_0 = M(1 + i)^0 - \frac{R}{i} \text{ from (4)}$$

Therefore $M = P_0 + \dfrac{R}{i}$

Substituting this into equation (4) we get:

$$P_n = \left(P_0 + \frac{R}{i}\right)(1 + i)^n - \frac{R}{i} \tag{5}$$

Equation (5) is the generalised formula from which all the other formulae of mathematics of finance can be obtained.

If $R = 0$, equation (5) becomes the compound interest formula:

$$P_n = P_0(1 + i)^n \tag{6}$$

Expressing P_0 in equation (6) as the dependent variable, we get the present value formula:

$$P_0 = P_n(1 + i)^{-n} \tag{7}$$

If P_0 in equation (5) is zero, it becomes the formula for the sum of an annuity of R per period:

$$P_n = \frac{R}{i}(1 + i)^n - \frac{R}{i}$$

$$= \frac{R[(1 + i)^n - 1]}{i} \tag{8}$$

The sum of an annuity of \$1 per period then, of course

$$= \frac{(1 + i)^n - 1}{i}$$

Equation (8) can be stated as

$$P_0(1 + i)^n = \frac{R[(1 + i)^n - 1]}{i}$$

Expressing P_0 as the dependent variable, we obtain the present value of an annuity of R per period:

$$P_0 = \frac{R[1 - (1 + i)^{-n}]}{i} \tag{9}$$

The present value of a perpetual annuity of R per period is then:

$$\lim_{n \to \infty} P_0 = \frac{R}{i} \tag{10}$$

Equation (5) can be solved for R when the other variables are known and $P_0 = 0$. R becomes the constant annual sinking fund requirement that must be invested at an interest rate of i per annum so as to arrive at the amount P_n (usually the loan to be repaid) at the end of the nth period:

$$R = \frac{iP_n}{(1 + i)^n - 1} \tag{11}$$

As a matter of fact any variable in equation (5) can be expressed as a function of the remaining variables. The variable to be ascertained is the dependent variable and the independent variables become known constants. In this way equation (5) can be used without further reduction to solve many problems involving mathematics of finance. Thus instead of memorizing a list of formulae, only one must be remembered. The others are easily obtained without much effort.

APPENDIX B

B.1. SOME AXIOMS OF PROBABILITY

1.1. The collection of all possible elementary outcomes of a random experiment which can be repeated under a given set of identical conditions is called the sample space of the experiment.

If S is the sample space and $E \subset S$, then $P(E)$ is the probability set function of the outcome of the random experiment, that is, $P(E)$ is the probability that the outcome is an element of E, which is termed an event.

If all the n elementary outcomes of the random experiment are designated $E_1, E_2, E_3, E_4, \ldots, E_n$:

$$P(E_i) \geq 0 \tag{1}$$

$$P(E_1) + P(E_2) + \cdots + P(E_n) = P(S) = 1 \tag{2}$$

$$P(E_1 \cup E_2 \cup E_3 \cup \cdots \cup E_n) = P(E_1) + P(E_2) + P(E_3) + \cdots + P(E_n) \tag{3}$$

where $E_i \cap E_j = 0$ = the null set and $i \neq j$

If $\bar{E}$ is designated as the complement of E, then $S = E \cup \bar{E}$ and $E \cap \bar{E} = 0$, so that

$$P(E) = 1 - P(\bar{E}) \tag{4}$$

since $P(E) + P(\bar{E}) = P(S) = 1$

$$\text{If } E = 0,\ P(E) = P(O) = 1 - P(S) = 0 \tag{5}$$

If $E_i \subset S$, $E_j \subset S$, and $E_i \subset E_j$,

then

$$P(E_i) \leq P(E_j) \tag{6}$$

$$P(O) \leq P(E_j) \leq P(S),\ j = 1, 2, \ldots, n$$

so that

$$O \leq P(E_j) \leq 1 \tag{7}$$

For any two events E_i, E_j, $(i \neq j)$ both being subsets of S,

$$P(E_i \cup E_j) = P(E_i) + P(E_j) - P(E_i \cap E_j) \tag{8}$$

And $P(E_i \cup E_j) = P(E_i) + P(E_j)$ (9)

if $P(E_i \cap E_j) = 0$, that is, if E_i and E_j are mutually exclusive.

The conditional probability of E_i given E_j is designated as $P(E_i/E_j)$:

$$P(E_i/E_j) = \frac{P(E_i \cap E_j)}{P(E_j)} \tag{10}$$

$$P(E_i/E_j) = P(E_i) \tag{11}$$

if E_i and E_j are independent.

1.2. If the random variable X represents the outcome of a random experiment whose sample space is S, then $p(x)$ is called the probability density function of X when

$$p(x) \geq 0,\ x \in S,$$

and

$$\sum_S p(x) = 1 \tag{12}$$

if X is discrete,
And

$$\int_S f(x)\, dx = 1 \tag{13}$$

if X is continuous.

B.2. MATHEMATICAL EXPECTATIONS

2.1. Expected Value

If X is a random variable having probability density function $p(x)$ and $f(X)$ is a function of X, then the mathematical expectation of

$f(X)$ is:

$$E[f(X)] = \sum_x f(x)p(x) \tag{14}$$

if X is discrete, and

$$= \int_{-\infty}^{\infty} f(x)p(x)\, dx \tag{15}$$

is X is continuous.

Generally, if $X_1, X_2, \ldots, X_n$ are random variables having probability density function $p(x_1, x_2, \ldots, x_n)$ and $f(X_1, X_2, \ldots, X_n)$ is a function of the variables, then the mathematical expectation of $f(X_1, X_2, \ldots, X_n)$ is:

$$E[f(X_1, X_2, \ldots, X_n)] = \sum_{x_n} \cdots \sum_{x_1} f(x_1, x_2, \ldots, x_n)p(x_1, x_2, \ldots, x_n) \tag{16}$$

if the variables are discrete, and

$$= \int_{-\infty}^{\infty} \cdots \int_{-\infty}^{\infty} f(x_1, x_2, \ldots, x_n)p(x_1, x_2, \ldots, x_n)\, dx_1 dx_2 \ldots dx_n \tag{17}$$

if the variables are continuous.

If $f(X) = X$, which is a discrete random variable having probability density function $p(x)$, then the mathematical expectation, called the expected value, of X is:

$$\mu_x = E(X) = \sum_x xp(x) \tag{18}$$

The observed mathematical expectation or sample arithmetic mean of X with a random sample size of n is:

$$\bar{X} = \sum_{i=1}^{n} X_i p_i(x) \tag{19}$$

$$\bar{X} = \frac{1}{n} \sum_{i=1}^{n} X_i \qquad \text{if } p(x) = \frac{1}{n} \tag{20}$$

2.2. Variances and Covariances

If $f(X) = (X - \mu_x)^2$ where X is a discrete random variable having probability density function $p(x)$, then the expected value of $f(X)$, called the variance of X is:

$$\begin{aligned} E[f(X)] &= \sum_x (x - \mu_x)^2 \, p(x) \\ &= E[(x - \mu_x)^2] \\ &= E(X^2) - \mu_x^2 \\ &= \sigma_x^2 \end{aligned} \tag{21}$$

The observed variance of X with a random sample of size n is:

$$S_x^2 = \sum_{i=1}^{n} (X_i - \bar{X})^2 \, P_i(x) \tag{22}$$

$$S_x^2 = \frac{1}{n-1} \sum_{i=1}^{n} (X_i - \bar{X})^2 \qquad \text{if } p(x) = \frac{1}{n} \tag{23}$$

If X, Y, and Z are random variables having joint probability density function $p(x, y, z)$ and $f(X, Y, Z)$ is a function of X, Y, Z; μ_x, μ_y, and μ_z are the expected values of X, Y and Z respectively; and σ_x^2, σ_y^2 and σ_z^2 are their variances respectively, then the following mathematical expectations, called covariances, can be calculated:

The covariance of X and Y is:

$$\begin{aligned} \sigma_{XY}^2 &= \sum_x \sum_y (x - \mu_x)(y - \mu_Y) p(x, y) \\ &= E[(X - \mu_x)(Y - \mu_Y)] \\ &= E(XY) - \mu_x \, \mu_Y \end{aligned} \tag{24}$$

where

$$E(XY) = \sum_x \sum_y xyp(x, y)$$

The covariance of X and Z is:

$$\sigma_{XZ}^2 = E[(X - \mu_x)(Z - \mu_z)] = E(XZ) - \mu_x \mu_z \tag{25}$$

And the covariance of Y and Z is:

$$\sigma_{YZ}^2 = E[(Y - \mu_Y)(Z - \mu_z)] = E(YZ) - \mu_Y \mu_Z \tag{26}$$

The observed covariance of Y and Z with random sample sizes of n is:

$$\begin{aligned} S_{YZ}^2 &= E[(Y - \bar{Y})(Z - \bar{Z})] \\ &= \frac{1}{n-1}\left[\sum_{i=1}^{n} (Y_i - \bar{Y})(Z_i - \bar{Z})\right] \end{aligned} \tag{27}$$

The correlation coefficient of X and Z is:

$$\rho_{XZ} = \frac{\sigma_{zx}^2}{\sigma_x \sigma_z} \tag{28}$$

2.3. Linear Transformations and Combinations

If X is a random variable with mean μ_x and variance σ_x^2, then

$$Y = a + bX$$

has mean

$$\mu_Y = a + b\mu_x \tag{29}$$

and variance

$$\sigma_Y^2 = b^2 \ \sigma_x^2 \tag{30}$$

$$\sigma_Y = |b| \ \sigma_x \tag{31}$$

If the observed mean and variance of X with a random sample size of n are $\bar{X}$ and S_{XX}^2 respectively, then

$$Y_i = a + bX_i$$

has mean

$$\bar{Y} = a + b\bar{X} \tag{32}$$

and variance

$$S_{YY}^2 = b^2 S_{XX}^2 \quad (33)$$

$$S_Y = |b| S_X \quad (34)$$

If X and Y are two random variables, the following results hold:

$$E[aX + bY] = aE(X) + bE(Y) \quad (35)$$

$$\text{Variancc } (aX + bY) = a^2\ \sigma_x^2 + b^2\sigma_Y^2 + 2ab\sigma_{xY}^2 \quad (36)$$

$$E(X + Y) = E(X) + E(Y) \quad (37)$$

$$\text{Variance } [X + Y] = \sigma_x^2 + \sigma_Y^2 + 2\sigma_{xY}^2 \quad (38)$$

If X and Y are independent

$$\sigma_{xY}^2 = 0 \quad (39)$$

B.3. SOME DISTRIBUTIONS

3.1. Normal

A continuous random variable X is said to have a normal distribution with mean μ and variance σ^2 if its probability density function is:

$$p(x) = \frac{1}{\sigma\sqrt{2\Pi}}\, e^{-1/2\left(\frac{x-\mu}{\sigma}\right)^2} \quad (40)$$

where $\Pi = 22/7$

and $e = \lim_{n\to\infty}\left(1 + \frac{1}{n}\right)^n$

The random variable Z,

$$Z = \frac{X - \mu}{\sigma} \quad (41)$$

has a standard normal distribution with $\mu = 0$ and $\sigma^2 = 1$ and its probability density function is:

$$p(z) = \frac{1}{\sqrt{2\Pi}} e^{-(1/2)Z^2} \tag{42}$$

3.2. Chi-square

When w independent standard normal variables are squared and added, the result is the Chi-square variable with w degrees of freedom:

$$\chi_w^2 = \sum_{i=1}^{w} Z_i^2 \tag{43}$$

having the following properties:

$$E(\chi_w^2) = w \tag{44}$$

$$\begin{aligned} \text{Variance } (\chi_w^2) &= w \text{ variance } (z^2) \\ &= 2w \end{aligned} \tag{45}$$

If χ_w^2 is divided by the w degrees of freedom the result is the modified Chi-square variable:

$$C_w^2 = \frac{\chi_w^2}{w} \tag{46}$$

3.3. Student's t

If a standard normal variable z is divided by $\sqrt{C_w^2}$, the result is a student's t variable with w degrees of freedom:

$$t_w = \frac{z}{\sqrt{C_w^2}} \tag{47}$$

t_w tends to z as w increases;

z can be virtually used in lieu of t_w when w is large, say $w \geq 30$.

In regression analysis with m regressors and n observations, when s^2 is used instead of the unknown σ^2 and for testing hypotheses or estimating confidence interval for a single parameter, say a_i, then:

$$t_{n-m} = \frac{\hat{a}_i - a_i}{\sqrt{\dfrac{S^2}{\sum x_i^2}}} \tag{48}$$

with $(n - m)$ degrees of freedom.

3.4. F

If one modified Chi-square variable C_w^2 is divided by another C_v^2 with w and v degrees of freedom respectively, the result is an F variable with w and v degrees of freedom:

$$F_{w,v} = \frac{C_w^2}{C_v^2} \tag{49}$$

In regression analysis with m regressors and n observations, when s^2 is used instead of the unknown σ^2, and for testing hypotheses or estimating confidence interval for k parameters, then:

$$F_{k,\,n-m} = \frac{1}{kS^2}\left[(\hat{A} - A)^T(X^TX)(\hat{A} - A)\right] \tag{50}$$

with k, and $(n - m)$ degrees of freedom and where the linear dependence relation is of the form:

$$\begin{aligned} Y &= a_1 + a_2x_2 + \cdots + a_mx_m + e \\ &= XA + e \text{ in matrix notation} \end{aligned}$$

B.4. LINEAR REGRESSION

4.1. Least-squares

If X and Y are two variables whose dependence relation is linear in the form:

$$Y = a + bX + e \tag{51}$$

where e is a random disturbance with zero mean and variance σ^2, and if there are n observations on (X, Y), the least-squares method of determining the parameter estimates $\hat{a}$ and $\hat{b}$ is to minimize the sum of the squares of the errors.

$$\text{Minimize} \quad \left[\sum_{i=1}^{n} \hat{e}_i^2 = \sum_{i=1}^{n} (Y_i - \hat{a} - \hat{b}X_i)^2\right] \tag{52}$$

Expressing both Y_i and X_i as deviations from their expected values gives:

$$\text{Minimize} \quad \sum_{i=1}^{n} (y_i - \hat{b}x_i)^2 = f(\hat{b}) \tag{53}$$

where $y_i = (Y_i - \bar{Y})$ and $x_i = (X_i - \bar{X})$.

The necessary conditions for a minimum are:

$$\frac{df(\hat{b})}{d\hat{b}} = -2x_i \sum_{i=1}^{n} (y_i - \hat{b}x_i) = 0$$

and

$$\frac{d^2f(b)}{d\hat{b}^2} = \sum_{i=1}^{n} x_i^2 > 0 \tag{54}$$

Equation (54) gives the estimated $\hat{b}$:

$$\hat{b} = \frac{\sum x_i y_i}{\sum x_i^2} \tag{55}$$

Reverting $y_i = \hat{b}x_i$ to the original expression gives:

$$Y_i - \bar{Y} = \hat{b}(X_i - \bar{X}) \text{ from which } \hat{a} = \bar{Y} - \hat{b}\bar{X} \tag{56}$$

The best fit regression line is therefore:

$$\hat{Y} = \hat{a} + \hat{b}X \tag{57}$$

4.2. Correlation Coefficient and Determination

It can be proved that the coefficient of correlation between X and Y, which measures the degree of co-variation or moving together of X and Y is:

$$r_{XY} = \frac{\sum x_i y_i}{\sqrt{\sum x_i^2 \sum y_i^2}} \tag{58}$$

The coefficient of determination is:

$$r_{XY}^2 = \frac{\sum (\hat{Y}_i - \bar{Y})^2}{\sum (Y_i - \bar{Y})^2} = \frac{\text{explained variation of Y}}{\text{total variation of Y}} \tag{59}$$

4.3. Properties

It can be proved that both $\hat{a}$ and $\hat{b}$ are unbiased minimum variance estimators (best linear unbiased estimators) of a and b respectively if the assumption is made that the errors e_i are independent random variables normally distributed and independent of the x_i which may be fixed or random provided its distribution is independent of a, b or σ^2. The following properties then hold:

$$\begin{aligned} E(\hat{a}) &= a \\ E(\hat{b}) &= b \\ \text{variance } (\hat{a}) &= \frac{\sigma^2}{n} \\ \text{variance } (\hat{b}) &= \frac{\sigma^2}{\sum x_i^2} \end{aligned} \tag{60}$$

where σ^2 is the variance of e, that is, of Y. The unbiased estimator of σ^2 is:

$$S^2 = \frac{1}{n-2} \sum_{i=1}^{n} [Y_i - \hat{a} - \hat{b}X_i]^2 = \frac{1}{n-2} \sum (Y_i - \hat{Y}_i)^2 \tag{61}$$

with $(n - 2)$ degrees of freedom. The loss of the two degrees of freedom results from the necessity of calculating $\hat{a}$ and $\hat{b}$. Equations (55) and (58) give:

$$\frac{\hat{b}}{r_{XY}} = \sqrt{\frac{\sum y_i^2}{\sum x_i^2}}$$
$$= \frac{S_Y}{S_X}$$

Hence,

$$\hat{b} = r_{XY}\frac{S_Y}{S_X} \qquad (62)$$

where S_Y and S_X are the observed standard deviations of Y and X respectively.

Thus $\hat{b} = 0$ if there is no correlation between X and Y.

4.4. Interval Estimation

If the assumptions mentioned previously hold, interval estimation can be validly made about the parameters a, b, Y and others.

$\hat{b}$ may be standardized to obtain:

$$z = \frac{\hat{b} - b}{\sqrt{\frac{\sigma^2}{\sum x_i^2}}} \qquad (63)$$

where z, is normally distributed with mean zero and variance 1. But when S^2 is substituted for the unknown σ^2, the standardized $\hat{b}$ loses its normal distribution and has instead the student's t distribution with $(n - 2)$ degrees of freedom:

$$t = \frac{\hat{b} - \mathrm{b}}{\sqrt{\frac{S^2}{\sum x_i^2}}} \qquad (64)$$

The interval $(-t_{.025}, t_{.025})$ with $t_{.025}$ designating the t value leaving $2\frac{1}{2}\%$ of the distribution in the upper-tail is called a random variable, and may be expressed as the probability

$$P(-t_{.025} < t < t_{.025}) = .95 \tag{65}$$

Substituting t with equation (64) gives:

$$P\left(-t_{.025} < \frac{\hat{b} - b}{\sqrt{\dfrac{S^2}{\sum x_i^2}}} < t_{.025}\right) = .95 \tag{66}$$

$$P\left(\hat{b} - t_{.025}\frac{S}{\sqrt{\sum x_i^2}} < b < \hat{b} + t_{.025}\frac{S}{\sqrt{\sum x_i^2}}\right) = .95 \tag{67}$$

The 95% confidence interval for b is therefore:

$$b = \hat{b} \pm t_{.025}\frac{S}{\sqrt{\sum x_i^2}} \tag{68}$$

Similarly, the 95% confidence interval for a is:

$$a = \hat{a} \pm t_{.025}\frac{S\sqrt{\sum X_i^2}}{\sqrt{n\sum x_i^2}} = \hat{a} \pm t_{.025}S\sqrt{\frac{1}{n} + \frac{\bar{X}^2}{\sum x_i^2}} \tag{69}$$

The 95% confidence interval for the mean value of Y_0 is:

$$\mu_{Y_0} = \mu_{\hat{Y}_0} \pm t_{.025}S\sqrt{\frac{1}{n} + \frac{x_0^2}{\sum x_i^2}} \tag{70}$$

where $\mu_{\hat{Y}_0} = \hat{a} + \hat{b}x_0$
$x_0 = (X_0 - \bar{X})$, X_0 being given.

The 95% confidence interval for an individual Y_0 is:

$$Y_0 = \hat{Y}_0 \pm t_{.025}\, S\sqrt{\frac{1}{n} + \frac{x_0^2}{\sum x_i^2} + 1} \tag{71}$$

For equations 68 to 71, $t_{.025}$ is obtained from Student's t Critical One-tail test table with $(n - 2)$ degrees of freedom.

4.5. Testing Hypotheses

A two-sided test of a hypothesis can be carried out by simply ascertaining whether the hypothesis is found within the confidence interval. For instance, if the null hypothesis

$$H_0 : b = 0, \tag{72}$$

is tested against the two-sided alternative

$$H_1 : b \neq 0, \tag{73}$$

then H_0 must be rejected at the 5% significance level if the null hypothesis of zero is not found in the confidence interval, otherwise it is accepted.

Suppose the null hypothesis

$$H_0 : b = 0, \tag{74}$$

is tested against the one-sided alternative,

$$H_1 : b > 0 \tag{75}$$

Here the comparison of

$$t = \frac{\hat{b}}{\sqrt{\dfrac{S^2}{\sum x_i^2}}} \tag{76}$$

must be made with the critical $t_{.05}$ value from Student's t Critical One-tail test table with $(n - 2)$ degrees of freedom.

If $t >$ this critical $t_{.05}$ value, H_0 must be rejected, otherwise it is accepted.

It must be pointed out that the final decision of accepting or rejecting must not be based on the mechanical testing of hypotheses alone; sound judgment and thorough understanding of the model tested as well as any prior experience should play an important role in the final decision-making.

B.5. MULTIPLE REGRESSION

5.1. Least-squares

If $Y, X_2, X_3, \ldots, X_m$ are m variables whose dependence relation is linear in the form:

$$Y = a_1 + a_2X_2 + \cdots + a_mX_m + e \tag{77}$$

where e is a random disturbance with zero mean and variance σ^2 and if there are n observations on $(Y, X_2, X_3, \ldots, X_m)$, the least-squares method of determining the parameter estimates a_i, $(i = 1, 2, \ldots, m)$ is to minimize the sum of the squares of the errors, e_i.

The n observations may be written in matrix notation as:

$$Y = XA + e \tag{78}$$

where

$$\begin{aligned} Y &= [Y_1, Y_2, \ldots, Y_n]^T \\ A &= [a_1, a_2, \ldots a_m]^T \\ e &= [e_1, e_2, \ldots e_n]^T \\ X &= \begin{bmatrix} 1 & X_{12} & \cdots & X_{1m} \\ 1 & X_{22} & \cdots & X_{2m} \\ \vdots & & & \\ 1 & X_{n2} & \cdots & X_{nm} \end{bmatrix} \end{aligned}$$

Minimize $$M[= \hat{e}^T\hat{e} = (Y - X\hat{A})^T(Y - X\hat{A})] \tag{79}$$

Equating to zero the partial derivatives of M with respect to $\hat{A}$ gives:

$$\frac{\partial M}{\partial \hat{A}} = -2X^TY + 2X^TX\hat{A} = 0$$

Hence, $$\hat{A} = (X^TX)^{-1}X^TY \tag{80}$$

The estimated (best fit) multiple regression is therefore:

$$\hat{Y} = X\hat{A} \tag{81}$$

5.2. Properties

The following properties can be proved:

$$\begin{aligned} E(Y) &= XA \\ \text{co-variance } (e) &= \text{co-variance } (Y) = \sigma^2 I \\ E(\hat{A}) &= A \\ \text{co-variance } (\hat{A}) &= .\sigma^2 (X^T X)^{-1} \end{aligned} \tag{82}$$

According to the Gauss-Markov Theorem, the least-squares estimators $\hat{A}$ are unbiased minimum variance estimators. They are the best linear unbiased estimators.

5.3. Correlation Coefficient and Determination

The multiple correlation coefficient R is:

$$R = \sqrt{\frac{\sum(\hat{Y}_i - \bar{Y})^2}{\sum(Y_i - \bar{Y})^2}} \tag{83}$$

The coefficient of determination is:

$$\begin{aligned} R^2 &= \frac{\sum(\hat{Y}_i - \bar{Y})^2}{\sum(Y_i - \bar{Y})^2} \\ &= \frac{(\hat{Y} - \bar{Y})^T(\hat{Y} - \bar{Y})}{(Y - \bar{Y})^T(Y - \bar{Y})} \\ &= \frac{\text{explained variation of } Y}{\text{total variation of } Y} \end{aligned} \tag{84}$$

The partial correlation of Y and X_2 estimates the degree of co-variation or moving together of Y and X_2 after removing the influence of $X_3, \ldots, X_m$ from both Y and X_2.

If there are only three variables X_2, X_3 and Y, then the partial correlation of Y and X_2 is:

$$r_{YX_2} \cdot X_3 = \frac{r_{YX_2} - r_{YX_3} r_{X_2X_3}}{\sqrt{1 - r^2_{X_2X_3}} \sqrt{1 - r^2_{YX_3}}} \tag{85}$$

If there is no correlation between Y and X_3 and between X_2 and X_3, then

$$r_{YX_2} \cdot X_3 = r_{YX_2} \tag{86}$$

since

$$r_{YX_3} = r_{X_2X_3} = 0$$

5.4. F-statistic

It can be shown that the following variable has an F distribution with k and $(n - m)$ degrees of freedom, where m is the total number of variables in the model, k is the number of parameters to be tested, and n is the number of observations:

$$F = \frac{1}{S^2 k} [(\hat{A} - A)^T (X^T X)(\hat{A} - A)] \tag{87}$$

$$\text{where } S^2 = \frac{1}{n - m} (Y - \hat{Y})^T (Y - \hat{Y}) \tag{88}$$

with $(n - m)$ degrees of freedom since m estimated parameters $\hat{A}$ have been calculated; S^2 is the unbiased estimator of the unknown σ^2.

If all the parameters are tested, a joint test F-statistic is often expressed as:

$$F = \frac{\text{variance explained by regression}}{\text{unexplained variance}}$$

$$= \frac{1}{S^2 m} [(\hat{Y} - \bar{Y})^T (\hat{Y} - \bar{Y})] \tag{89}$$

$$= \frac{R^2/(m - 1)}{(1 - R^2)/(n - m)} = \frac{R^2(n - m)}{(1 - R^2)(m - 1)} \tag{90}$$

S^2 being the unexplained variance, and only $a_2, \ldots, a_m$ are tested.

5.5. Interval Estimation

From equation (87) the probability statement may be made:

$$P\left[\frac{1}{S^2k}(\hat{A} - A)^T(X^TX)(\hat{A} - A) \leq F_{\alpha/2}\right] = (100)(1 - \alpha)\% \quad (91)$$

A (100)(1 − α) per cent confidence interval for the mean value of Y_0 may be made from equation (91) as:

$$U_{Y_0} = \hat{Y}_0 \pm t_{\alpha/2}S\sqrt{X_0(X^TX)^{-1}\ X_0^T} \quad (92)$$

where $t^2_{\alpha/2} = F_{\alpha/2}$,
$\hat{Y}_0 = X_0\ \hat{A}$ from equation (81) and X_0 is given.

Similarly, a (100)(1 − α) per cent confidence interval for an individual Y_0 is:

$$Y_0 = \hat{Y}_0 \pm t_{\alpha/2}S\sqrt{X_0(X^TX)^{-1}\ X_0^T + 1} \quad (94)$$

where $\hat{Y}_0 = X_0\ \hat{A}$ with X_0 given.

A (100)(1 − α) per cent confidence interval for an individual a_i is:

$$a_i = \hat{a}_i \pm s_i\ t_{\alpha/2} \quad (95)$$

where $s_i = (\sqrt{(X^TX)_i^{-1}}\ S)$ is the estimated standard error of a_i and $(X^TX)_i^{-1}$ is the ith diagonal element of $(X^TX)^{-1}$.

For equations (92) to (95), $t_{\alpha/2}$ is obtained from Student's t Critical One-tail test table with $(n - m)$ degrees of freedom.

5.6. Testing Hypotheses

A two-sided test of a hypothesis can be carried out by simply ascertaining whether the hypothesis is found within the confidence interval. For instance if the hypothesis

$$H_0: a_i = h, \tag{96}$$

is tested against the two-sided alternative

$$H_1: a_i \neq h, \tag{97}$$

then H_0 must be rejected at the α significance level if the hypothesis of h value is not found in the confidence interval.

If the null hypothesis,

$$H_0: \ a_i = 0, \tag{98}$$

is tested against the one-sided alternative

$$H_1: \ a_i > 0, \tag{99}$$

then H_0 must be rejected if

$$t = \left| \frac{\hat{a}_i}{s_i} \right| > \text{the critical } t \text{ value} \tag{100}$$

with t having $(n - m)$ degrees of freedom.

If the separate tests for the significance of the individual coefficients a_i lead us to accept all the null hypotheses, we may not necessarily reject the regression relationship itself because multicollinearity may exist to a very great extent. A joint test for the significance of the entire regression taking into account all the coefficients is carried out using the F-statistic in equation (90).

If the null hypothesis

$$H_0: \ A = 0, \tag{101}$$

is tested against the alternative,

$$H_1: \ A \neq 0, \tag{101}$$

then the H_0 must be rejected if

$F >$ the critical α point of F where the critical α point of F is obtained from the F table with (m) and $(n - m)$ degrees of freedom.

5.7. Linearity and Normal Distribution

The basic assumption of the multiple regression explained above is linearity in the sense that the dependent variable Y is linearly related to the independent variables, X_i. Sometimes a non-linear relationship can be transformed into a linear one and multiple regression analysis can still be performed. For valid tests of significance and confidence interval estimates, the assumption that the random disturbance e_i are normally distributed with zero mean and constant variance σ^2 must hold. The normal distribution assumption can usually be made to hold by increasing n.

5.8. Multi-collinearity

If the columns of X in equation (78) are nearly linearly dependent, the problem of multi-collinearity exists. This is not very serious if the objective is merely to predict Y_0. But as multi-collinearity increases, the reliability of the estimators $\hat{a}_i$ of a_i decreases, and the separate influences of the independent variables on Y are extremely difficult to estimate; the influence on Y of one regressor may be wrongly attributed to another if both regressors are highly correlated. If there is perfect collinearity in the sense that X^TX is singular, then $(X^TX)^{-1}$ does not exist and A can hardly be estimated. Regressors should therefore be as mutually uncorrelated as possible.

The problem of multi-collinearity does not exist if the columns of X are orthogonal in the sense that (X^TX) is a diagonal matrix. In the absence of multi-collinearity, the relevance of regressors can be more easily determined, their confidence intervals are made more precise, and the inclusion or exclusion of certain regressors will not affect the coefficients $\hat{A}$ already calculated.

5.9. Autocorrelation

This problem may arise involving time series where e_t at time t is correlated with e_{t-1}, e_{t-2}, and so on. Thus the assumption of its independence of one another is violated. One method of detecting autocorrelation is the use of the Durbin-Watson statistic. The presence of autocorrelation renders estimates of R^2, confidence interval estimates and tests of significance unreliable.

5.10. Heteroscedasticity

If the variance σ^2 of the errors e_i is not constant, the problem of heteroscedasticity arises. Its presence can be detected by the Durbin-Watson statistic. Heteroscedasticity, if uncorrected, is serious because variances are not valid and test of significance are not reliable.

Methods and approaches dealing with problems of heteroscedasticity, autocorrelation, multi-collinearity, non-linearity and simultaneous equations are beyond the scope of this appendix.

B.6. SELECTED BIBLIOGRAPHY

1. A.G. Goldberger: Econometric Theory.
2. Hoel: Elementary Statistics.
3. D.S. Huang: Regression and Econometric Methods.
4. J. Johnston: Econometric Methods.
5. E. Malinvaud: Statistical Methods of Econometrics.
6. H. Theil: Principles of Econometrics.
7. S.S. Wilks: Mathematical Statistics.
8. R.J. Wonnacott and T.H. Wonnacott: Econometrics.
9. G.U. Yule and M.G. Kendall: An Introduction to the Theory of Statistics.

APPENDIX C

Table 1

$$\frac{1}{(1+i)^n} = \text{Present Value of \$1}$$

n \ i	1%	2%	3%	4%	5%	6%	8%	10%	12%	14%	15%	16%	18%	20%	22%	24%
1 . . .	0.990	0.980	0.971	0.962	0.952	0.943	0.926	0.909	0.893	0.877	0.870	0.862	0.817	0.833	0.820	0.807
2 . . .	0.980	0.961	0.943	0.925	0.907	0.890	0.857	0.826	0.797	0.769	0.756	0.743	0.718	0.694	0.672	0.650
3 . . .	0.971	0.912	0.915	0.889	0.864	0.810	0.794	0.751	0.712	0.675	0.658	0.611	0.609	0.579	0.551	0.524
4 . . .	0.961	0.924	0.888	0.855	0.823	0.792	0.735	0.683	0.636	0.592	0.572	0.552	0.516	0.482	0.451	0.423
5 . . .	0.951	0.906	0.863	0.822	0.784	0.747	0.681	0.621	0.567	0.519	0.497	0.476	0.437	0.402	0.370	0.341
6 . . .	0.942	0.888	0.837	0.790	0.746	0.705	0.630	0.564	0.507	0.456	0.432	0.410	0.370	0.335	0.303	0.275
7 . . .	0.933	0.871	0.813	0.760	0.711	0.665	0.583	0.513	0.452	0.400	0.376	0.354	0.314	0.279	0.249	0.222
8 . . .	0.923	0.853	0.789	0.731	0.677	0.627	0.540	0.467	0.404	0.351	0.327	0.305	0.266	0.233	0.204	0.179
9 . . .	0.914	0.837	0.766	0.703	0.615	0.592	0.500	0.424	0.361	0.308	0.284	0.263	0.225	0.191	0.167	0.144
10 . . .	0.905	0.820	0.744	0.676	0.614	0.558	0.463	0.386	0.322	0.270	0.247	0.227	0.191	0.162	0.137	0.116
11 . . .	0.896	0.804	0.722	0.650	0.585	0.527	0.429	0.350	0.287	0.237	0.215	0.195	0.162	0.135	0.112	0.094
12 . . .	0.887	0.788	0.701	0.625	0.557	0.497	0.397	0.319	0.257	0.208	0.187	0.168	0.137	0.112	0.092	0.076
13 . . .	0.879	0.773	0.681	0.601	0.530	0.469	0.368	0.290	0.229	0.182	0.163	0.145	0.116	0.093	0.075	0.061
14 . . .	0.870	0.758	0.661	0.577	0.505	0.442	0.340	0.263	0.205	0.160	0.141	0.125	0.099	0.078	0.062	0.049
15 . . .	0.861	0.743	0.642	0.555	0.481	0.417	0.315	0.239	0.183	0.140	0.123	0.108	0.081	0.065	0.051	0.040
16 . . .	0.853	0.728	0.623	0.534	0.458	0.394	0.292	0.218	0.163	0.123	0.107	0.093	0.071	0.054	0.042	0.032
17 . . .	0.844	0.714	0.605	0.513	0.436	0.371	0.270	0.198	0.146	0.108	0.093	0.080	0.060	0.045	0.034	0.026
18 . . .	0.836	0.700	0.587	0.494	0.416	0.350	0.250	0.180	0.130	0.095	0.081	0.069	0.051	0.038	0.028	0.021
19 . . .	0.828	0.686	0.570	0.475	0.396	0.331	0.232	0.164	0.116	0.083	0.070	0.060	0.043	0.031	0.023	0.017
20 . . .	0.820	0.673	0.554	0.456	0.377	0.312	0.215	0.149	0.104	0.073	0.061	0.051	0.037	0.026	0.019	0.014
21 . . .	0.811	0.660	0.538	0.439	0.359	0.294	0.199	0.135	0.093	0.064	0.053	0.044	0.031	0.022	0.015	0.011
22 . . .	0.803	0.647	0.522	0.422	0.342	0.278	0.184	0.123	0.083	0.056	0.046	0.038	0.026	0.018	0.013	0.009
23 . . .	0.795	0.634	0.507	0.406	0.326	0.262	0.170	0.112	0.074	0.049	0.040	0.033	0.022	0.015	0.010	0.007
24 . . .	0.788	0.622	0.492	0.390	0.310	0.247	0.158	0.102	0.066	0.043	0.035	0.028	0.019	0.013	0.008	0.006
25 . . .	0.780	0.610	0.478	0.375	0.295	0.233	0.146	0.092	0.059	0.038	0.030	0.024	0.016	0.010	0.007	0.005

Table 2

$$\frac{1}{i}\left[1 - (1 + i)^{-n}\right] = \text{Present Value of \$1 Received Annually}$$

n \ i	1%	2%	3%	4%	5%	6%	8%	10%	12%	14%	15%	16%	18%	20%	22%	24%
1 . . .	0.990	0.980	0.971	0.962	0.952	0.943	0.926	0.909	0.893	0.877	0.870	0.862	0.847	0.833	0.820	0.807
2 . . .	1.970	1.942	1.914	1.886	1.859	1.833	1.783	1.736	1.690	1.647	1.626	1.605	1.566	1.528	1.492	1.457
3 . . .	2.941	2.884	2.829	2.775	2.723	2.673	2.577	2.487	2.402	2.322	2.283	2.246	2.174	2.106	2.042	1.981
4 . . .	3.902	3.808	3.717	3.630	3.546	3.465	3.312	3.170	3.037	2.914	2.855	2.798	2.690	2.589	2.494	2.404
5 . . .	4.853	4.713	4.580	4.452	4.330	4.212	3.993	3.791	3.605	3.433	3.352	3.274	3.127	2.991	2.864	2.745
6 . . .	5.795	5.601	5.417	5.242	5.076	4.917	4.623	4.355	4.111	3.889	3.784	3.685	3.498	3.326	3.167	3.020
7 . . .	6.728	6.472	6.230	6.002	5.786	5.582	5.206	4.868	4.564	4.288	4.160	4.039	3.812	3.605	3.416	3.242
8 . . .	7.652	7.325	7.020	6.733	6.463	6.210	5.747	5.335	4.968	4.639	4.487	4.344	4.078	3.837	3.619	3.421
9 . . .	8.566	8.162	7.786	7.435	7.108	6.802	6.247	5.759	5.328	4.946	4.772	4.607	4.303	4.031	3.786	3.566
10 . . .	9.471	8.983	8.530	8.111	7.722	7.360	6.710	6.145	5.650	5.216	5.019	4.833	4.494	4.192	3.923	3.682
11 . . .	10.368	9.787	9.253	8.760	8.306	7.887	7.139	6.495	5.938	5.453	5.234	5.029	4.656	4.327	4.035	3.776
12 . . .	11.255	10.575	9.954	9.385	8.863	8.384	7.536	6.814	6.194	5.660	5.421	5.197	4.793	4.439	4.127	3.851
13 . . .	12.134	11.348	10.635	9.986	9.394	8.853	7.904	7.103	6.424	5.842	5.583	5.342	4.910	4.533	4.203	3.912
14 . . .	13.004	12.106	11.296	10.563	9.899	9.295	8.244	7.367	6.628	6.002	5.724	5.468	5.008	4.611	4.265	3.962
15 . . .	13.865	12.849	11.938	11.118	10.380	9.712	8.559	7.606	6.811	6.142	5.847	5.576	5.092	4.676	4.315	4.001
16 . . .	14.718	13.578	12.561	11.652	10.838	10.106	8.851	7.824	6.974	6.265	5.954	5.668	5.162	4.730	4.357	4.033
17 . . .	15.562	14.292	13.166	12.166	11.274	10.477	9.122	8.022	7.120	6.373	6.047	5.749	5.222	4.775	4.391	4.059
18 . . .	16.398	14.992	13.754	12.659	11.690	10.828	9.372	8.201	7.250	6.467	6.128	5.818	5.273	4.812	4.419	4.080
19 . . .	17.226	15.678	14.324	13.134	12.085	11.158	9.604	8.365	7.366	6.550	6.198	5.878	5.316	4.844	4.112	4.097
20 . . .	18.046	16.351	14.877	13.590	12.462	11.470	9.818	8.514	7.469	6.623	6.259	5.929	5.353	4.870	4.460	4.110
21 . . .	18.857	17.011	15.415	14.029	12.821	11.764	10.017	8.649	7.562	6.687	6.312	5.973	5.384	4.891	4.476	4.121
22 . . .	19.660	17.658	15.937	14.451	13.163	12.042	10.201	8.772	7.645	6.743	6.859	6.011	5.410	4.909	4.488	4.130
23 . . .	20.456	18.292	16.444	14.857	13.489	12.303	10.371	8.883	7.718	6.792	6.399	6.044	5.432	4.924	4.499	4.137
24 . . .	21.243	18.914	16.936	15.247	13.799	12.550	10.529	8.985	7.784	6.835	6.434	6.073	5.451	4.937	4.507	4.143
25 . . .	22.023	19.523	17.413	15.622	14.094	12.783	10.675	9.077	7.843	6.873	6.464	6.097	5.467	4.948	4.514	4.147

Table 3

$$P(X \le x) = N(x) = \frac{1}{\sqrt{2\pi}} \int_{-\infty}^{x} e^{-z^2/2}\, dz = \frac{1}{\sqrt{2\pi}} \int_{0}^{x} e^{-z^2/2}\, dz + 0.5$$

x	0	1	2	3	4	5	6	7	8	9
0.0	.5000	.5040	.5080	.5120	.5160	.5199	.5239	.5279	.5319	.5359
0.1	.5398	.5438	.5478	.5517	.5557	.5596	.5636	.5675	.5714	.5754
0.2	.5793	.5832	.5871	.5910	.5948	.5987	.6026	.6064	.6103	.6141
0.3	.6179	.6217	.6255	.6293	.6331	.6368	.6406	.6443	.6480	.6517
0.4	.6554	.6591	.6628	.6664	.6700	.6736	.6772	.6808	.6844	.6879
0.5	.6915	.6950	.6985	.7019	.7054	.7088	.7123	.7157	.7190	.7224
0.6	.7258	.7291	.7324	.7357	.7389	.7422	.7454	.7486	.7518	.7549
0.7	.7580	.7612	.7642	.7673	.7704	.7734	.7764	.7794	.7823	.7852
0.8	.7881	.7910	.7939	.7967	.7996	.8023	.8051	.8078	.8106	.8133
0.9	.8159	.8186	.8212	.8238	.8264	.8289	.8315	.8340	.8365	.8389
1.0	.8413	.8438	.8461	.8485	.8508	.8531	.8554	.8577	.8599	.8621
1.1	.8643	.8665	.8686	.8708	.8729	.8749	.8770	.8790	.8810	.8830
1.2	.8849	.8869	.8888	.8907	.8925	.8944	.8962	.8980	.8997	.9015
1.3	.9032	.9049	.9066	.9082	.9099	.9115	.9131	.9147	.9162	.9177
1.4	.9192	.9207	.9222	.9236	.9251	.9265	.9279	.9292	.9306	.9319
1.5	.9332	.9345	.9357	.9370	.9382	.9394	.9406	.9418	.9429	.9441
1.6	.9452	.9463	.9474	.9484	.9495	.9505	.9515	.9525	.9535	.9545
1.7	.9554	.9564	.9573	.9582	.9591	.9599	.9608	.9616	.9625	.9633
1.8	.9641	.9649	.9656	.9664	.9671	.9678	.9686	.9693	.9699	.9706
1.9	.9713	.9719	.9726	.9732	.9738	.9744	.9750	.9756	.9761	.9767

Table 3 (*cont.*)

x	0	1	2	3	4	5	6	7	8	9
2.0	.9772	.9778	.9783	.9788	.9793	.9798	.9803	.9808	.9812	.9817
2.1	.9821	.9826	.9830	.9834	.9838	.9842	.9846	.9850	.9854	.9857
2.2	.9861	.9864	.9868	.9871	.9875	.9878	.9881	.9884	.9887	.9890
2.3	.9893	.9896	.9898	.9901	.9904	.9906	.9909	.9911	.9913	.9916
2.4	.9918	.9920	.9922	.9925	.9927	.9929	.9931	.9932	.9934	.9936
2.5	.9938	.9940	.9941	.9943	.9945	.9946	.9948	.9949	.9951	.9952
2.6	.9953	.9955	.9956	.9957	.9959	.9960	.9961	.9962	.9963	.9964
2.7	.9965	.9966	.9967	.9968	.9969	.9970	.9971	.9972	.9973	.9974
2.8	.9974	.9975	.9976	.9977	.9977	.9978	.9979	.9979	.9980	.9981
2.9	.9981	.9982	.9982	.9983	.9984	.9984	.9985	.9985	.9986	.9986
3.0	.9987	.9987	.9987	.9988	.9988	.9989	.9989	.9989	.9990	.9990
3.1	.9990	.9991	.9991	.9991	.9992	.9992	.9992	.9992	.9993	.9993
3.2	.9993	.9993	.9994	.9994	.9994	.9994	.9994	.9995	.9995	.9995
3.3	.9995	.9995	.9995	.9996	.9996	.9996	.9996	.9996	.9996	.9997
3.4	.9997	.9997	.9997	.9997	.9997	.9997	.9997	.9997	.9997	.9998
3.5	.9998	.9998	.9998	.9998	.9998	.9998	.9998	.9998	.9998	.9998
3.6	.9998	.9998	.9999	.9999	.9999	.9999	.9999	.9999	.9999	.9999
3.7	.9999	.9999	.9999	.9999	.9999	.9999	.9999	.9999	.9999	.9999
3.8	.9999	.9999	.9999	.9999	.9999	.9999	.9999	.9999	.9999	.9999
3.9	1.0000	1.0000	1.0000	1.0000	1.0000	1.0000	1.0000	1.0000	1.0000	1.0000

Table 4

$$P(T \leq -t) = 1 - P(T \leq t)$$

n	$t_{.995}$	$t_{.99}$	$t_{.975}$	$t_{.95}$	$t_{.90}$	$t_{.80}$	$t_{.75}$	$t_{.70}$	$t_{.60}$	$t_{.55}$
1	63.66	31.82	12.71	6.31	3.08	1.376	1.000	.727	.325	.158
2	9.92	6.97	4.30	2.92	1.89	1.061	.816	.617	.289	.142
3	5.84	4.54	3.18	2.35	1.64	.978	.765	.584	.277	.137
4	4.60	3.75	2.78	2.13	1.53	.941	.741	.569	.271	.134
5	4.03	3.36	2.57	2.02	1.48	.920	.727	.559	.267	.132
6	3.71	3.14	2.45	1.94	1.44	.906	.718	.553	.265	.131
7	3.50	3.00	2.36	1.90	1.42	.896	.711	.549	.263	.130
8	3.36	2.90	2.31	1.86	1.40	.889	.706	.546	.262	.130
9	3.25	2.82	2.26	1.83	1.38	.883	.703	.543	.261	.129
10	3.17	2.76	2.23	1.81	1.37	.879	.700	.542	.260	.129
11	3.11	2.72	2.20	1.80	1.36	.876	.697	.540	.260	.129
12	3.06	2.68	2.18	1.78	1.36	.873	.695	.539	.259	.128
13	3.01	2.65	2.16	1.77	1.35	.870	.694	.538	.259	.128
14	2.98	2.62	2.14	1.76	1.34	.868	.692	.537	.258	.128
15	2.95	2.60	2.13	1.75	1.34	.866	.691	.536	.258	.128
16	2.92	2.58	2.12	1.75	1.34	.865	.690	.535	.258	.128
17	2.90	2.57	2.11	1.74	1.33	.863	.689	.534	.257	.128
18	2.88	2.55	2.10	1.73	1.33	.862	.688	.534	.257	.127
19	2.86	2.54	2.09	1.73	1.33	.861	.688	.533	.257	.127
20	2.84	2.53	2.09	1.72	1.32	.860	.687	.533	.257	.127
21	2.83	2.52	2.08	1.72	1.32	.859	.686	.532	.257	.127
22	2.82	2.51	2.07	1.72	1.32	.858	.686	.532	.256	.127
23	2.81	2.50	2.07	1.71	1.32	.858	.685	.532	.256	.127
24	2.80	2.49	2.06	1.71	1.32	.857	.685	.531	.256	.127
25	2.79	2.48	2.06	1.71	1.32	.856	.684	.531	.256	.127
26	2.78	2.48	2.06	1.71	1.32	.856	.684	.531	.256	.127
27	2.77	2.47	2.05	1.70	1.31	.855	.684	.531	.256	.127
28	2.76	2.47	2.05	1.70	1.31	.855	.683	.530	.256	.127
29	2.76	2.46	2.04	1.70	1.31	.854	.683	.530	.256	.127
30	2.75	2.46	2.04	1.70	1.31	.854	.683	.530	.256	.127
40	2.70	2.42	2.02	1.68	1.30	.851	.681	.529	.255	.126
60	2.66	2.39	2.00	1.67	1.30	.848	.679	.527	.254	.126
120	2.62	2.36	1.98	1.66	1.29	.845	.677	.526	.254	.126
∞	2.58	2.33	1.96	1.65	1.28	.842	.674	.524	.253	.126

Source; R.A. Fisher and F. Yates, Statistical Tables for Biological, Agricultural and Medical Research (6th edition, 1963), Table III, Oliver and Boyd Ltd., Edinburgh.

Table 5

F Distribution Critical Points 5%

N = degrees of freedom for numerator D = degrees of freedom for denominator

D \ N	1	2	3	4	5	6	8	12	16	20	30	40	50	100	∞
1	161.40	199.50	215.70	224.60	230.20	234.00	238.90	243.90	246.30	248.00	250.10	251.10	252.20	253.00	254.30
2	18.51	19.00	19.16	19.25	19.30	19.33	19.37	19.41	19.43	19.45	19.46	19.46	19.47	19.49	19.50
3	10.13	9.55	9.28	9.12	9.01	8.94	8.85	8.74	8.69	8.66	8.62	8.60	8.58	8.56	8.53
4	7.71	6.94	6.59	6.39	6.26	6.16	6.04	5.91	5.84	5.80	5.75	5.71	5.70	5.66	5.63
5	6.61	5.79	5.41	5.19	5.05	4.95	4.82	4.68	4.60	4.56	4.50	4.46	4.44	4.40	4.36
6	5.99	5.14	4.76	4.53	4.39	4.28	4.15	4.00	3.92	3.87	3.81	3.77	3.75	3.71	3.67
7	5.59	4.74	4.35	4.12	3.97	3.87	3.73	3.57	3.49	3.44	3.38	3.34	3.32	3.28	3.23
8	5.32	4.46	4.07	3.84	3.69	3.58	3.44	3.28	3.20	3.15	3.08	3.05	3.03	2.98	2.93
9	5.12	4.26	3.86	3.63	3.48	3.37	3.23	3.07	2.98	2.93	2.86	2.82	2.80	2.76	2.71
10	4.96	4.10	3.71	3.48	3.33	3.22	3.07	2.91	2.82	2.77	2.70	2.67	2.64	2.59	2.54
11	4.84	3.98	3.59	3.36	3.20	3.09	2.95	2.79	2.70	2.65	2.57	2.53	2.50	2.45	2.40
12	4.75	3.89	3.49	3.26	3.11	3.00	2.85	2.69	2.60	2.54	2.46	2.42	2.40	2.35	2.30
13	4.67	3.81	3.41	3.18	3.03	2.92	2.77	2.60	2.51	2.46	2.38	2.34	2.32	2.26	2.21
14	4.60	3.74	3.34	3.11	2.96	2.85	2.70	2.53	2.44	2.39	2.31	2.27	2.24	2.19	2.13
15	4.54	3.68	3.29	3.06	2.90	2.79	2.64	2.48	2.39	2.33	2.25	2.21	2.18	2.12	2.07

Table 5 (*cont.*)

D \ N	1	2	3	4	5	6	8	12	16	20	30	40	50	100	∞
16	4.49	3.63	3.24	3.01	2.85	2.74	2.59	2.42	2.33	2.28	2.20	2.16	2.13	2.07	2.01
17	4.45	3.59	3.20	2.96	2.81	2.70	2.55	2.38	2.29	2.23	2.15	2.11	2.08	2.02	1.96
18	4.41	3.55	3.16	2.93	2.77	2.66	2.51	2.34	2.25	2.19	2.11	2.07	2.04	1.98	1.92
19	4.38	3.52	3.13	2.90	2.74	2.63	2.48	2.31	2.21	2.15	2.07	2.02	2.00	1.94	1.88
20	4.35	3.49	3.10	2.87	2.71	2.60	2.45	2.28	2.18	2.12	2.04	1.99	1.96	1.90	1.84
22	4.30	3.44	3.05	2.82	2.66	2.55	2.40	2.23	2.13	2.07	1.98	1.93	1.91	1.84	1.78
24	4.26	3.40	3.01	2.78	2.62	2.51	2.36	2.18	2.09	2.03	1.94	1.89	1.86	1.80	1.73
26	4.23	3.37	2.98	2.74	2.59	2.47	2.32	2.15	2.05	1.99	1.90	1.85	1.82	1.76	1.69
28	4.20	3.34	2.95	2.71	2.56	2.45	2.29	2.12	2.02	1.96	1.87	1.81	1.78	1.72	1.65
30	4.17	3.32	2.92	2.69	2.53	2.42	2.27	2.09	1.99	1.93	1.84	1.79	1.76	1.69	1.62
40	4.08	3.32	2.84	2.61	2.45	2.34	2.18	2.00	1.90	1.84	1.74	1.69	1.66	1.59	1.51
50	4.03	3.18	2.79	2.56	2.40	2.29	2.13	1.95	1.85	1.78	1.69	1.63	1.60	1.52	1.44
60	4.00	3.15	2.76	2.53	2.37	2.25	2.10	1.92	1.81	1.75	1.65	1.59	1.56	1.48	1.39
70	3.98	3.13	2.74	2.50	2.35	2.23	2.07	1.89	1.79	1.72	1.62	1.56	1.53	1.45	1.35
80	3.96	3.11	2.72	2.48	2.33	2.21	2.05	1.88	1.77	1.70	1.60	1.54	1.51	1.42	1.32
100	3.94	3.09	2.70	2.46	2.30	2.19	2.03	1.85	1.75	1.68	1.57	1.51	1.48	1.39	1.28
150	3.91	3.06	2.67	2.43	2.27	2.16	2.00	1.82	1.71	1.64	1.54	1.47	1.44	1.34	1.22
200	3.89	3.04	2.65	2.41	2.26	2.14	1.98	1.80	1.69	1.62	1.52	1.45	1.42	1.32	1.19
400	3.86	3.02	2.62	2.39	2.23	2.12	1.96	1.78	1.67	1.60	1.49	1.42	1.38	1.28	1.13
∞	3.84	2.99	2.60	2.37	2.21	2.09	1.94	1.75	1.64	1.57	1.46	1.40	1.32	1.24	1.00

INDEX

N.B. References are to paragraphs

INDEX TO APPENDICES